Specific Targeted Research Project on the Formation of Europe:
Prehistoric Population Dynamics and the Roots of Socio-Cultural Diversity

Institute of Archaeology
Jagiellonian University

I0096082

The First Neolithic Sites in Central/South-East European Transect

Volume V

Settlement of the Linear Pottery Culture in Southeastern Poland

Agnieszka Czekaj-Zastawny

BAR International Series 2049
2009

Published in 2016 by
BAR Publishing, Oxford

BAR International Series 2049

The First Neolithic Sites in Central/South-East European Transect

ISBN 978 1 4073 0625 4

© A Czekaj-Zastawny and the Publisher 2009

Text translated by Jerzy Kopacz

Catalogue translated by Agnieszka Czekaj-Zastawny (aga@archeo.pan.krakow.pl)

BAR Publishing is the trading name of British Archaeological Reports (Oxford) Ltd.
British Archaeological Reports was first incorporated in 1974 to publish the BAR
Series, International and British. In 1992 Hadrian Books Ltd became part of the BAR
group. This volume was originally published by Archaeopress in conjunction with
British Archaeological Reports (Oxford) Ltd / Hadrian Books Ltd, the Series principal
publisher, in 2009. This present volume is published by BAR Publishing, 2016.

Printed in England

BAR
PUBLISHING

BAR titles are available from:

BAR Publishing
122 Banbury Rd, Oxford, OX2 7BP, UK
EMAIL   info@barpublishing.com
PHONE   +44 (0)1865 310431
FAX   +44 (0)1865 316916
www.barpublishing.com

From the series editor

The modelling of the process of Neolithization – one of the basic tasks of the FEPRE project – requires to built a complete database i.e. not only the register of radiocarbon dates but also the inventory of the FTN sites: both those excavated as well as those recorded in the course of surface surveys. In view of the fact that in the Neolithization of Europe the axis running from the Balkans to the Carpathians is of essential importance we have decided to make up the inventory of FTN sites along this axis. Within the territory from 41 to 51 degrees latitude north the following sheets have been taken into account: E – Bulgaria, D – Romania, C – Eastern Hungary, B – Eastern Slovakia, A – Southeastern Poland (see map). The result are five volume catalogue of FTN sites with the following contents:

1. General information about cultural evolution at the onset of Neolithic in a given territory: taxonomic definitions, stratigraphic sequences, seriations, basic data on settlement, material culture, subsistance economy;

2. Additional data on cultural and economic problems specific for a given region;

3. A list of radiometric dates,

4. A catalogue of sites in alphabetical order.

Site catalogues are made up of the following data categories:

Identification and location of sites:

Name of a site (and number on the map)

1. Administrative unit appropriate to a given site;

2. River basin

3. Geographical coordinates

4. Geomorphological situation (river basin, location in relation to the land relief)

A. Information on excavated sites:

1. Name(s) of researcher(s) responsible for the excavation;

2. Date of excavation (years);

3. Bounded research area: excavated and surveyed;

4. Type and number of features;

5. Relative chronology based on archaeological seriation and absolute chronology; number of settlement phases;

B. Information on sites recognized on the basis of surface finds

1. Area of occurrence of portable finds;

2. Taxonomic attribution and – when possible – chronological framework of sites.

C. The most important references.

Each volume deals with a different taxonomic unit representing FTN in a given territory:

Volume 1 – Bulgaria – sites of the Monochrome and the Early Painted Pottery Phase (Karanovo I type)

Volume 2 – Romania (Transilvania and Banat) – sites of the Early Phase (with white-painted pottery) of Criş-Körös Culture,

Volume 3 – Eastern Hungary (Tisza basin) – sites of the Körös-Starčevo Culture,

Volume 4 – Eastern Slovakia – sites of the Early Phase of the Eastern Linear Pottery Culture,

Volume 5 – South-Eastern Poland – LBK sites.

The database and the analysis of archaeological records provides the most up-to-date groundwork for the construction of the model on Neolithization of Central Europe within the framework of the FEPRE project; it is also aimed at any other modeling of these processes.

Janusz K. Kozłowski

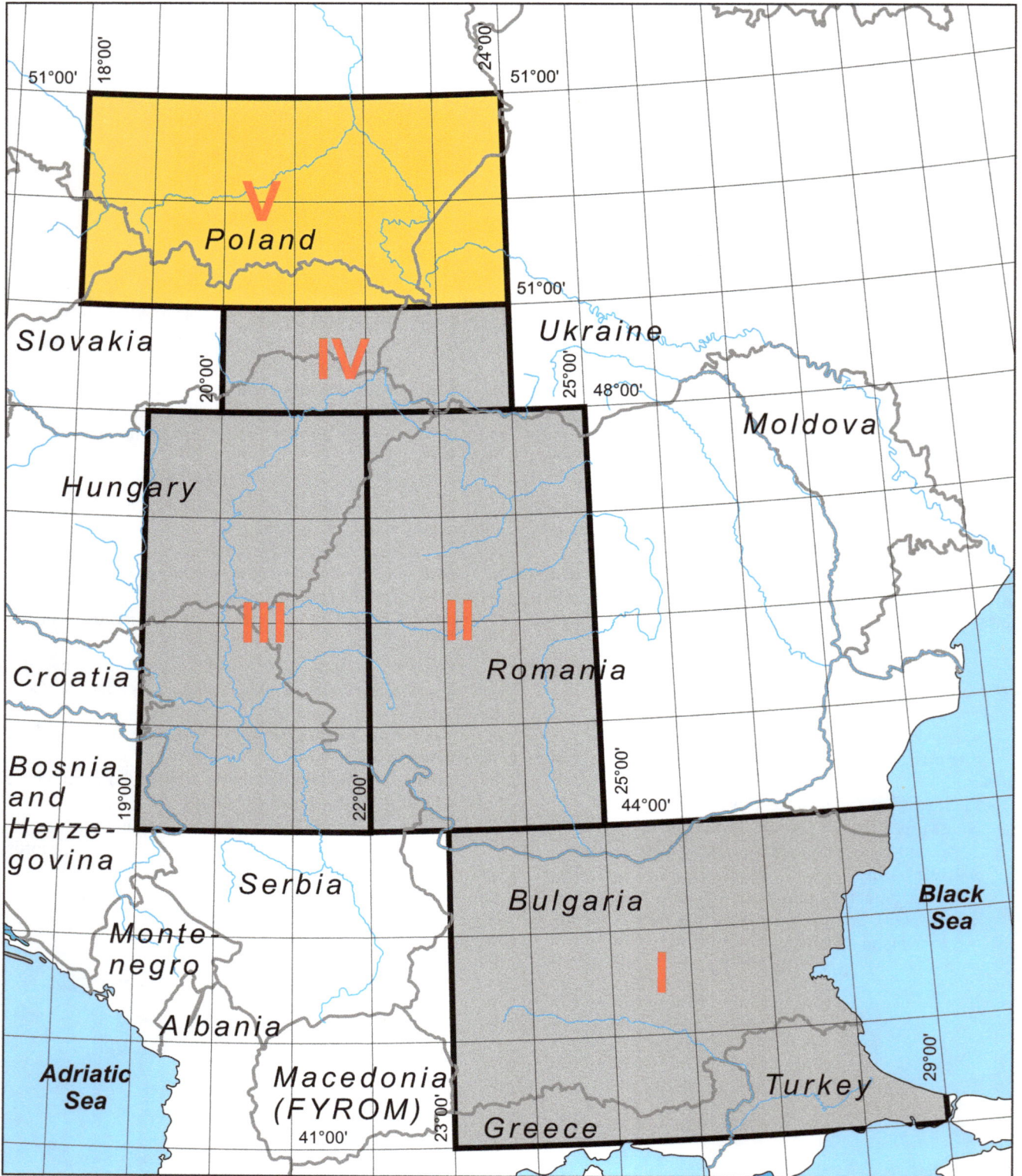

51°00' 18°00' 24°00' 51°00'

V
Poland

Slovakia
IV
51°00'

Ukraine
20°00'
25°00'
48°00'

Moldova

Hungary

III
II

Croatia
Romania

Bosnia
and
Herze-
govina
19°00'
22°00'
25°00'
44°00'

Serbia

Bulgaria
Black
Sea

Monte-
negro

I

Albania

Adriatic
Sea

Macedonia
(FYROM)
23°00'
29°00'
41°00'

Turkey

Greece

Agnieszka Czekaj-Zastawny

SETTLEMENT OF THE LINEAR POTTERY CULTURE IN SOUTHEASTERN POLAND

CONTENTS

Please note that full-size versions of the images shown at the back of this book are available to download from www.barpublishing.com/additional-downloads.html

1. INTRODUCTION

1.1. Objectives of the work

Last a few dozen years has witnessed a multi-aspect research on the Linear Pottery Culture (LBK). Studies of that type have a long history, especially in southeastern Poland. They have been focused mainly on loess areas in the western part the Lesser Poland Upland. Their results constitute until today a basis for the knowledge of earliest farmers territories in our country. In contrast, other regions remained less recognized until very recent years.

Evidences for studying the Linear Pottery Culture are very rich. Nowadays – in the time of intensive research linked – among others – with rescue excavations on multiple construction works – augmentation of data in incomparably bigger them in previous dozens of years. However, the most important in this respect is the AZP Project (Archaeological Picture of Poland) which encompassed until today more than 90 per cent of the territory of Poland. Comparing with the situation in 1980s the number of Linear Pottery sites increased almost eight times. For example, in the Raba River basin there have been confirmed a presence of a few dozen sites, while in 1970s only one small concentration of 5 settlement points was known (Kulczycka-Leciejewiczowa 1973b, 21, fig. 1). In 1980s on the whole territory of the southeastern Poland only 115 sites were registered (Kruk 1980, map 1) – today we have them 793 (**Catalogue**).

This work aims at a few objectives. Firstly, it is orderly presenting all evidences obtained until today, including the most recent discoveries. They fall into three categories. The most numerous come from AZP research. There have been catalogued all site of the culture in question discovered during surface survey on the area of our interest. Evidences from older excavations fall into the second category. Finally, we have the third category that includes the most recent unpublished discoveries obtained by means of regular excavations. Most of them were made of the line of Freeway A-4 under construction, between cities of Kraków and Tarnów, covered by wide-area rescue research. All these data draw a new settlement picture of the Linear Pottery Culture in the upper Vistula. Moreover, previously recognized concentrations appear to be bigger than expected.

Having such a vast scope of evidence basis available for analysis I was able to assume the next task, i.e. a reconstruction of the settlement basis of Linear Pottery communities. To obtain this goal it was necessary to put forward scores of detailed questions related to forms of the settlement, their structures, spatial economy, and space utilization. In cases of domestic sites an attempt has been made to reconstruct their architecture, functionality of structures and their close vicinity. The research has also encompassed the geography of the Linear Pottery Culture by analyzing distribution of settlement points, characters of the sites, criteria of selection settlement places, as well as spatial organization and relations between individual sites. In this case my considerations were based mainly on evidences from surface survey and confirmed – to the best possible extent – by materials obtained by the material obtained during systematic excavations. All issues presented above are focused on presentation of the settlement region of the Linear Pottery Culture in the upper Vistula basin on the background of other settlement centers of the culture in question.

The monographic work includes also a part devoted to burials of the Linear Pottery Culture. As so-far, this question has not been yet comprehensively discussed. The first ellaboration devoted to this topic, based on evidences from southeastern Poland, will be published soon (Czekaj-Zastawny, *in press*).

1.2. Spatial and chronological scope of the work

The research encompassed the upper Vistula basin from the sources of this river to the confluence of the San River (Fig. 1). This area is generally referred as southeastern Poland. Its natural borders, formed by Vistula and its tributaries, draw the settlement region of the Linear Pottery Culture in this part of Poland.

The chronological scope includes the whole period of existence of the Linear Pottery Culture in the upper Vistula basin. We find here all development stages of this culture recognized in other parts of Poland – in relative chronology – from the Proto-Note (Gniechowice) Phase to the younger stage of Phase III-Železovce (ŽIIb). Therefore, the beginning of the Linear Pottery Culture in the area of our interest corresponds with the Bíňa Phase in Slovakia and Phase A of the Vinča culture (Pavúk 1980). Due to insufficient number of radiocarbon dates the absolute chronology of the developing period of the Linear Pottery Culture can by drawn only generally – from about 5500 to 4900 BC.

1.3. Natural environment of the research area

Geographical scope of the work encompasses the upper Vistula basin in southwestern Poland, a region morphologically very diverse. It is bordered from the north by vast plains of Mazovia and Polesie. Towards the south it merges with the Carpathian Foothills, up to the northern borders of the range itself. The southernmost and – at the same – the highest parts of the research are: the Orava–Podhale Basin with the northern fringe of the Tatra Mts., the Sanok-Turcza Mts., and the Western Bieszczady Mts.

The river network in southeastern Poland was developed earlier then in other parts of the country. Generally, it was formed in the Late Pliocene and Eo-Pleistocene. Exceptional in this respect is the Sandomierz Basin which during these periods belonged to the Dnister River drainage area. Altogether, the river network in southern Poland is well developed, due to an intensive precipitation and a diverse morphology (Dynowska 1991, 371–372). The river network encompasses basins of the Vistula and their main tributaries: the Nida, Szreniawa, Kamienna, Soła, Skawa, Raba, Dunajec, Wisłoka, Wisłok, San, as well upper basins of the Wieprz and Bug Rivers. Outline of the drainage area of the Vistula is asymmetric and more developed on the right-hand side of the river, especially in its upper course. Until the regulation of the river in the mid 19th century, it had a meandrous character. Areas of a glen character can be found at outlets of the mountainous tributaries, e.g. the Soła, and Dunajec. Prior to regulation, the width of the Vistula riverbed varied from 20–50 m in the Oświęcim Basin to 200 m in the Sandomierz Basin (Starkel 2001, 15–16).

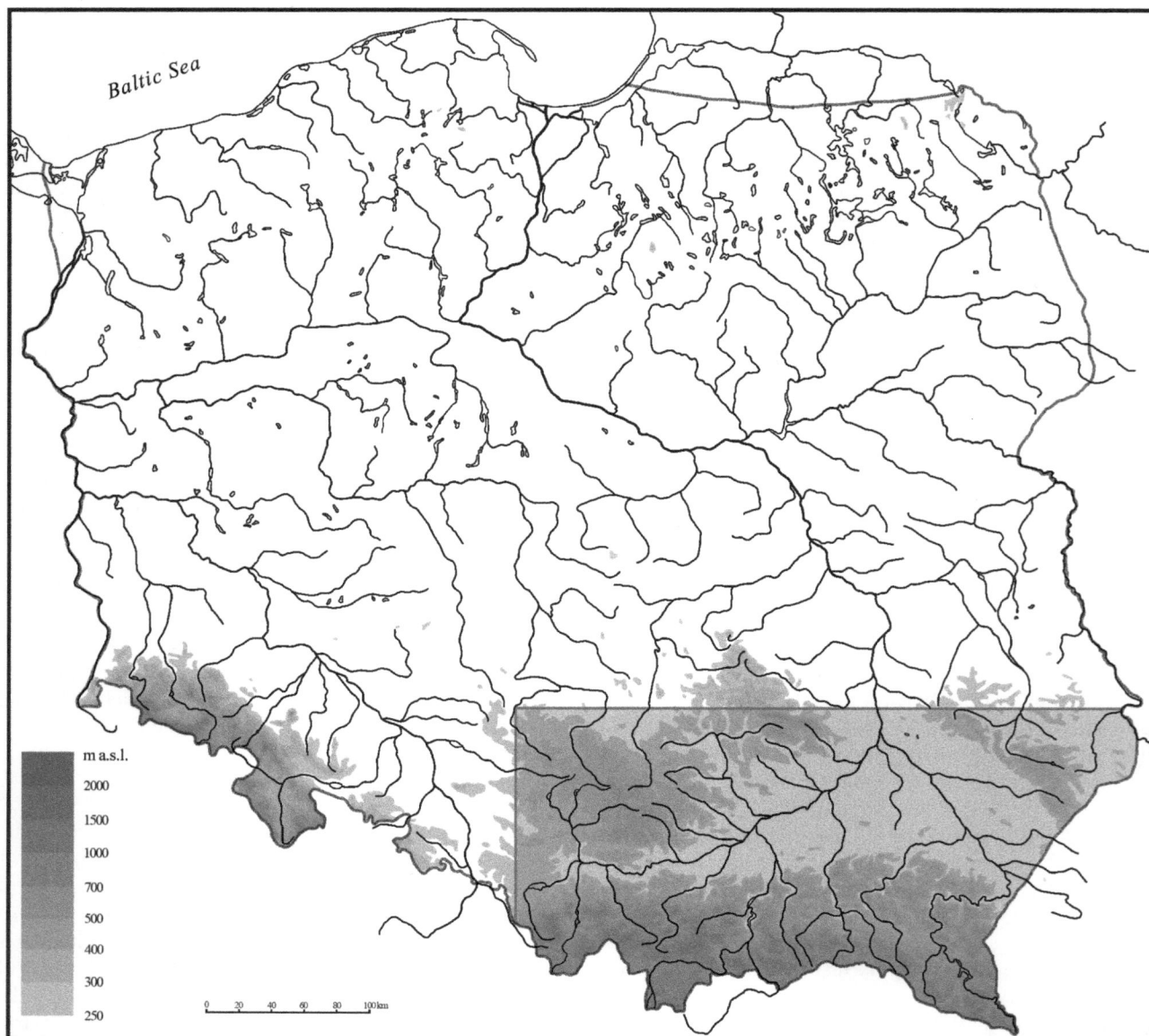

Fig. 1. Research area – upper Vistula basin. Drawn by I. Jordan

The soil cover of the area in question was developing in relation to the climate, rock bedding, and natural vegetation. The latter – stabilized in the Holocene – encompassed mainly complexes of multi-species deciduous and deciduous-coniferous forests. Brown soils (over 50%) and podsols are dominant (about 25%; Prusinkiewicz & Bednarek 1991, 389).

1.4. Natural conditions during the time of the Linear Pottery Culture

The natural environment today differs very much from that prevailing during the time of development of the Linear Pottery Culture. We should remember about transformations related to the natural evolution of the environment and about human impacts upon it. The situation today can be taken as a starting point for the reconstruction of the natural environment during the Atlantic Phase of the Holocene. The most stable elements are: river network, terrain relief, and soils, genetically diversified. Quite different things are changes of the soil fertility due to their degradation. We omit here – as not relevant to the Holocene – today's characteristics of the vegetation and climate. They are also subjected to easily observable transformations.

Terrain relief is an element that transforms very slowly. Therefore, we can say that it has not been changed very much from the time of our interest.

At the beginning of the Holocene, with disappearance of frozen grounds, transformations of hill slopes slowed down. In contrast, the erosion and the gravitation, related to processes of deepening of valley floors, became more significant. The "forested period" of Holocene is distinctive by intensive sinking of rainfall water into the soil and intensive leaching of the latter (Starkel 1991a, 140–144). The Atlantic Phase which followed a period of mild and dry climate, was convenient for a development black soils on loess uplands (Jersak & Śnieszko 1983). Flowing waters craved suffosian channals which deepened the network of loess gorges, some of them of the earlier origin. During the Holocene the gorges were gradually filled up. On karst areas, sink holes and karst valleys were developing. Denudation processes were not intensive and slopes remained basically unchanged. On elevated places of floors of small valleys accumulation prevailed. A development of pit bogs can be also observed. These relief-shaping processes coincided with the Neolithic settlement. The deforestation disturbed water circulations and increased the surface flow and washing (Starkel 1991a, 140–144). Traces of these processes can be observed at the edge base of the loess terrace at Pleszów (Godłowska *et al.* 1987). However, during the time of LBK development anthropogenic transformations of the natural environment were relatively small, in comparison with younger stage of the Neolithic (Kruk 1983).

Soils were elements of natural environment extremely important for agricultural communities. Throughout the time they have been subjected to transformations and their agricultural properties changed very much. The original value of soils can be reconstructed on the basis of their natural-genetic classification.

Recurring cycles of glacial and interglacial periods interrupted the soil development. As a result, we have soils of various age and origin. The majority of them developed at the turn of the Vistulian and the Holocene. Peat-bogs and bog-soils were formed in depressions. They were accompanied by clayey-boggy soils, muds, and wash soils. Typical elements of that period were long-lasting bogs and marshes in depressions and on elevated flats. On areas deprived of ground and surface waters, accumulation of black soil humus can be observed. There were also soils of the the Early Holocene origin – well developed aeruginous soils, podsols, boggy soils, gley soils, and undeveloped soils. In forested areas podsol processes were active (Kowalkowski 1991).

In the upper Vistula basin an important role in soil-forming processes was played by the loess bedrock, but also by the climate and vegetal cover. In such conditions brown and buff soils developed. Today they constitute over 50% of all soils on the whole Polish territory (Prusinkiewicz & Bednarek 1991, 388–389). It has been accepted that their original extent was much bigger then today and that throughout the time it diminished on behalf of degraded soils and young skeletal soils (Kruk 1973, 143–149). The prevalence of brown soils over other soils at the time of the LBK development was probably even bigger. Also the extent black soils, at that time more homogenous, was wider.

Climate is the main non-anthropogenic element influencing transformations of the natural environment – terrain relief, vegetation, waters, and soils. During the Neolithic its impact was bigger than today, as human influences upon it were practically non-existing.

The developing sequence of LBK falls entirely into the Atlantic Phase of the Holocene, dated to 8400–5000 BP (Starkel 1991b, fig. 45). At the beginning of this Phase (8500–8000 BP) deep changes of air circulation over Europe took place – from the south to the west (Ralska-Jasiewiczowa & Starkel 1991, 179). As a result, humid airs of the Atlantic origin became dominant over the continent. The average temperature was 1–2°C higher then today, so was the precipitation. The thermal situation at that time was very stable. Only at the turn of the Atlantic and Sub-Boreal Periods the climate became cooler.

Comprehensive analyses of Holocene climatic changes in Poland are based on soil profiles dated by the isotope method $\delta^{18}O$. Dates have been obtained from river and lake sediments, and from pollen samples (Ralska-Jasiewiczowa & Starkel 1991, 179). The Atlantic climate, thermally stable, featured nevertheless warm and wet cycles. About 8500–8000 BP southern Poland witnesses an increase amount of violent floods and slope processes (registered in profiles of river valleys) became very active. The invasion of alder is another indicator of wet climate. The western circulation brought mild winters. Composition of forest complexes from 7700–5000 BP, as well as the presence of grape-vine in southern Poland, indicate that the temperature was 1–2°C higher then today. Precipitation was higher by 10–15%, and evaporation – due to the high temperature – by 20–30% (Ralska-Jasiewiczowa & Starkel 1991, 179). Only at the end of the Atlantic Phase the average temperature slightly decreasedd (Kruk 1973, 122–123).

Vegetal cover is an element of natural environment subjected to very deep transformations. Early farmers entered areas ecologically stable and almost completely forested. They occupied mainly ground covered by multi-species deciduous forests, especially in the zone of low terraces.

In early stages of the Atlantic Phase all component of stenothermal deciduous forests were already present on Polish territories. They were gradually developing until the balance with actual climatic and biotopic conditions was reached. New complexes, optimal for local conditions, are referred as climax complexes. They were very stable. Under a compact cover of tree-tops, a specific micro-climate developed. It was hardly influenced from outside. Atlantic forest of uplands and hills in southern Poland were dominated by elm and hazel. It may indicate that on these areas forests were less compact then in the north of the country. In depressions of the Low Beskid Mts., which served as routes of northern migrations of stenothermal deciduous trees, multi-species forests of the lowland type (with high share of linden developed. In the eastern part of the Carpathians, black alder complexes entered the areas of peat-bogs (Ralska-Jasiewiczowa 1991, 114–118).

An evaluation of the potential natural vegetation of loess uplands was presented by J. Kruk and L. Przywara (Kruk & Przywara 1983). The authors propose a theoretical reconstruction of the situation of vegetal complexes without any human influences. It is close to the natural environment encountered on these areas by LBK people.

We can assume the coexistence of various vegetal landscapes, developing on high river terraces, low slopes above valleys, and on edges and slopes of loess uplands, today occupied by complexes wet forests, "...(zones B and C) there were developing complexes with oak (*Quercus*), linden (*Tilia*), maple (*Acer*), and hazel (*Corylus avellana*). Oak and pine (*Pinus*) probably constituted mixed forests on dry parts of water dividers (zone D) and on sandy loess. Trees such as ash (*Fraxinus excelsior*) and elm (*Ulmus*) could have formed complexes of the *Alno-Padion* type – in river valleys, on wet soils and in places exposed to floods (zone A). Willow (*Salix*) and poplar (*Populus*) grew probably in complexes similar *Salicion*, typical to fertile alluvial soils on areas seasonally floods. On forest borders, species related to *Rosacea* might have formed (with other components) brush complexes of the *Prunetalia* type, often related to human economic activities (Milisauskas, Kruk *et al.* 2004). According to Kruk and Przywara (1983) wet forests growing on loess uplands were most important in the scope extent – were. They were followed by mixed forests, riverine forests, and alder forests. Xerothermic complexes were rare.

On the territory of our interest three types of vegetal landscapes coexisted: wet forests – on slopes of loess hills of limestone or Cretaceous bedrock, on sandy-clayly flats, and on marl flat hilltops; sylvan forests – on ridges of loess uplands and loamy sands on flats; riverine forests on areas seasonally flooded and in wet river valleys.

Changes of the vegetal cover on the Vistula terrace near Cracow during the LBK period can be observed on pollen profiles from Kraków-Pleszów (Godłowska *et al.* 1987).

Natural resources. They include, first of all, raw materials utilized in the Early Neolithic – flint and possibly salty springs. Their presence in areas of intensively cultivation is significant. We assume that they were, together with fertile soils, very important factors in settlement development of the region.

The Cracow-Częstochowa Upland was the main source of siliceous raw material for the area of the upper Vistula basin. It is abundant with deposits of flints of various age (mainly Jurassic), representing several varieties of different chipping properties. The Upland is built of Upper Jurassic limestones. The most important are platy limestones – primary rocks of Upper Jurassic flints (Lech 1981). The Upper Jurassic sediments are bordered from the west by older formations containing flints other varieties, jaspers, and cherts. In the eastern part of the Cracow Upland, along its southern borders and in the Nida Basin, Jurassic limestones are covered by Cretaceous sediments. They contained Jurassic and Cretaceous flints and cherts – all in secondary positions (Lech 1981).

Salt springs are located on the other side of the Vistula. They are related the presence on this area salt, salty loams, gypsum, and anhydrites, lixiviated by penetrating waters (Bukowski 2003). Salty springs are spread mainly in the area extending from Sidziny, through Swoszowice, Barycz, Wieliczka, up to Przebieczany. They can be also found between Łężkowice and Bochnia (Bukowski 2003, fig. 3).

2. LINEAR POTTERY CULTURE IN SOUTHEASTERN POLAND

The Linear Pottery Culture, included by G. Child to his *Danubian Ia* Period (Childe 1929, 36–47), is in southeastern Poland the earliest Neolithic unit of the southern origin. In relation to the division into geographic-cultural zones, the territory in question belongs to the eastern zone of LBK milieu (Coudart 1998).

LBK appeared in Poland as early as in the first phase of its expansion. It spread into area between the upper Odra basin and the Western Volhynian Upland and – to the north – to Kuyavia and the Chełmno region. It is commonly accepted that groups of people of the culture in question penetrated here from territories of Bohemia and Moravia by two routes: through the Moravian Gates and through the Kłodzko Basin (Kozłowski 1998). However, there are evidences that trans-Carpathian routes *via* mountain passes were also utilized. For example, in Gwoździec on the Wiśnicz Foothills a domestic site from the early phase of LBK with elements of Alföld culture has been discovered (Kukułka 2001, 11–40). It is not an isolated discovery – multiple settlement points indicate the presence of a concentrated LBK settlement in this area.

The chronological division of LBK in southeastern Poland is based on systems developed for Bohemia and southwestern Slovakia by Soudský (1954) and Neustupy (1956). The most actual division into periods takes into account mainly changes of pottery ornamentation (and – in smaller degree – forms of vessels), but also relations with territories of southwestern Slovakia, which influenced the LBK development on the area of our interest. It is as follows (Fig. 2): the earliest phase (called Proto-Music Note), corresponding with assemblages of the Flomborn Phase in Rhineland, the A-Phase in Bohemia and Moravia, and the Bíňa Horizon in southwestern Slovakia (Kulczycka-Leciejewiczowa 1979, 51; Pavúk 1980, 7–90), is sub-divided into Sub-Phases Ia – Gniechowice, and Ib – Zofipole (Kulczycka-Leciejewiczowa 1964, 47–67; 1979, 19–164; 1983, 67–97). According to the newest hypothesis of J. Pavúk, Proto-Music Note assemblages of Phase Ia should be rather linked with the horizon of Milanovce (Pavúk 2004). It is related to the presence in Phase Ia of the *barbotino* ornamentation and motifs of rows of fingertip impressions beneath vessel rims, typical for the Milanovce Phase (Pavúk 2004, 78). Phase II (Middle) – Music Note – has been divided into three Sub-Phases, corresponding with the development of LBK in southwestern Slovakia: NI – Early, NII – Classic, NIII – Late (Kadrow 1990, 9–76), or into the Early and Late Music Note Sub-Phases (Godłowska 1991, 7–68). As in southwestern Slovakia (Pavuk 1969, 269–367) we can also subdivide Phase III (Late) – Želiezovce into: ŽI, ŽIIa, ŽIIb (as so far ŽIIb has been recognized only in the Cracow area and in Rzeszów), and – hypothetically (it is unknown in Poland) ŽIII (Godłowska 1992, 152–153; Kadrow 1990, 9–76).

If observations in the scope of taxonomy and chronology of LBK in upper Vistula basin are compatible with the classic schemes, the question of disintegration of the culture in question in southeastern Poland presents a problem. In the literature we can find several hypotheses on this issue (Kaczanowska 1990, 71–97), two of them being still considered as acceptable. As we have said, in the area of our interest (e.g. on site complex at Targowisko, Kłaj commune) there are known materials of the Želiezovce Phase IIa and IIb, among them pottery fragments with red-painted bands (Czerniak *et al.* 2006, 542). In contrast, elements related to the younger stage of the Želiezovce Phase (ŽIII) are absent.

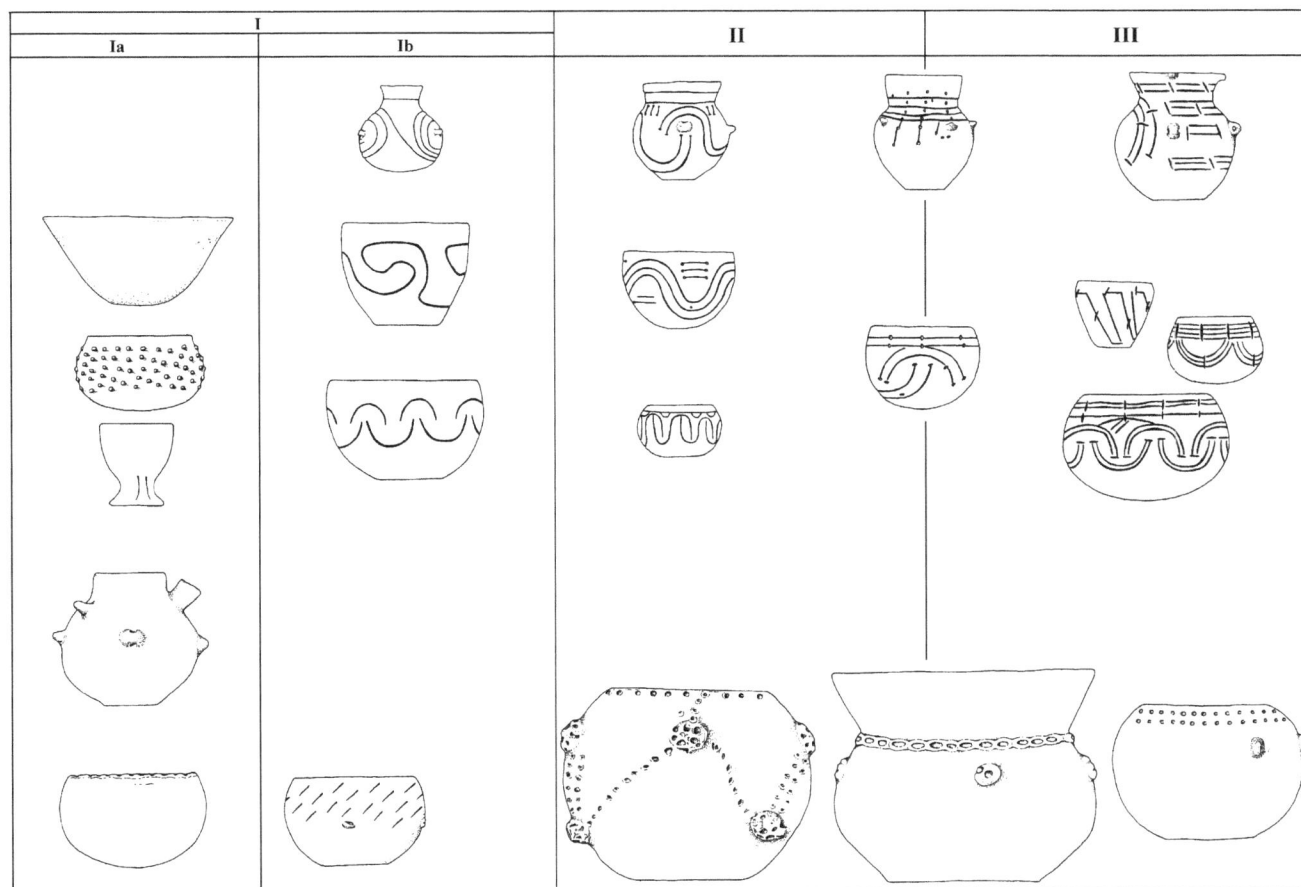

Fig. 2.   Pottery forms typical for main chronological phases of LBK in southeastern Poland. Drawn by J. Ożóg

We do not have also any Proto-Lengyel elements that, if present, would indicate a local "floating" transition the next stage of development related to the Samborzec-Opatów group of the Lengyel culture (Kaczanowska 1990, 71–97).

Consequently, the first theory suggests a settlement gap between LBK and the Lengyel culture. After disintegration of LBK the next colonization wave should have been related to immigrants from the south – the bearers of the already crystallized Lengyel culture (Kulczycka-Leciejewiczowa 1979, 19–164; Kaczanowska 1990, 71–97; Kamieńska & Kozłowski 1990, 14–16; Kozłowski 2004).

The second presented theory assumes the settlement continuation and development of cultural units related to the so-called Lengyel-Polgár circle. They should have emerged under influences of the Lengyel and Tisza-Polgár culture, and – in a small degree – of the Stroked Band Pottery culture and groups of Late LBK. Development of the Samborzec group was influenced by the Lengyel culture, and that of the Malice culture – the Tisa culture. In both cases influences from the Stroked Band Pottery were only minor (Kadrow & Zakościelna 2000, 187–255). The theory of the settlement continuation is compatible with recent studies of A. Kulczycka-Leciejewiczowa (2002).

3. SETTLEMENT OF EARLIEST FARMING COMMUNITIES

3.1. Settlement extent and its organization

The settlement region in the upper Vistula basin has in most parts natural borders separating it from other LBK centers in Europe. Only the eastern reach of the research area, corresponding with the state border, is not very clear. It is not bordered by areas void of settlement, but rather continue up to the Dnister basin. It seems that a "floating" border between both regions runs between a settlement center around Rzeszów and that in the vicinity of Przemyśl.

In the area of our interest there have been registered so-far 793 settlement points (cf. *Catalogue*; Czekaj-Zastawny 2000b; 2001; 2008a). They are distributed unevenly. Most of them concentrate on the left-hand side of the Vistula basin. Sites on the right bank of this river are much less frequent. Sites are located mainly on Vistula tributaries; while the Vistula valley itself was much less settled (only two bigger concentrations are known from there). Everywhere we can observe areas with saturated with settlement points, separated one from another by zones of much less settlement, or even deprived of it. The biggest concentration of sites in the entire region is that in the vicinity of Cracow.

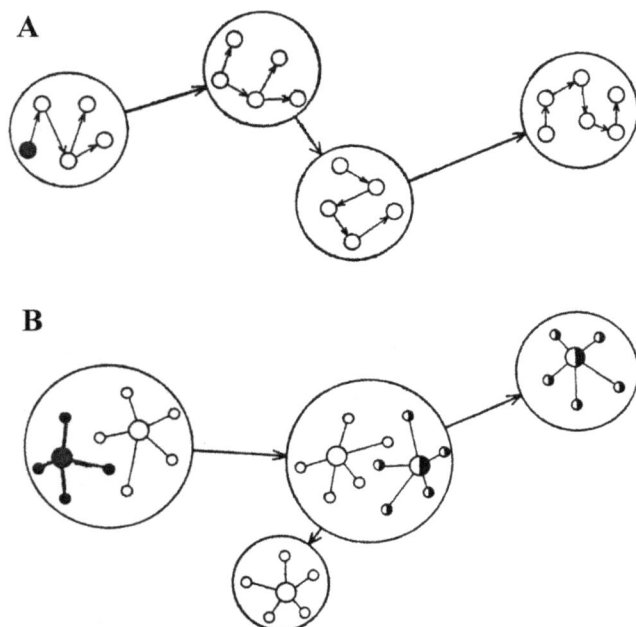

Fig. 4. Models of basic settlement units and settlement network development. Circles symbolize concentrations of archaeological sites (**A**) and/or true microorganisms of spatial utilizations (**B**); (after Kruk 1980)

It spreads on both banks of Vistula, between basins of Rudawa, Nidzica, and Raba rivers (Fig. 3).

Regular distribution of points of settlement can be observed also in macro-regional scale, mainly as concentrations of sites in river valleys of Vistula tributaries. We find here zones of a dense concentration of settlement points separated, as in the whole region, by areas unsettled or of a very scattered settlement. Such a distribution of sites, recognized in the whole researched area as typical for LBK, has an exception in the Dłubnia River valley, where pattern of sites is more uniform.

Basing on detailed analyses of settlement regions we can conclude that a great amount of new data from the upper Vistula basin confirms LBK settlement model drawn by J. Kruk (1973; 1980).

LBK settlement reveals tendency to grouping settlement points. It is best visible in the basin of the Nidzica River, and least on the right-hand bank of Vistula in the area of Brzezie. An average value calculated for the whole upper Vistula region (R = 0.614) indicates that LBK sites are grouped in two ways (Fig. 4): as concentrations of permanent habitation sites of equal status (A), and as microregions comprising one or few settlements, camp sites, and settlement traces (B). At present we can say that both models (Kruk 1980) are equally important – most often they appear together (e.g. on the Dłubnia River near Iwanowice), although on same areas one model prevails over the other (e.g. on the right-hand bank of Vistula – model A in the area of Brzezie, model B – in the area of Łoniowa). This picture differs slightly from that drawn on the basis of research in 1970s and 1980s (Kruk 1980, 84), when the second model was considered more probable. It seems that, apart from Early Neolithic traditions maintained throughout the whole

LBK sequence, a settlement organization in any region was influenced by natural conditions. The first described model refers to areas rich with natural resources, such as Iwanowice (flint deposits) and Brzezie regions (salty springs). It is confirmed by a relatively short equidistance radius, related to settlement density and presence of many permanent domestic sites.

Natural conditions, besides influencing settlement organization pf LBK people, had their impact on settlement distribution, both in regional and local scales. In the whole upper Vistula basin we observe a predominance of sites located on loess soils. It is the main and constant tendency in Early Neolithic settlement. Extent of most settlement concentrations corresponds with loess covers with very few exceptions. Location of settlement points on specific soils, as well as extent of various soil types (in percentage) in the close vicinity of sites indicate that only areas of highest productive potentials were utilized. This tendency can be observed in relation to sites of all three types, i.e. domestic sites, camps, and settlement traces. It is a rather surprising observation, especially in relation to settlement traces spread over vast areas with diverse soils. Different locations have sites in areas, where settlement traces have been registered mostly on topographic forms not occupied by permanent settlement. It suggests early penetration of early farming people was directed mainly to patches of fertile soils, even if topography of the place excludes a stable habitation. The goal of this penetration was to find a suitable farming land.

On the whole researched of the upper Vistula basin sites related to river basins overwhelmingly prevail. They are situated mainly on low terraces and on valley edges, then on valley sides and on upper terraces. Only few sites locate on valley beds, originally probably on small elevations subsequently leveled by river accumulation and side erosion. In comparison with river valley, settlement points of upland location are much less frequent (only 20 per cent). Some of them are situated immediately above valleys – in upland border zones, on hilltops and on promontories. Others lie even deeper – on watersheds, on flats and slopes of ridges and in dry valleys.

Significant is locations of sites of specific types. We find permanent domestic sites locate mainly on lower terraces and on river valley borders. Location of camps is similar, yet valley slopes were more often used. In relation to settlement points the situation is different. Apart from terraces and valley edges they often appear – as we have said – in areas seldom utilized by domestic sites and camps, i.e. on slopes and valley beds. Numerous settlement traces have been also located in zones of upper landscape, not related to river valleys, most often on watersheds.

Important elements of natural environment, considerably influencing settlement, are natural resources, such as flint and salty springs. Deposits of siliceous raw material partially correspond with areas of intensive LBK settlement in upper Vistula basin, between rivers of Rudawa and Szreniawa. Similarly, on the other side of Vistula, the area of salty springs between Bochnia and Wieliczka reveals a dense LBK settlement with a great number of permanently settled sites with houses of the post construction.

Concluding, a tendency for settlement concentration in areas of high environmental potentials, mentioned already on the occasion of discussion of the settlement organization, can be observed in the whole upper Vistula basin. All analyzed elements indicate that development of the biggest (in the scope of area and density) settlement center between rivers of Rudawa, Raba, and Nidzica, was related to natural resources. They were, apart from fertile soils, river network, and – probably – floral habitat and convenient climate, deposits of siliceous raw material and salty springs.

3.2. Domestic site and camp – building-up and space organization

In the upper Vistula basin, long-lasting settlement (the presence of long houses of the post construction) has been confirmed on almost half of excavated sites (64, out of 130; Czekaj-Zastawny 2008a). The ration calculated for sites recognized only by surface survey is different, but statistics based on data obtained by excavations is more reliable.

Available data suggest that among settlement forms functioning throughout the development sequence of LBK, permanent domestic sites prevailed by far over camps. However, if we take into account a diverse functionality of camps and frequency of possible various activities that were being accomplished some distance away from permanently settled sites, and also a smaller chance to discover a camp than a site, the situation might have been different.

3.2.1. Domestic sites

Long houses of the post construction were typical elements of every permanently settled site, no matter of natural conditions (Fig. 5). Interred features were never erected. It seems that constructions of that type were "reserved" only for camps. Structures discovered during earlier excavations of domestic sites and interpreted as dug-in dwellings were, in fact, remains of constructional pits accompanying houses erected above the ground. They are usually better preserved – due to their dimensions – than postholes. Therefore, we often register then even if accompanied postholes disappeared due to erosion.

Space organization of settlement

LBK settlements in the upper Vistula basin were in most cases open. They were usually composed of 3–4 households (8 at most). Houses were built in a distance no shorter than 45–50 meters one another, to provide a space for necessary near-house utility pits. It has been calculated on the basis of date available in this work that a domestic site of 3–4 households (*i.e.* houses, yards, and outside zones occupied by utility features) covered the area of *ca.* 1 hectare.

Analyses of elements included in settlement spatial organization, such as intentional location of specific utility features in required quantity, functional division of the area utilized by the site, and orientation of all structures according to N–S axis, indicate that the settlement area was to a certain extent intentionally built and organized. On certain sites we can also assume intentional location of individual households. It can be well observed on Site 17 at Brzezie, where houses of subsequent constructional phases locate in

three parallel rows along W–E axis. As a rule on each site we find one house (occasionally two) of exceptional length, *i.e.* over 30 meters. It is always a tripartite construction – Type 1 after Modderman (Modderman 1986; 1988).

Typical medium-size settlement sites in the upper Vistula basin are located most often on flats of the lower terrace of the river or on its edge, with easy access to the water. The area exploited by inhabitants of the site, either to build settlement structure, or to other economic activities, can be divided into three zones.

The outer zone – outside of the build-up area, used by all inhabitants, was within a radius of 1.35–1.5 from the settlement. It served as farming and grazing ground, and as a resource of building materials. It was a zone of intensive economic use, concentrating basic activities related to exploitation of environmental resources.

Within the outer zone, in the close vicinity of houses, on easy, sunny slopes and in relatively dry part of the river valley floor (on fen soils), there were cultivated fields of the garden type. Corn fields, utilizing mainly brown soils, were located in upper parts of the terrace, within a radius of *ca.* 0.5 km from the domestic site, cutting into multi-species deciduous forests. This area was sufficient for husbandry purpose. Extent of the utilized land was in this case twice as big and covered the area within the radius of at least 1 km from the domestic site. It served as a pasture ground, where animals grazed on fallowing fields and on clearings next to forests. The area necessary for maintaining herds (summer grazing and winter food) is estimated for few dozen hectares (about 90). It is very probable that husbandry and land cultivation were being carried out also in more distant areas (several kilometers from the site). Such a presumption is based on the presence of camps that might have served for that purpose. The close vicinity of the site (possibly also the cultivated fields) was also utilized as a resource for obtaining building materials required in house constructions.

The inner zone – within the domestic around households. The zone was occupied by various utility features common for all inhabitants. Recognized/examined on few sites due to peripheral location in relation to houses, it can be reconstructed on the basis of the research of Site 4 in Kraków-Olszanica (Milisauskas 1986) and a few other sites outside Poland (e.g. Lüning 1982; Modderman 1986; 1988).

In the inner economic zone, on the area of several thousands sq. meters, there were numerous features of various use, such as storage pits, ovens built of clay, bigger hearths, etc. Ovens served probably for cooking meals – in accompanying pits there have been found remains of cereals and weeds. We can assume that big fireplaces and pottery kilns were also located there.

The central zone – households. It was a zone of individual household activities inside or outside of houses, in a distance up to 25 m from them.

House interiors can be divided into three functional parts (Lüning 1982; Modderman 1986; 1988; Fig. 6). The middle part served for domestic (domestic-working) purpose. It was the biggest part of the house and provided sufficient room for everyday activities. Occasionally it also served as burial place for defunct inhabitants. The northern

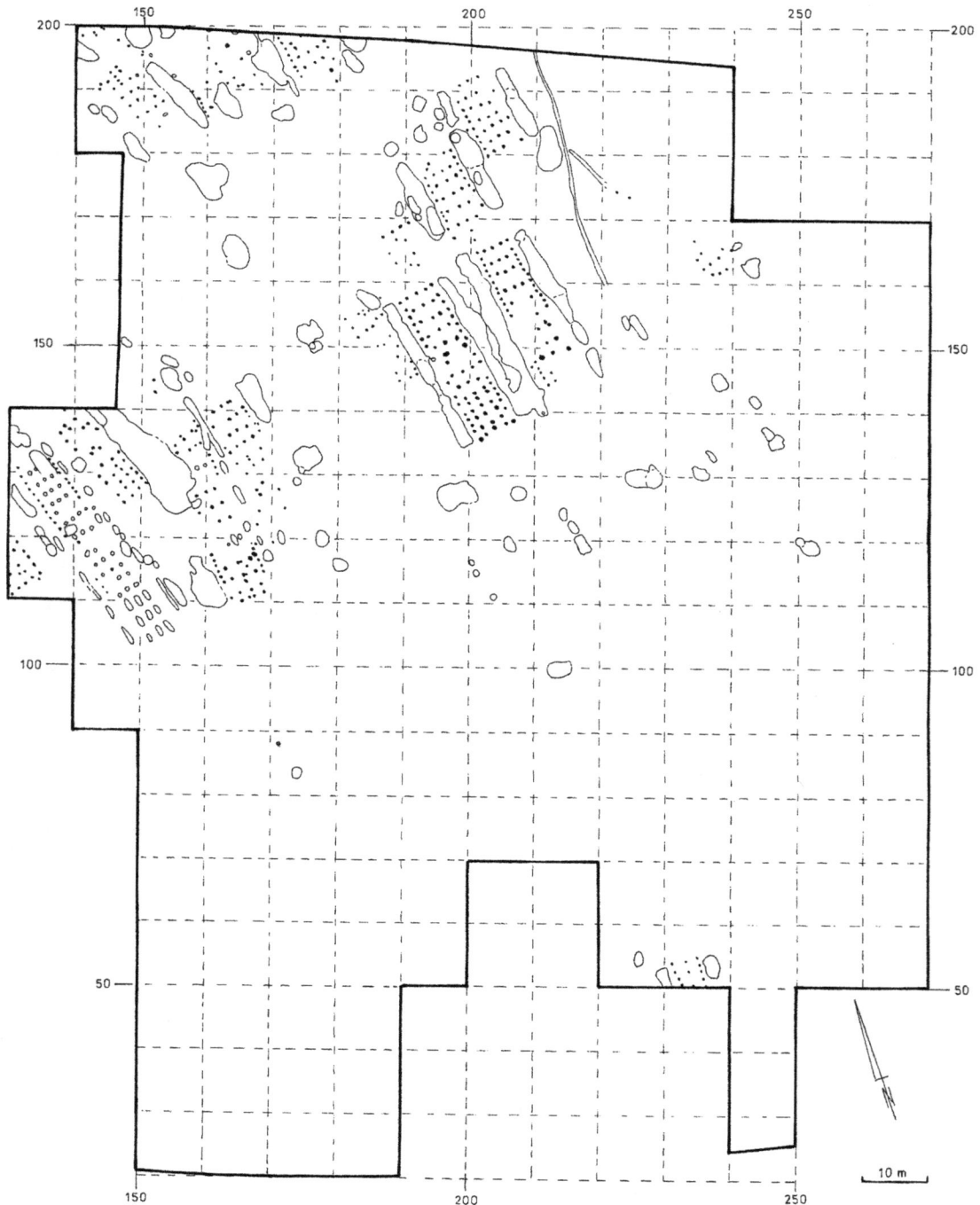

Fig. 5. Brzezie, Site 17, Kłaj commune, Małopolskie voivodship. Location of LBK features within the area excavated in 2000-2004. Drawn by I. Jordan

part was occupied by domestic animals or (according to some authors) served as living-sleeping space. The southern part, occasionally with upper floor supported by double or single densely placed posts, was used as storage. Also the area outside of the house was functionally divided. Its northern part served mainly for stone chipping. We find here also storage pits and hearths. The southern part was related to activates that required using pottery (preparing meals, eating, cleaning the house; Lüning 1982; Modderman 1986; 1988). Each household has its own features required for daily works (*pit complexes*, *pits*, *small pits*). Fea-

tures of other types (*storage pits, ovens, offering pits*) could have been commonly used by several households (Pavlů *et al.* 1986, 360).

Building-up

Within the same domestic sites we find houses of various types and sizes, of various layout and deviation from the main N axis. Such diversity can be observed on all sites, no matter of their chronological position (Fig. 7).

Length of majority of examined construction is between 11 and 27.5 m. Most frequent house length (16 cases)

14

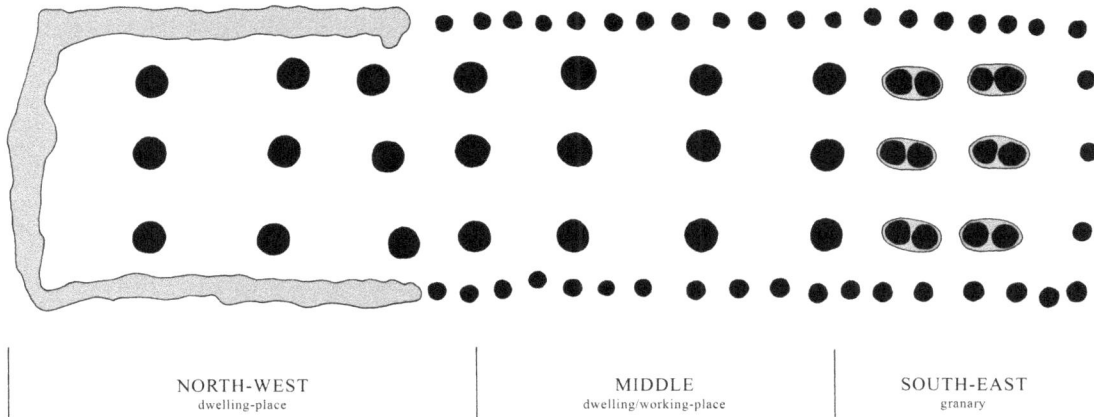

NORTH-WEST
dwelling-place

MIDDLE
dwelling/working-place

SOUTH-EAST
granary

Fig. 6. Possible functional division of LBK house (drawn by I. Jordan after Lüning 1982; Modderman 1988)

was 12–20.5 m, while the average width was 6–6.5 m. The length/with ration of individual houses appear to be accidental. The shortest among analyzed structures was the house from Targowisko 12/13 – 6 m long. The longest house – 43 m long, was registered in Kraków-Olszanica 4. It had also an additional utility space on the second floor.

Precise measuring of the analyzed constructions proves that the rule of the rectangular outlines is not quite correct in relation to LBK houses. On the ground of differences of widths of northern and southern walls three type of house outlines have been distinguished: rectangular, pseudo-rectangular, and slightly trapezoid (Fig. 8). On the first glance all houses seem to be rectangular. Differences between widths of a house measured in its three parts never exceed

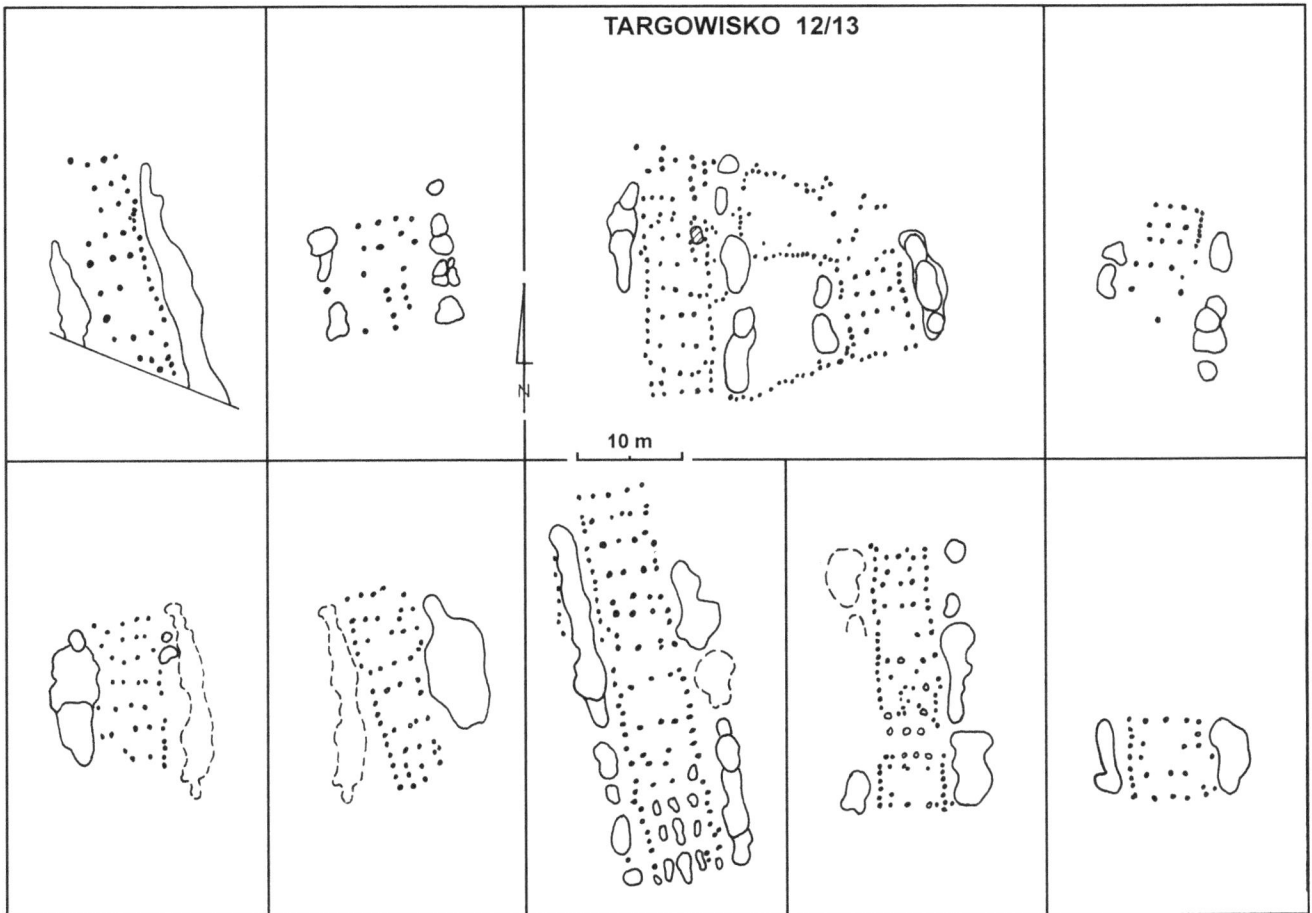

TARGOWISKO 12/13

10 m

Fig. 7. Targowisko, Site 12/13, Kłaj commune. Outlines of analyzed houses. Drawn by E. Osipowa

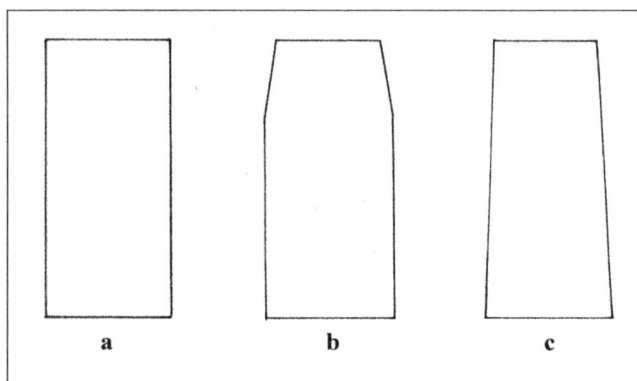

Fig. 8. Types of house outlines distinguished on analyzed sites: **a** – rectangular, **b** – pseudo-rectangular, **c** – quasi-trapezoid (drawn by E. Osipowa after Coudart 1998, fig. 7)

50 cm and – considering the length of the construction – are almost imperceptible. Differentiation of layouts of LBK houses in the upper Vistula basin is by no means exceptional in the whole reach of the culture in question and analogies to them can be found in other parts of Europe (Coudart 1998; Pavlů 2000, 188–190, fig. 6.0.3.a).

Variety of orientation of houses from the N–S axis observed on examined sites is also a wide-spread feature. The most common (observed in 95 houses) is the NW–SE axes,

with various deviations to the north. Much less frequent (7 houses) is the NE–SW orientation. The exact N–S orientation has been observed only twice.

Post structures

On the basis of well preserved postholes we can observe several constructional regularities (Czekaj-Zastawny 2008a). Depth and diameter of holes in separate (five) rows are diversified. Both inner rows of posts, which formed constructional frames of longer walls, were always less interred and smaller then those in three inner rows which served as supports the roof. They were also more liable to destruction. Differences of depths between outer and inner postholes are usually 30–40 cm. Similarly – the diameters of outer holes is smaller then inner the inner holes. Observing examples of postholes in which we can distinguish the post pit and the post proper, we can say that diameter of outer posts was 20–30 cm and diameter of their pits 25–50. Analogous calculations for three inner rows are: 30–60 cm and 50–80 cm (Fig. 9). Houses with a reinforcement in the southern part are slightly different. Besides features described above they have rectangular pits with double posts. They are the biggest and deepest constructional features. On 11 excavated sites there were discovered 8 houses with double posts, always in their southern parts. It is assumed (e.g. Lüning 1982, 16–18; Coudart 1998) that this part of the house needed a reinforcement because of the presence of an additional storey (garret).

Fig. 9. Vertical cross-section of a house with various depths of inner and outer postholes. Elaborated by A. Czekaj-Zastawny, realized by Ł. Wójcik

Houses were constructed on even ground which was cleared of humus. Such a surface can served as a mud floor. It has been confirmed by discoveries from Lower Silesia, where an original utilization floor was registered in two houses of the Stroked Band Pottery culture (Romanow 1977).

Entrance

The analyzed constructions do not give much clue about location of the entrance. Posts of shorter walls are always wider spaced. Northern walls are occasionally built from tightly fitted beams inserted into the foundation groove. On this ground we presume that LBK houses had the entrance in the southern or southeastern part of the house (Modderman 1988, 94). Besides, the presence of constructional pits along longer walls rather excludes any entrance from these sides. Experimental reconstruction of a long house (Modderman 1988) indicates that the southern entrance was optimal due to its exposure to sunshine. This hypothesis is again confirmed by the examples from Lower Silesia, first of all from Strachów (Houses IV and VI; Kulczycka-Leciejewiczowa 1993) and Skoroszowice (House 1; Wojciechowski 1981). Location of the entrance has been also reconstructed on some sites in northern France and Belgium – on the basis of distribution of artifacts interpreted as a household waste (Boiron 2006).

Reparations

It is assumed that LBK houses could survive 25–50 years (Coudart 1998, 61–62) and that throughout their existence they underwent several reparations. An example of it can be found in Brzezie 17, were broken or cracked posts were reinforced by additional well fitted posts (Fig. 10). Replacement of all posts was also feasible, although not conformed by material evidences. Whole walls and roof were probably also subjected to reparations.

Roof construction

We do not possess any more detailed data related to the roof construction. Positioning of posts indicates that the roof, probably of the span type, rested on three rows of posts. The ridge-rafter construction was probably used as a simple and strong base for straw or reed cover. More advanced reconstruction are based on architectural rules and ethnographical analogies (Milisauskas 1986; more detailed Coudart 1998, Chapter 3.1.2, 62–67). They indicate that the sloping angle of the roof was 45° (Soudsky 1969; Modderman 1988, 90–93). All constructional hypotheses find their confirmations in models of Neolithic houses discovered on few sites throughout Europe, which depict and ridge beams. In all cases the roof slope was 45° (Fig. 11).

It appears that roof edges hand over the constructional pits along house walls and were occasionally supported by additional posts. Short rows of such postholes (diameter of 5–20 cm) were discovered in Brzezie 17, Targowisko 12/13, and Zagórze 2. In Brzezie 17 traces of posts were found also on the bottom of the constructional pit. There were also discovered vestiges of a small "annex" attached the western wall of one of the houses – two "columns" (each composed of four posts of diameter of 10–15 cm) between three constructional pits. The "columns" served probably as supports for a roof extension that protected a space outside of the house (Fig. 12).

Buliding material

Building material used for constructing houses can be determined by charcoal particles recovered from postholes and from daub clay fragments.

The analyses indicate that house framed were most often built of oak (data from Kraków-Olszanica, Bylany, Langweiler; Milisauskas 1986; Soudsky & Pavlů 1972). Construction of this kind of wood could survive up to 50 years. Convenient (in the scope of the size of trunk) was also maple, elm, and pine, discovered few sites (e.g. Hienheim and Olszanica). However, their resistance was up to 25 years. On LBK sites there were also discovered remains of birch, alder, ash, linden, poplar, and willow – the wood of the usefulness period not exceeding 12 years (Bakels 1978). It caperers the house frames were built entirely of oak, while other species were used for finishing works and the interior arrangement (e.g. for the plaiting).

Vegetal fragment and their impressions in daub clay indicate that the area between outer posts were filled by plaiting of thin twigs (Bakels 1978) and daubed by loess clay excavated from constructional pits along walls of the house under construction. For the site at Kraków-Olszanica calculations of the capacity these pits were made, in relation to the raw material required for daubing (Milisauskas 1986). They indicate that the amount of loess clay excavated from the pits was sufficient for daubing outer walls 2–2.5 m high with a layer 5–10 cm thick. Composition of constructional daub is often similar to the composition of the paste of thick walled kitchen pottery (admixture of rough chaff; e.g. Brzezie 17). We are not sure, however, if it was an intentional or accidental temper (daubing with clay prepared for pottery production or contamination with chaff from the close vicinity of the pits).

Classification of LBK constructions

For the analyzed sites we can apply a universal classification of LBK constructions worked out by Modderman (1986; 1988). As elsewhere in Europe, we distinguish the following types: 1 – tripartite long house, 2 – middle-size house with double partition, 3 – small house without partition.

Although construction from the upper Vistula basin are compatible with basic types of Modderman (1986; 1988), they reveal a certain specificity in of constructional details. Classification of houses applied in this work is based on Modderman's classification (Fig. 13). However, it does not include typology of the earliest (I) phase of LBK, as no constructional remains from that time have been registered. In relation to the Music Note Phase (II) and the Želiezovce Phase, all three basic Modderman's types are known from the upper Vistula basin. They correspond only with type of houses recognized in Bylany (Modderman 1986, fig. 29).

Concluding, it can be said that the concept of house construction was in LBC constant, despite a certain variability of constructional details. The observed differences are relatively minor, more of less the same on each site, and

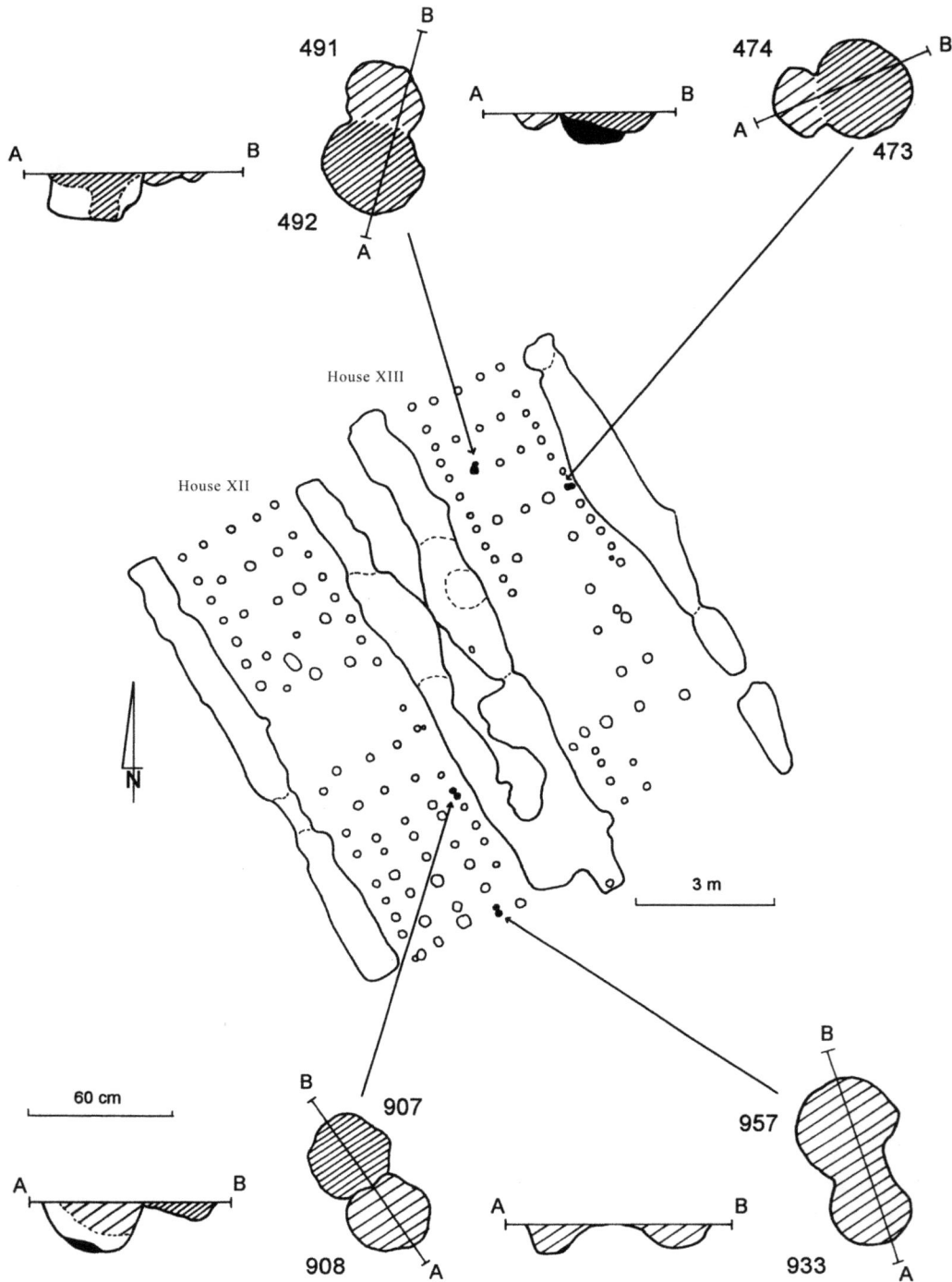

Fig. 10. Examples of reparation of posts from Site 17 at Brzezie, Kłaj commune. Drawn by A. Zastawny

well within the scale of variability in the whole extent of the culture in question. However, we cannot speak about uniformity of all construction types due to observed tendencies typical to specific territories. Constructions from the upper Vistula basin are close to their counterparts from other areas of the same eastern geo-cultural zone of LBK, *i.e.* Lesser Poland, Slovakia, Moravia, Silesia (?), Kuyavia, and – to a certain degree – from the central zone (Bohemia). In relation to the western zone and most of the central zone the differences are bigger.

3.2.2. Camps

The works presents also open camps and cave sites utilized by LBK people. On the research area traces of only 4 unquestionable (confirmed by excavations) open camps have been registered. Interpretation of sites of this type is very difficult, due to their low discoverability and chances of erroneous including into them other remains, e.g. destroyed domestic sites or settlement points.

The analyzed open camps were located in river valleys – on low terraces, close to domestic sites or in a distance of a

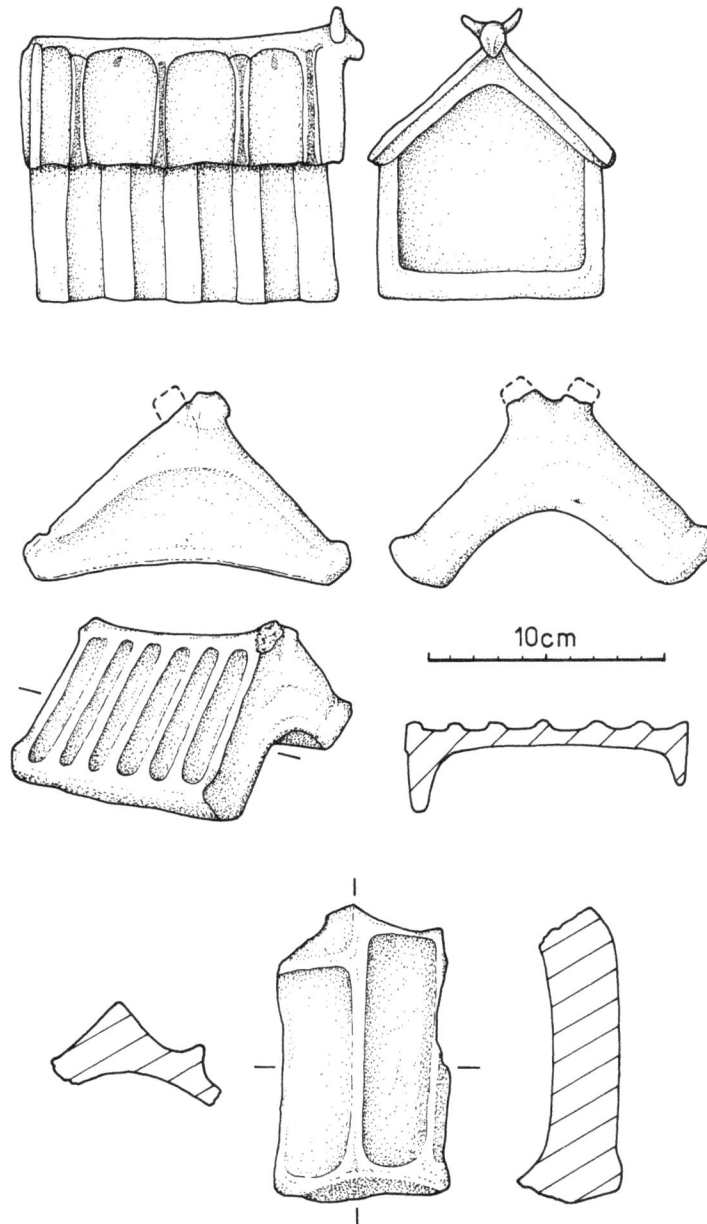

Fig. 11. Neolithic clay models of houses: A – St. Pölten-Galgenleithen, Austria (after Lenneis, Neugebauer-Maresch, Ruttkay 1999, 90-92, abb. 42:3), B – Střelice, Moravia, Czech Republic (after Podborský 1993, 138, obr. 81:16), C – Branč, Slovakia (after Vladár, Lichardus 1968, 323, abb. 74, 75). Drawn by J. Ożóg

few kilometers from them. They are distinctive by specific utilization of space, different than spatial organization of domestic sites. Camps were composed of a few (2–6) features grouped on a restricted area (25–90 sq. m). One of them was a small structure (300–600 × 240–560 cm), partially interred, probably serving for domestic purpose (dug-in dwelling or shack), of rectangular or oval outline, with flat bottom (Fig. 14). Post traces in these pits are probably remains of roof supports. Dwelling structures were accompanied by a few (1–5) small utility features, usually hearths and storage pits. Stratigraphic observations indicate that camps were used several times. Camp of a similar layout, composed of a hut and utility pits, are known also from

other regions of LBK milieu, e. g. in the upper Odra basin (Kulczycka-Leciejewiczowa 1993, 72).

Cave sites of LBK concentrate in the southeastern part of the Cracow-Częstochowa Upland. They are located immediately above valley floors of rivers: Prądnik, Sanka, Kobylanka, Bolechówka, and Kluczwoda. The biggest grouping of them is in the Prądnik valley, where LBK artifacts have been registered in 16 caves (Rook 1980). However, some of them are single finds that testify only a brief presence of man in a cave. Only six cases can be interpreted as places of a seasonal stay. In relation to four other caves (each of them yielded 3 potsherds) a character of human penetration is uncertain. Most abundant with artifacts were

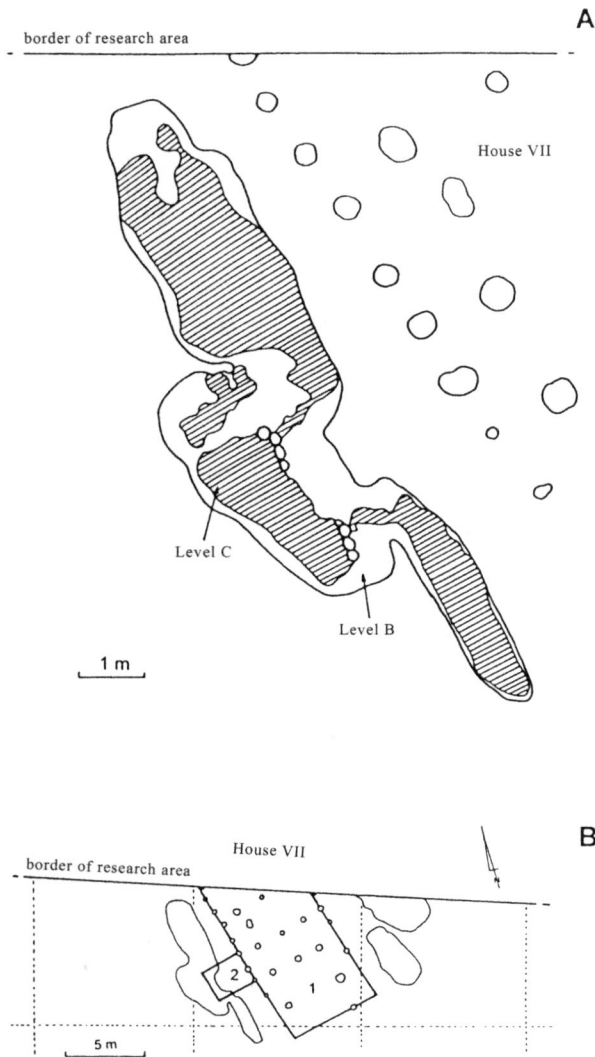

Fig. 12. Brzezie Site 17, Kłaj commune. Traces of an "annex" at the southern part of the western wall of House VII. Drawn by A. Zastawny

caves: Wierzchowska Górna, Maszycka, Górna w Ogrojcu, W Okopach Wielka Dolna, Ciemna-Oborzysko Wielkie, and Pod Słupami.

Spatial organization of camp sites is unknown. In most of caves where LBK materials were found, no observations on distribution or stratigraphy of artifacts have been made (Rook 1980). We can only assume that cave interiors and cave terraces were utilized mainly for burning fires.

Apart from sites presented above, certain settlement points listed in *Catalogue* as site of uncertain affiliation with LBK, might have served as camps. Especially, there are sites located in areas abundant with flint deposits and in between zones of intensive settlement. They have been distinguished by presence on the surface lithic artifacts featuring Early Neolithic characteristics. Some of them may be related to the Lengyel or Malice culture, other possibly indicate the presence of LBK camps located on routes between permanent sites and flint deposits.

Despite a small number of camps examined by excavations it seems probable that in the upper Vistula basin LBK sites of that type represent four categories. These categories do not attempt to classify camps, due very few excavated sites. Instead, they indicate possible multifunction of camps and various circumstances accompanying their appearance:

1) camps set immediately before building a permanent site in placed never settled before – to reconnaissance the area (Site 2 at Zagórze, Niepołomice commune);

2) camps set after the existing permanent site was moves to another place – to continue their economic activities (e.g. on new farming fields; Site 17–20 at Cracow-NH-Pleszów);

3) independent camps existing in places where no permanent site existed either earlier or later – utilized as permanent sites (farming fields or pasture grounds; Site 76 at Bracow-NH-Branice, Site 1 at Jurkowice, Opatów commune);

4) independent camps located between permanent sites and flint deposits – related to exploitation of stone raw material, and cave camps.

3.3. Chronology of Linear Pottery Culture settlement in the upper Vistula basin

Pottery typical for specific LBK chronology-style phases are known in the upper Vistula basin from ca. 20 per cent sites. On this basis it can be concluded that in the area in question there are represented all stages of LBK development recognized in Poland – from Phase Ia through younger part of Phase III-ŽIIb.

LBK sites of recognized relative chronology are distributed in southeastern Poland rather evenly, with the exception less recognized areas. There are known 28 sites with materials of Phase I – Pre-Music Note (12 with pottery of the Gniechowice Style, 16 with pottery of the Zofipole Style). Phases II – Music Note and III – Želiezovce are represented on most of sites (64 and 58 sites respectively).

The earliest developing phase is least represented (28 sites). Settlement points from Gniechowice and Zofipole stages of Phase I are distributed similarly. While they are known from almost whole LBK milieu, majority of them concentrate in the western part of the area of our interest. Materials from Phase Ia reflect strong relations with western Slovak territories. The beginning of the Linear Pottery Culture in the upper Vistula valley corresponds with the Milanovce Phase in Slovakia (Pavúk 2004). Settlement linked with its earliest stage was not intensive and can be interpreted as recognizing and tentative settling new areas. Its distribution indicates that penetration was focused mainly on territories of western Lesser Poland abundant with deposits of siliceous raw material. Later on it spread to the east and northeast. As we have already said, no C14 dates are available for Phase I of LBK in the upper Vistula basin (cf. Brzezie 17, Kłaj commune; Table 1). Therefore it can be presumed that the first developing stage of LBK lasted there about 250–200 years, *i.e. ca.* 5600–5400 BC.

On the territory of our interest most frequent is settlement from the Music Note Phase (64 sites). In contrast to the previous phase, we find Music Note materials in every settlement concentration in quantity corresponding with settlement concentration in a given area. Sites appear also on

Table 1. Radiocarbon dates from sites in the upper Vistula basin

BRZEZIE 17, KŁAJ COMMUNITY (after Czekaj-Zastawny 1008a)			
LABORATORY	**DATE**	**CALIBRATION** (after Ramsey 2005)	**SAMPLE**
Ki-9343	6230 ± 100 BP	5310-5050 BC (68.2%)	feature 90/B
Ki-9344	6155 ± 100 BP	5220-4960 BC (68.2%)	feature 1/B3
Ki-9345	6410 ± 100 BP	5480-5300 BC (68.2%)	feature 1
Ki-9346	6330 ± 100 BP	5470-5400 BC (12.6%) 5390-5210 BC (55.6%)	feature 1
Ki-11286	6215 ± 80 BP	5300-5240 BC (16.1%) 5230-5190 BC (11.7%) 5180-5060 BC (40.4%)	feature 238/C
Ki-11287	6180 ± 80 BP	5230-5010 BC (68.2%)	feature 238/C
Ki-11288	6130 ± 80 BP	5210-4980 BC (68.2%)	feature 317/B
Ki-11289	5830 ± 80 BP	4790-4590 BC (68.2%)	feature 499/B
Ki-11290	5780 ± 70 BP	4710-4540 BC (68.2%)	feature 158/B
Ki-11291	6140 ± 80 BP	5210-4990 BC (68.2%)	feature 238/C
Ki-11292	5840 ± 70 BP	4790-4610 BC (68.2%)	feature 317/B
Ki-11293	5720 ± 80 BP	4690-4480 BC (66.7%)	feature 238/B
Ki-11295	5640 ± 80 BP	4550-4360 BC (68.2%)	feature 216/B
Ki-11296	6190 ± 70 BP	5230-5040 BC (66.9%)	feature 377/A
Ki-11297	5660 ± 80 BP	4590-4440 BC (53.3%) 4430-4370 BC (14.9%)	feature 238/C
Ki-11298	6260 ± 80 BP	5320-5200 BC (44.5%) 5170-5070 BC (23.7%)	feature 317/B

KRAKÓW OLSZANICA 4 (after Milisauskas 1986)			
LABORATORY	**DATE**	**CALIBRATION** (after Ramsey 2005)	**SAMPLE**
M-2314	6700 ± 220 BP	5850-5460 BC (66.1%)	feature 12-69-D1
GrN-5384	6430 ± 75 BP	5480-5340 BC (68.2%)	feature 2-67-B1
M-2011	6300 ± 400 BP	5650-4750 BC (68.2%)	feature 1-67-B1 and 6-67-B1
M-2165	6150 ± 210 BP	5320-4830 BC (68.2%)	feature 1-68-B1
GX-2639	6095 ± 350 BP	5400-4600 BC (68.2%)	feature 10a-68-B1
M-1986	6020 ± 220 BP	5250-4650 BC (68.2%)	feature 1-67-B1
GX-2638	6000 ± 340 BP	5300-4500 BC (68.2%)	feature 57-68-B1
M-2320	5800 ± 210 BP	4950-4400 BC (68.2%)	feature 1-69-D1
GX-2640	5025 ± 260 BP	4250-3500 BC (68.2%)	feature 21-71-C1

areas previously not settled by the Linear Pottery culture. In that period LBK settlement in upper Vistula basin reached a maximal extent – Music Note materials are known from settlement points of most extreme areas of LBK milieu. The dates for that phase (*cf.* Table 1) indicate that the Classic Phase lasted about 300–350 years.

The next stage of LBK colonization in the upper Vistula basin is linked with the Želiezovce Phase. It is known from 58 sites. In contrast to the Music Note Phase that comprised the whole region in question, the settlement of the Želiezovce Phase is zonal and its settlement point do not extend

beyond the San River. Most of discovered sites are dated to the beginning of the Phase (ŽI) and to its developed stage (ŽIIA). On 11 sites there were discovered materials related the final stage of the Želiezovce Phase, *i.e.* ŽIIB. The youngest dates of the phase in questions are about 4700–4550 BC.

Number of Music Note and Želiezovce sites indicates that after the most intensive LBK settlement was during the Classic Phase and after that period it gradually diminished. Sites from Sub-Phase ŽIIB are less frequent than from early periods of LBK. Moreover, they yielded only a few pot-

Table 1. continued

KRAKÓW PLESZÓW 17 (after Godłowska *et al.*, 1987)			
PALYNOLOGICAL SETTLEMENT PHASE	**LBK CHRONOL. PHASES**	**DATE**	**CALIBRATION** (after Ramsey 2005)
II	Želiezovce	5905 ± 40 BP 5910 ± 40 BP 5985 ± 50 BP	4830-4810 BC (6.8%) 4800-4720 BC (61.4%) 4830-4720 BC (68.2%) 4940-4800 BC (68.2%)
I	Music Note	(earlier than) 6075 ± 40 BP 6255 ± 40 BP 6050 ± 40 BP	(earlier than) 5050-4930 BC (68.2%) 5300-5210 BC (68.2%) 5010-4890 BC (63.4%)

ŁONIOWA 8, DĘBNO COMMUNITY (after Valde-Nowak 2008a; 2008a)			
LABORATORY	**DATE**	**CALIBRATION** (after Ramsey 2005)	**SAMPLE**
Poz-15982ŁO-4	6230±40 BP	6300-5200 BC (45.1%) 5170-5070 BC (23.1%)	feature 111
Poz-15981ŁO-3	6340±40 BP	5370-5290 (91.2%)	feature 88
Poz-15979ŁO-2	6220±40 BP	5170-5070 (44.6%) 5230-5200 (13.0%) 5300-5260 BC (10.6%)	feature 23

ZWIĘCZYCA 3, BOGUCHWAŁA COMMUNITY (after Dębiec & Dzbyński 2007)			
LABOLATORY	**DATE**	**CALIBRATION** (after Ramsey 2005)	**SAMPLE**
Poz - 16475	6240±40 BP	5310-5200 BC (60.2%) 5150-5120 BC (4.1%) 5100-5080 BC (3.9%)	feature 36
Poz - 16477	6170±40 BP	5180-5060 BC (62.0%)	feature 36
Poz - 16478	6960± 60 BP	5900-5750 BC (68.2%)	feature 85
Poz - 16479	6070± 40 BP	5050-4930 BC (67.3%)	feature 116

ŻERKÓW 1, GNOJNIK COMMUNITY (after Valde-Nowak 2007)			
LABOLATORY	**DATE**	**CALIBRATION** (after Ramsey 2005)	**SAMPLE**
Poz-18662	6210 ± 40 BP	5180-5060 (56.3%) 5230-5190 (11.9%)	feature 21/06

sherds. Interesting is a certain increase of sites with long houses during the Želiezovce Phase. It suggests that small settlement points were being gradually replaced by bigger domestic sites.

As so-far no materials related to Sub-Phase ŽIII and to the Proto-Lengyel horizon (intermediate between LBK and the Lengyel culture in the Carpathian Basin) have been discovered. It seems that during that period there was in the upper Vistula basin a certain settlement gap (Kaczanowska 1990, 71–97).

On the entire research area the widest chronological span can be observed on settlement sites dated from IA to ŽIIB. Examples of settlements from various stages of LBK are also visible on sites of other types, i.e. seasonal camps and settlement traces (*cf. Catalogue*). Among open camps there are single sites dated to consecutives chronological phases of LBK, *i.e.* to the Pre-Music Note, Music Note, and Želiezovce, and one dated to the turn of the Music Note and Želiezovce Phases. Occupation of caves is also a feature of the whole development of the culture in question, starting from its earliest stage (I). Pottery of the Gniechowice Style has been found in two caves – that of the Music Note Phase also in two caves, while potsherds from the Želiezovce Phase are known from five caves. There are also a few finds of pottery with characteristic ornamentation in context of settlement traces – single fragments dated from the Pre-

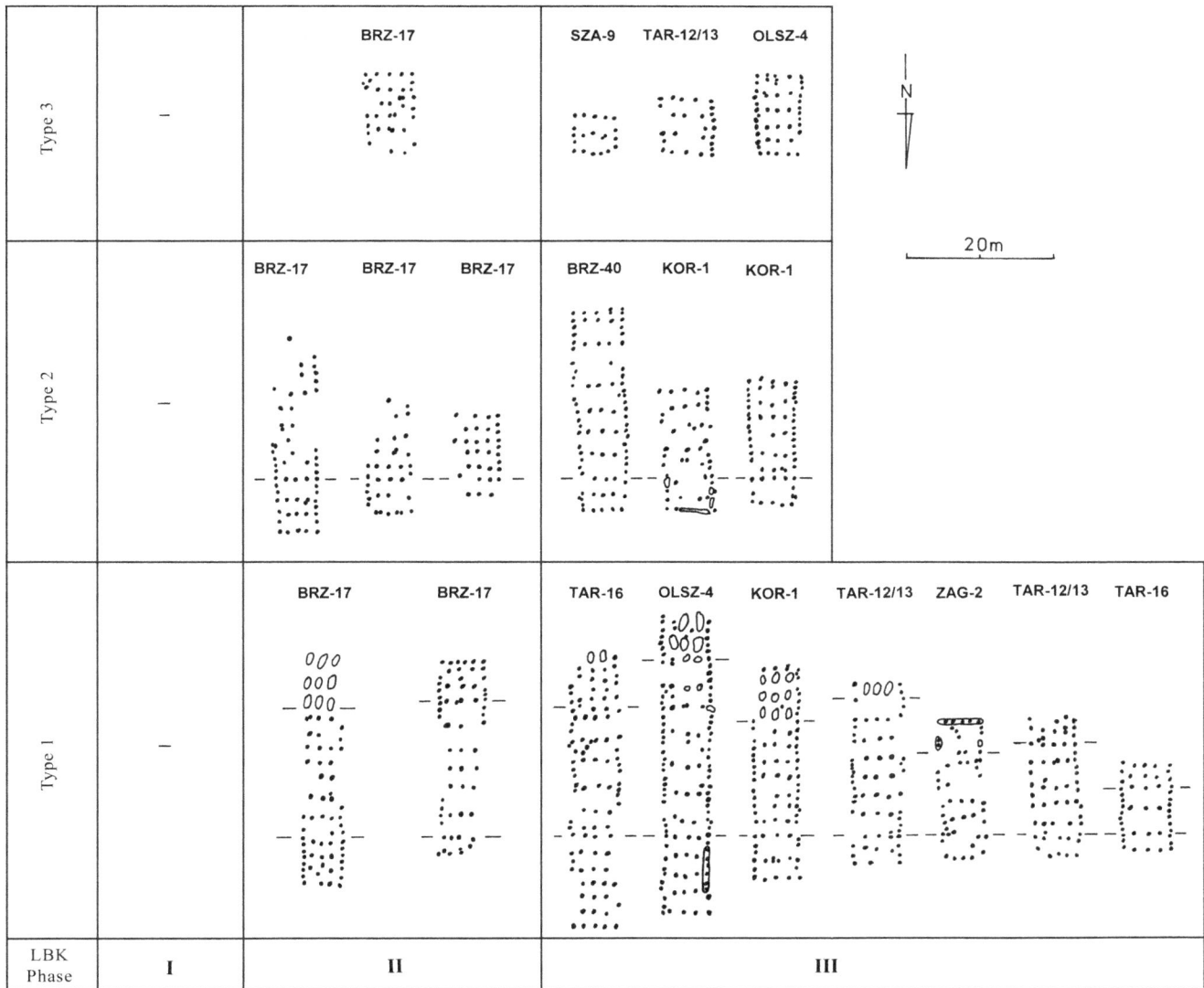

Fig. 13. Typology of outlines LBK houses A. Czekaj-Zastawny for upper Vistula basin (Czekaj-Zastawny 2008a). Drawn by E. Osipowa

Music Note and Music Note Phases, and two fragments from the Želiezovce Phase.

3.4. Linear Pottery Culture settlement in the upper Vistula basin and other settlement centers

Our studies clearly indicate that – on the background of major LBK regions in the western part of its extent, e.g. in the lower basin of Rhine (Lüning 1982) and the upper basin of Danube (Reinecke 1982), its settlement on upper Vistula is not less intensive – in the scope of density of sites, their character, function, layouts, and chronological span. The only observed difference is lack (as so-far) separate burial grounds accompanying big domestic sites.

Excavations of last forty years, especially on the Cracow section of Freeway A4 under construction, revealed the presence several settlement microregions with domestic sites with houses of the post construction. At present we can name a few dozens such sites, the most important being: Olszanica 4, Kraków-NH-Mogiła 62, Kraków-Górka Narodowa 9, Łoniowa 18, Gwoździec 2, Brzezie 17 and 40,

Szarów 9, Targowisko 11, 12/13, 14, 16, Zagórze 2, and also Kormanice 1 and 2, Łańcut 3, Olchowa 20, Rzeszów Staromieście 3, Rzeszów Piastów 16, Rzeszów WSK 34, and Albigowa 38. In the regional scale one of the most important results of this research is confirming basin the presence in the right-hand upper Vistula basin the developed settlement of the Linear Pottery Culture, comparable with that recognized on the left bank of the river.

The already mentioned concentration of settlement points near Brzezie, Targowisko, and Zagórze is comparable with the concentration in the valley of the Merzbach River (sites: Langweiler 2, 3, 8, 9, 16, and Niedermerz 4) on loess areas of the lower Rhine basin (Lüning 1982). It was composed of domestic areas of various sizes with post houses (Fig. 15). Sites on the right bank of the Vistula River are grouped between Zakrzowiec and Targowisko (valley of the Tusznica, tributary to Raba) in a distinctive microregional concentration of sites of various sizes (Fig. 16). However, it is much bigger – the Merzbach microregion is only 2.5 km long, while the Tusznica microregion extents

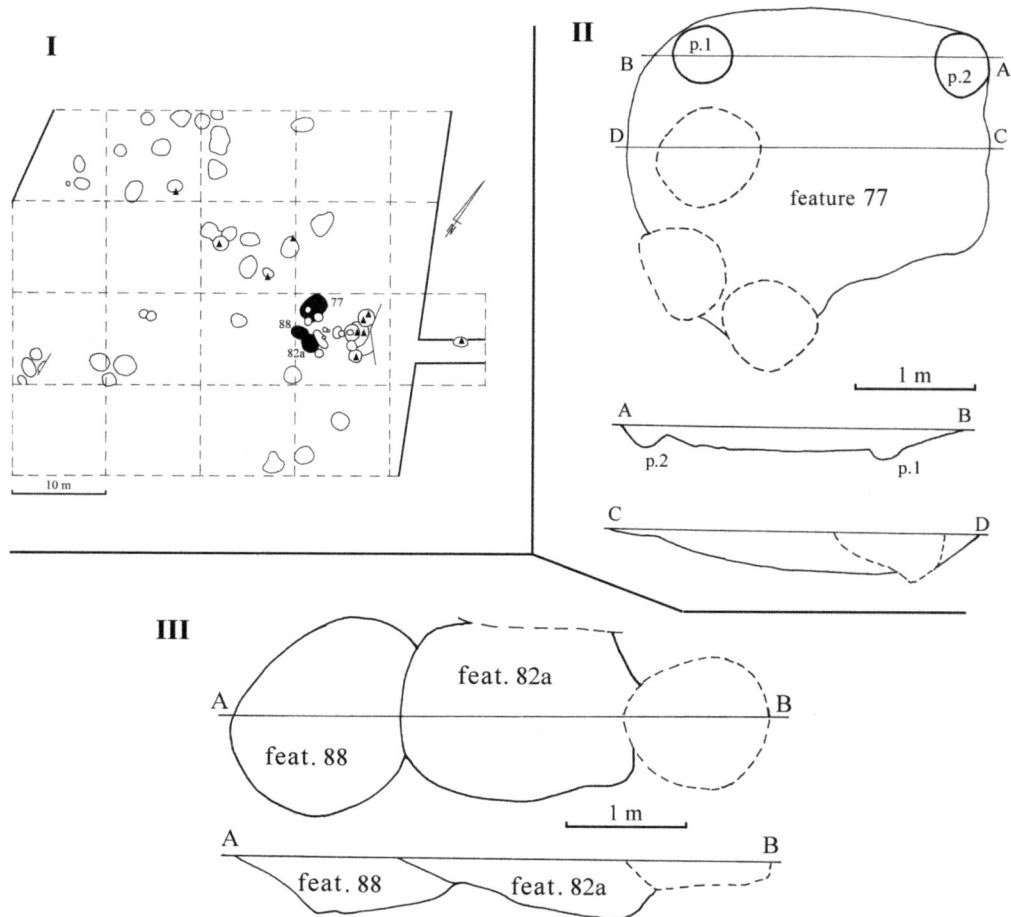

Fig. 14. Kraków-NH-Branice, Site 76. LBK camp: I – location of features and single pottery fragments, II – horizontal layout and cross-sections of feature 77, III – horizontal layout and cross-sections of features 88 and 82a (drawn by I. Jordan after Godłowska 1986)

up to 9 km. It determines not only the amount of settlement points, but also distances between sites. The latter concentration is composed of 12 domestic sites separated one from another by a distance of 200–1800 m, while the concentration on the Merzbach River includes 7 such sites spread by 100 to 300 m. Specific for the Merzbach region is the presence of fortified places and separate burial grounds, unknown on the right bank of the Vistula River. From the latter area we have only individual feature that can be tentatively interpreted as burials.

Site 17 at Brzezie yielded an exceptional construction – a palisade fragment. It was discovered near the site limits – remains of houses do not extend beyond that line (cf. Fig. 5). We are not sure if it was originally built in specific places only or rather encircled the whole site. Also the function of the palisade remains not obvious, as it the first construction of that type discovered on Polish territories. Moreover, it has not many analogies in LBK milieu outside of Poland. Examples of encircling sites by palisades of moats can be found in Lower Austria – Asparn/Schletz (Lenneis 2001), in Belgium – Darion (Keeley & Cahen 1989), in Baden-Wirtemberg – Vaihingen an der Enz (Krause 1999). It has been assumed that fortifications built within sites or in their vicinity are typical for northwestern

zones of LBK. While elements described as defenses (Kruk & Milisauskas 1999, 39; there further references) are being interpreted as refuges, functions of palisades or moats around sites are unclear. These constructions were not very solid (e.g. single-line palisade of wide-spaced posts). They might have served as enclosures to separate domestic animals (inside) from wild animals (outside), or perhaps they protected fields close to houses from animals (Modderman 1988, 102–103).

The other elements and the building system of permanent settlement sites recognized in the upper Vistula basin are the same as elsewhere in LBK. Typical is a general orientation of households (N–S with various deviation to NW–SE) and layouts of houses maintaining appropriate spacing (radius of about 25 around houses) necessary for household activities. As a rule domestic sites were long uses. It is reflected by several (dozen or so) building phases and significant "shifting" of built-us areas with the site (cf. in Bohemia – Bylany, in Slovakia – Štúrovo, in Poland – Kraków-Olszanica, Brzezie, in Germany – sites in the Merzbach River valley, in Austria – Neckenmarkt, Strögen; Pavlů 2000; Pavúk 1994; Milisauskas 1986; Lüning 1982; Lenneis 2001). Similar are also types and functions of utility features within individual households and those com-

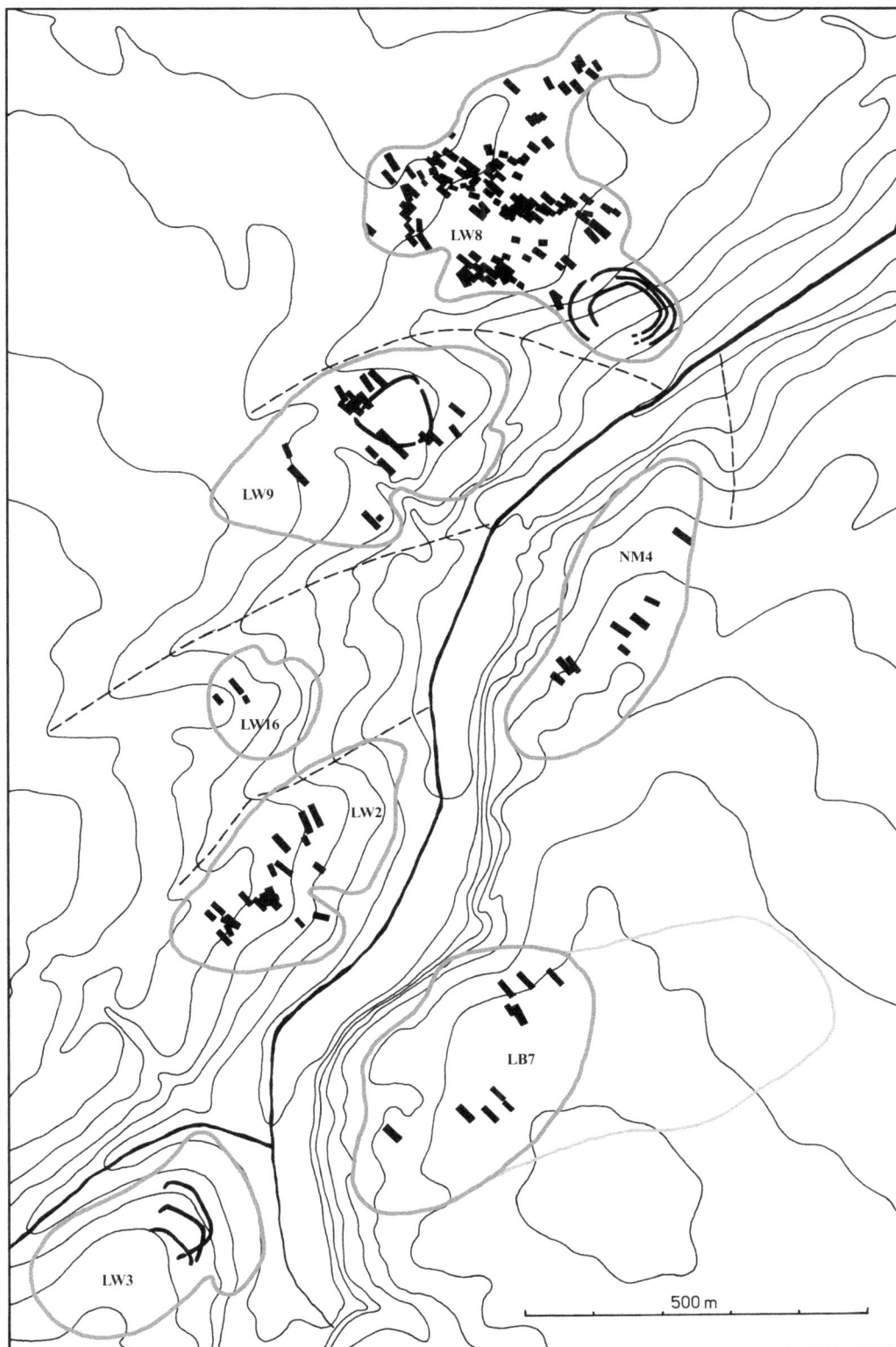

Fig. 15. Valley of the Merzbach River. Concentration of LBK settlements with long post houses (drawn J. Ożóg after Lüning 1982)

monly used by inhabitants of the site. Wells, known from several LBK sites (e.g. from Rhineland – Erkelenz-Kuckhoven, and Austria – Asparn; Kruk & Milisauskas 1999, 27) have not been so-far discovered in the upper Vistula basin.

Typology of post houses elaborated by Modderman (1986; 1988) is also applicable to the area of our interest, with only minor corrections related to specific local conditions. Typical are layouts of houses close to rectangular – pseudo-rectangular or slightly trapezoid. Analogical diver-

Fig. 16. Valley of the Tusznica River. Concentration of LBK settlements with long post houses (sites on Freeway A4 under construction, research 2000-2004). Drawn by A. Zastawny

sification in the whole LBK milieu has been observed by A. Coudart (1998). Only one examined house (on Site 17 at Brzezie, Kłaj commune) is not compatible with building rules of the Linear Pottery Culture. In this case we have vestiges of the construction composed of only three rows of posts. The house from Brzezie 17 has no analogies in whole LBK.

No LBK house dated to Phase I has been discovered in the upper Vistula basin. An attempt to reconstruct such a house was undertaken on Site at Stary Zamek in Silesia on the basis of near-house constructional pits (Kulczyka-Leciejewiczowa 1988, fig. 6). It was the so-called house with penthouses, close to Type 1 of Phase I of Modderman according to the Bylany typology (Modderman 1986, fig. 29) and to Type Ib of the same author according to Dutch typology (Modderman 1986, fig. 28). House from the Site at Stary Zamek was a typical 5-row structure, but had also additional rows of outer posts (one on the N side and one on the S side) set in narrow holes along the walls. These posts supported "penthouses". It cannot be determined if the

Fig. 17. View of a completed house of LBK. Reconstruction on the bases of data obtained from Site 17 at Brzezie, Kłaj commune. Elaborated by A. Czekaj-Zastawny, realized by Ł. Wójcik

house belonged to variant of the "Y" construction, recognized as typical for that period in the western part of the LBK extent (Modderman 1988, 98).

Constructions from younger phases (Music Note and Želiezovce; Fig. 17) in the upper Vistula basin correspond with Modderman's classification. We have here all three types of houses – long, medium, and small. However, detailed analyses indicate that they are compatible only with the classification elaborated for Bylany (Modderman 1986, fig. 29). On sites from the Music Note Phase no house with foundation groove in the northern part has been discovered. This feature is typical for the western extent of LBK (typology for Holland; Modderman 1986, fig. 28). Only few examples of such houses are known from the Želiezovce Phase. Construction with encircling groove (Type 1a; Modderman 1988), appearing in Holland in earlier and younger phases, have not been registered on the area of our research.

It should be noticed that types of houses in the upper Vistula basin do not differ from analogues construction from other parts of Poland, *i.e.* Kuyavia and Lower Silesia (Czerniak 1994; Kulczycka-Leciejewiczowa 1993; 1997; Zych 2002; Pyzel 2006).

As elsewhere, LBK settlement points in the upper Vistula basin are grouped on loess soils, the most fertile in a give region. This tendency has been confirmed on almost all well examined areas of LBK extent. Analyses of that kind have been done for territories of Austria (77.97% of LBK sites are on loess soils; Lenneis 2001) and southwestern Germany (85–100%; Sielmann 1971). Similar is the situation in the upper Odra basin, where sites locate mainly on brown and dusty soils developed on loess and loess-like sediments (Kulczycka-Leciejewiczowa 1993, table 4), and in the European Lowland (on black, gray, and brown soils; Kruk & Milisauskas 1999, 25; Pyzel 2006). Also in other European regions we found a specific relations between site location and soils (upper Elbe – *ca.* 50% sites on loess soils, middle Elbe – *ca.* 90%, Sollau – *ca.* 70%, Men, Rhine – *ca.* 90%, upper Danube – *ca.* 95%, middle Danube – *ca.* 70%; after Kulczycka-Leciejewiczowa 1993, fig. 10). Utilization of best soils has been observed also in northwestern Poland (Wiślański 1969), where LBK sites are mainly on black soils, brown soils, and podsols developed on dusty sediments of alluvial origin. On areas with prevailing sandy soils settlement points are registered only sporadically and always close to minor more fertile patches (fen soils, dehydrated soils, *etc.*; Wiślański 1969, 63–64, table III).

Selection of convenient topographic location for settlement also followed similar criteria. Sites were located almost exclusively in river valley, most often low – on low terraces and on valley borders, where multi-specious de-

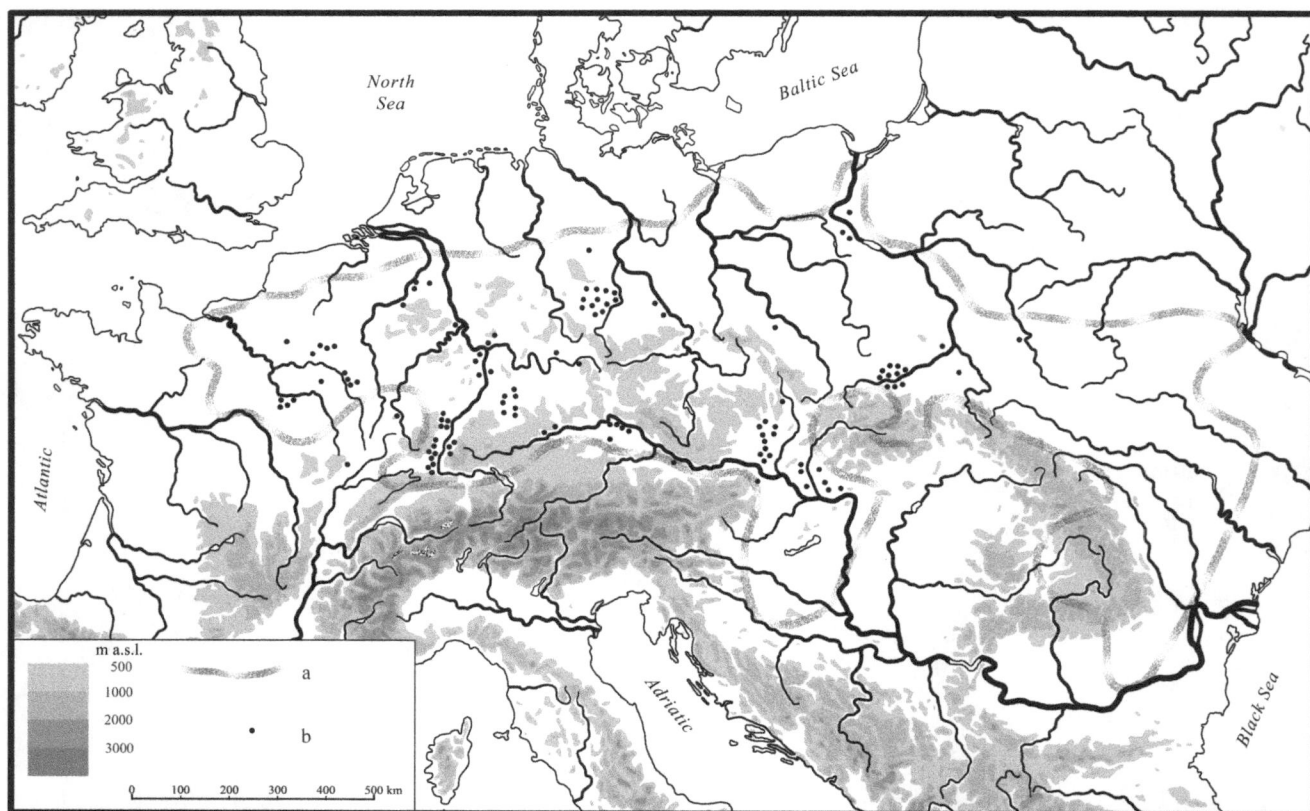

Fig. 18. Location of the most important sites with LBK graves in Europe: a – maximal extent of LBK; b - LBK sites witch graves. Drawn by A. Zastawny (after Jeunesse 1997, complemented by the author)

ciduous forests prevailed. Preferred were places with easy access to water, in a distance no bigger than 500 m from the river. Confirmation of such preferences can be found in many areas occupied by LBK (Sielman 1971; Howel 1983; Rulf 1983; Lüning 2000), even on the European Lowland, where topographic forms are less developed than on uplands. For example, in northwestern Poland LBK sites are usually located in lower parts of low terraces of bigger river valleys (53.33%), then on elevated places over bogs and streams without developed valleys (33.33%). Much more settlement points (11.66%) can be found on edges of bigger valleys and high lake shores. Exceptional (1.66%) is location on inclinations and edges of small valley and lake shores (Wiślański 1969, table II).

As a conclusion of the discussion on settlement preference of LBK people we can revoke the statement of A. Kulczycka-Leciejewiczowa (1993) that the most convenient for Early Neolithic settlers were areas of natural environment with multi-specious deciduous forests (with oak and linden). Such a habitat reflected environmental conditions that "revealed its value for settlement purpose" (Kulczycka-Leciejewiczowa 1993, 49).

4. FUNERARY RITE OF THE LINEAR POTTERY CULTURE

From the whole territory encompasses in the period between the mid of the 6th till the mid of the 5th cent. BC by

the LBK settlement – from the Paris Basin to Volhynia, there are known a few thousands of settlement points of the culture in question. Burial were discovered on about 100 sites (Fig. 18). There are individual graves and vast burial ground containing up to 300 graves (e.g. Wandersleben in central Germany – 311 graves; Jeunesse 1997, 152). A total, more then 2500 graves LBK are known.

In comparison with funerary sites from Central and Western Europe, burials of the Linear Pottery Culture in Poland are very infrequent. Until recently there were known only individual graves or very small concentrations of them, located within settlement sites or on their outskirts. The excavations of 2008 change considerably this picture, as the first in Poland LBK cemetery was discovered. From loess uplands of Lesser Poland (were the majority of LBK funerary objects are located), a few well recognized settlement centers of this culture have been recognized (Czekaj-Zastawny 2008a). Yet, the number of graves is relatively very small. On the whole territory of southeastern Poland graves of the Linear Pottery Culture are known from 13 sites only (Fig. 19). They are: Aleksandrowice (3 graves), Brzezie (3 graves), Łoniowa (1 grave), Modlniczka (38 cremation graves), Olchowa (1 grave), Samborzec (5 graves), Szczotkowice (1 grave), and Targowisko (1 grave). All grave listed above have been discovered in last 40 years. The richest of them (from Szczotkowice) was discovered accidentally in 1961 during a road construction. In last few years graves at Aleksandrowice, Brzezie, Targowisko,

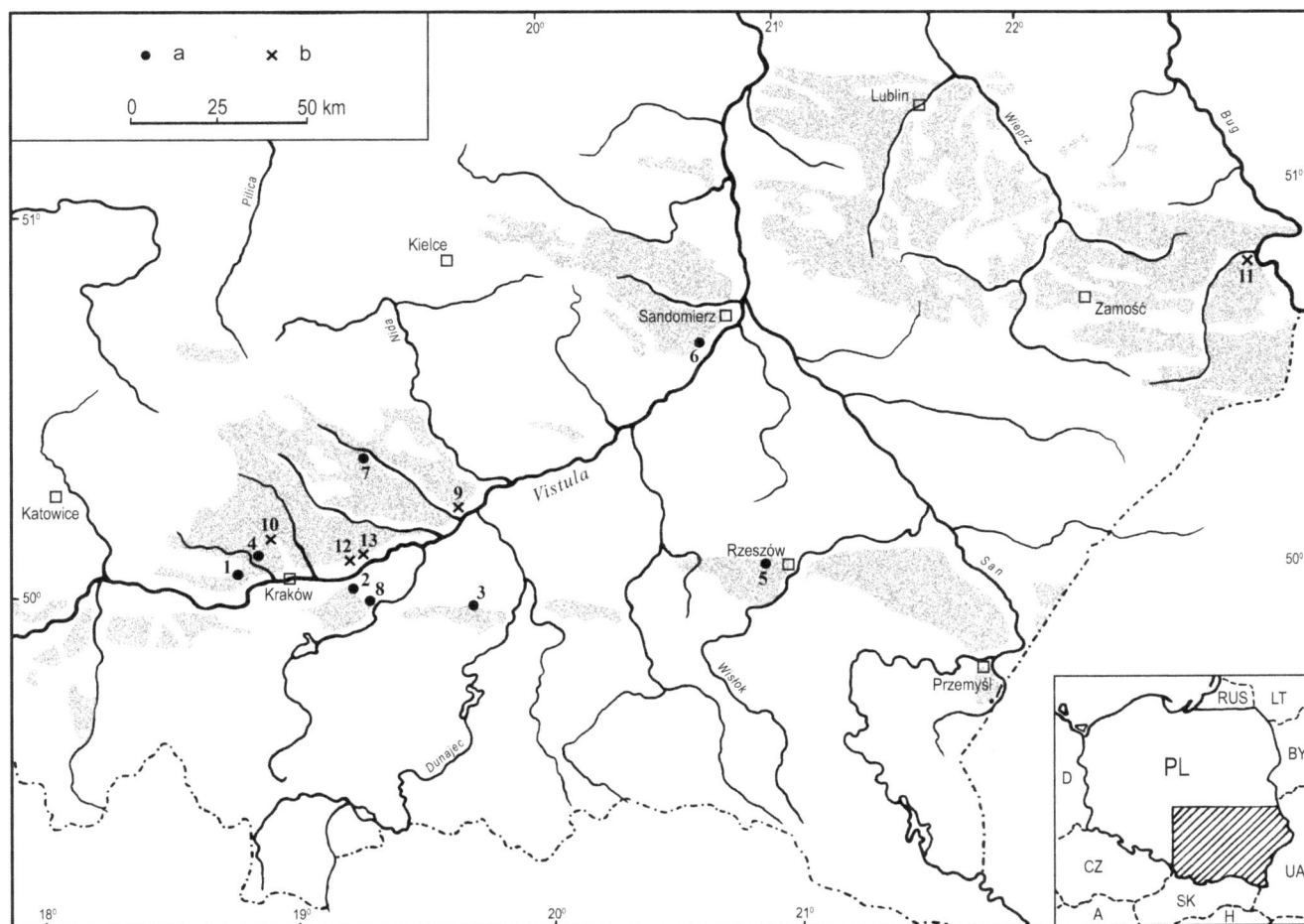

Fig. 19. Map of funerary sites of the Linear Pottery Culture in southeastern Poland: a – graves; b – presumable graves; 1 – Aleksandrowice, Site. 2, 2 – Brzezie, Site 17, 3 – Łoniowa, Site 18, 4 – Modlniczka, Site 2, 5 – Olchowa, Site 20, 6 – Samborzec, Site 1, 7 – Szczotkowice, Site 1, 8 – Targowisko, Site 16, 9 – Bejsce, 10 – Giebułtów, Site 1, 11 – Gródek, Site 2, 12 – Igołomia, Site 1, 13 – Złotniki, Site 1. Drawn by I. Jordan

Olchowa, and Łoniowa were discovered. The most recent find (2008) is that from Modlniczka.

4.1. Context and location of funerary finds

In the whole LBK milieu three type of location of grave in relation to the settlement sites have been distinguished (Jeunesse 1997, 43–44): cemeteries proper (Type 1), individual burials on settlement sites (Type 2), and small grave concentrations within a settlement site or on its outskirts (Type 3). Burials can be also found in a not typical context, e.g. in ditches encircling settlement sites and in caves.

Among Polish LBK funerary sites one falls into Type 1 and several into Type 2. Many sites, due to an inadequate state of research, can be classified as belonging either to Type 3 or to Type 1.

We can positively determine the funeral context of following sites: Modlniczka (Type 1), Łoniowa, Olchowa, Samborzec, Targowisko, Igołomia-Zofipole (Type 2), and Brzezie (Type 3). In other cases multiple interoperations are possible (Aleksandrowie and Giebułtów – Type 1 or 3; Szczotkowice, Bejce, Gródek, and Złotniki – type unknown).

Type 1, exceptional in Poland, is known only from one site – Modlniczka. It is a cemetery located in a low part of the valley of a local creel valley – wet and covered by alluvial sediments, a few hundred meters from a settlement site (located on the upper terrace). On the site in question, 38 cremation graves of LBK were spread on the area of a few hundred ares, without any distinctive concentration. A few burials were also discovered in a ditch running across the site (Czekaj-Zastawny et al. in press).

Type 2 – individual graves within a site, has been registered in Łoniowa, Olchowa, Samborzec, Targowisko, and Igołomia-Zofipole. The context of graves from Brzezie is also unquestionable. They fall into Type 3, i.e. small concentrations of burials related to a settlement site, located within it or on its outskirt. In Brzezie the burials were spread on the excavated area of 5.5 hectares. In this case, the research positively delimited the southwestern, southern, and southeastern parts of the site. Three burials were located at its southeastern borders, outside the zone of houses and utility structures. They had almost the same orientation and outlines typical for grave pits.

The location of the grave from Łoniowa – in relation to a nearby post house – is very interesting. According to the excavator of the site (Valde-Nowak 2008a, 51–54) the grave and the house are contemporaneous. This observation, first of that kind, is very significant of the analysis of the LBK domestic architecture. Certain similarities to the situation observed in Łoniowa can be found on sites Brzezie 17 and 40, and in Targowisko 12/13, presently being worked out. On both sites at Brzezie a few pits – similar to that from Łoniowa but without artifacts – were discovered within long houses. In Targowisko, a grave located in a house (in its central part, at the eastern wall) was discovered. It is probably contemporary with the house but this hypothesis should be confirmed by future detailed analyses.

The more precise interpretation of burials within the settlement sites presented above is at present impossible due to incomplete analyses of the recovered materials. Assuming that domestic features co-existed with graves, we can only describe only the spatial relations between them. In the case of locations of Type 2 (individual graves with settlement sites), burial can be usually found near the houses, very close to the constructional pits.

Topographic location of the described funerary sites (with the exception of Modlniczka) is typical for LBK settlement on the area of our interest (Kruk 1973; Czekaj-Zastawny 2008a, 104–107). In this respect there are no differences between sites with and without burials. Almost all analyzed sites are located on slopes or flats of low terraces of water courses. They can be also found on promontories at outlets of creeks into bigger rivers (Aleksandrowice, Olchowa), on rounded edges of river terraces (Szczotkowice, Gródek, Złotniki, Igołomia-Zofipole) and on flats near creeks (Brzezie). The location of the site at Samborzec is slightly different – on a highland slope, close to the outlet of a small river to the Vistula. The site at Łoniowa is exceptional due to its quasi-mountainous location – in the uppermost part of the Dunajec valley, near a water divider. It has no analogies in the whole LBK milieu in the upper Vistula region.

4.2. Construction and types of graves

Excavations on several sepulchral sites testify about a biritual character of graves of the Linear pottery culture, with inhumations prevailing over cremations. However, in some region both rituals appear in the same frequency, no matter of the developing phase of the culture in question. In southeastern Poland the presence of inhumation and cremation graves on the same site has not been confirmed. The only cremation burial discovered during older excavation (from Gródek on Bug river; describes as a "possible of LBK") was found on an Early Medieval settlement site, beneath of settlement pit, on the depth of 148–150 cm. In this case burnt bones and LBK potsherds rested in the untouched sediments and no outline of a grave pit was visible (Kempisty 1962, 284–285). The already mentioned cemetery at Modlniczka contained 38 cremation burials in round pits of diameters up to 40 cm (Czekaj-Zastawny et al. in press). Among 27 graves identified as "inhumations", 12 did not contained human remains. Absence of bones can be explained by high soil acidity, although a case of symbolic burials cannot be excluded. The latter appear sporadically in LBK – in Germany, Denmark, and in Slovakia. From

Aiterhofen, Bavaria, 36 cenotaphs are known, 10 of them with grave goods (Nieszery 1995; Jeunesse 1997, 62).

Double and multiple graves are very rare in the whole extent of LBK (e.g. a few double graves from Aiterhofen and 2 triple graves from Nitra). On the area of our interest all graves with preserved human remains are single burials in purposely dug pits. Burials in utility pits have not been registered, although in two cases (Olchowa and Złotniki) grave pits were located within bigger non-domestic features.

The analyzed grave pits are very simple. Those with inhumation burials have usually an oval outline, or perhaps rectangular with rounded corners. Dimensions of grave pits depended on the height of the dead and the body position. More frequent pit dimensions are: length 120–185 cm, width 68–120 cm. The biggest one was discovered in Łoniowa – in the uppermost part it was regularly rectangular, 260 × 200 cm. It had a specific feature – in its eastern part the bottom formed a step 20 cm high, upon which a set of stone artifacts was placed.

Depth of grave pits varied between 15 and 100 cm. This element, because of various erosion, is not significant in our analyses. The vertical cross-section of pits was usually basin-like, with flat bottom. In most cases no traces of additional constructions were discovered. Only two graves from Aleksandrowice (features no. 2541 and 2542) revealed the presence of posts (Czekaj-Zastawny 2000a; 2008c). In the first feature there were visible traces of four posts – three at the corners and one in the middle of the longer (southern) side (Fig. 20). The postholes had round outlines and were 30 cm deep (measuring from the level on which they become visible). Feature no. 2542 revealed during the exploration the presence of small dark spots, symmetrically spaced along longer sides of the pit (three on each side) – possible vestiges of a wooden construction (Fig. 21). On upper exploration levels they had circular outlines, but on lower level their shape changed into semi-oval (opposite to the situation in feature no. 2541). It is possible it was the construction composed of six small poles, inserted into the ground outside of the grave pit.

In the whole LBK extent graves with traces of wooden constructions are rare finds. Besides the example presented above, postholes linked with graves were discovered in Sondershausen (burials 24 and 28), Arnstadt (burial 8), and in Mulhouse-Est (burials 2 and 14). All these structures are interpreted as grave pit roofing (Kahlke 1954, 68, fig. 16; Jeunesse 1997, 60–61). There are not definite proofs confirming the use of stone in constructions of graves. The information about the existence of such a construction in Szczotkowice is questionable (accidental discovery during a road construction – information about it are from the workers who also returned recovered from the grave).

Fills of the presented graves are similar. In most cases their homogenous character indicates that the pits were filled at one time, using for that purpose earth from the close vicinity (with small potsherds, daub, and charcoal). It is especially true for graves within settlement sites. A different situation was registered in Aleksandrowice, where no artifacts were found fills of the grave pits. Their profiles revealed two layers corresponding with two filling phase:

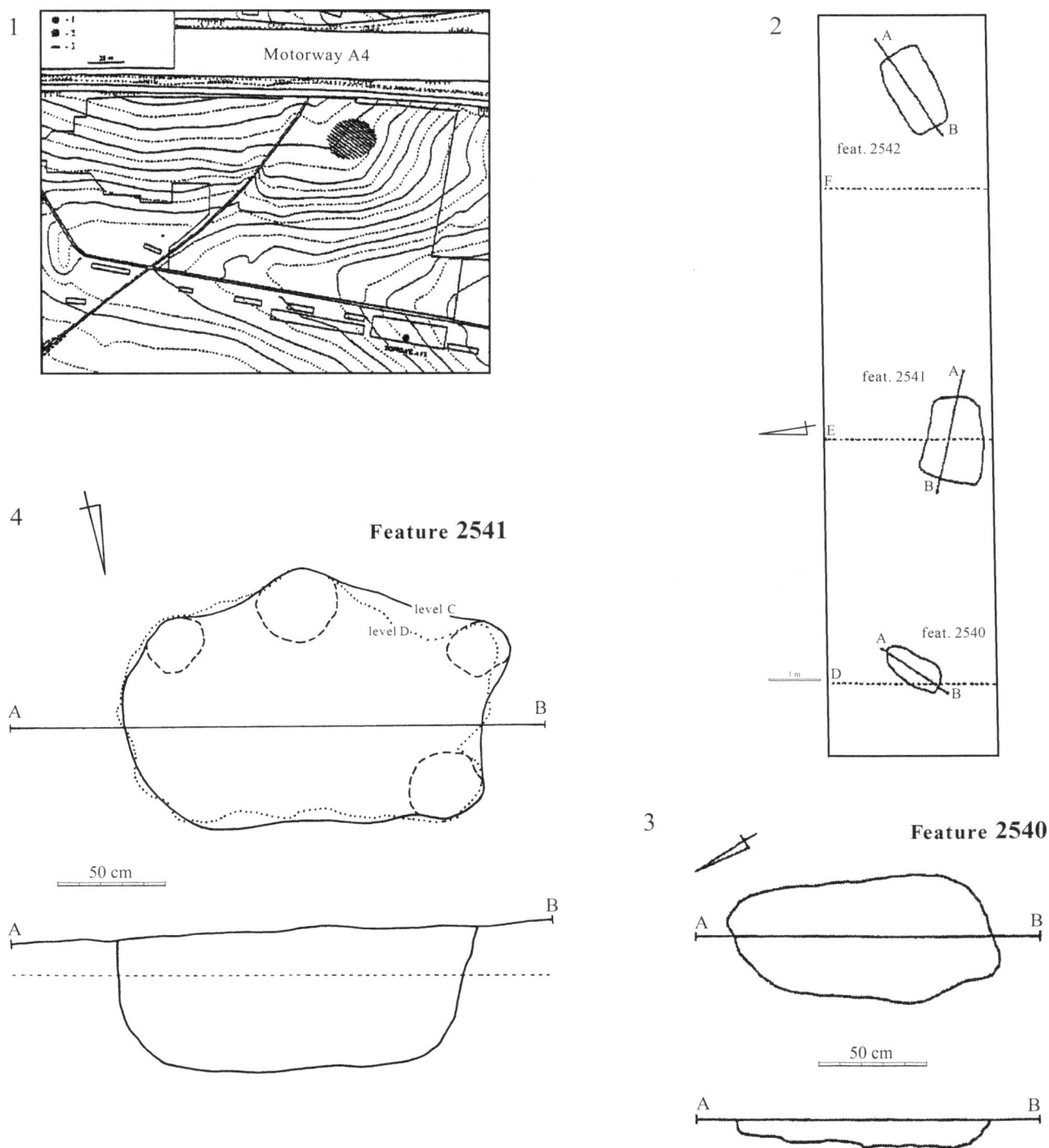

Fig. 20. Aleksandrowice, Site 2. 1 – location of graves (1) in sounding trenches (3) in relation to LBK settlement features (2); 2 – location of graves in a sounding trench; 3 – horizontal outline and cross-section of feature 2540; 4 – horizontal outline and cross-section of feature 2541. Drawn by A. Zastawny

clear and homogenous at the bottom (almost from the same time as the pit) and poorly distinctive in the upper part (basin like, related to the secondary filling). This observation can be taken as an argument for the existence in this place a whole (cf. the part related to location of the grave finds).

Orientation of grave pits is much diversified. As elsewhere on European LBK funerary site, no strict rules can be observed in this respect. On the same site grave can by orientated in various direction. In Aleksandrowice we have two graves orientated NE–SW, but a grave located in between (feature 2541) has the NW–SE orientation. Three graves from Samborzec were located along the N–S axis and two others – along the W–E axes. In Brzezie, all three graves were oriented NE–SW, one of them more towards

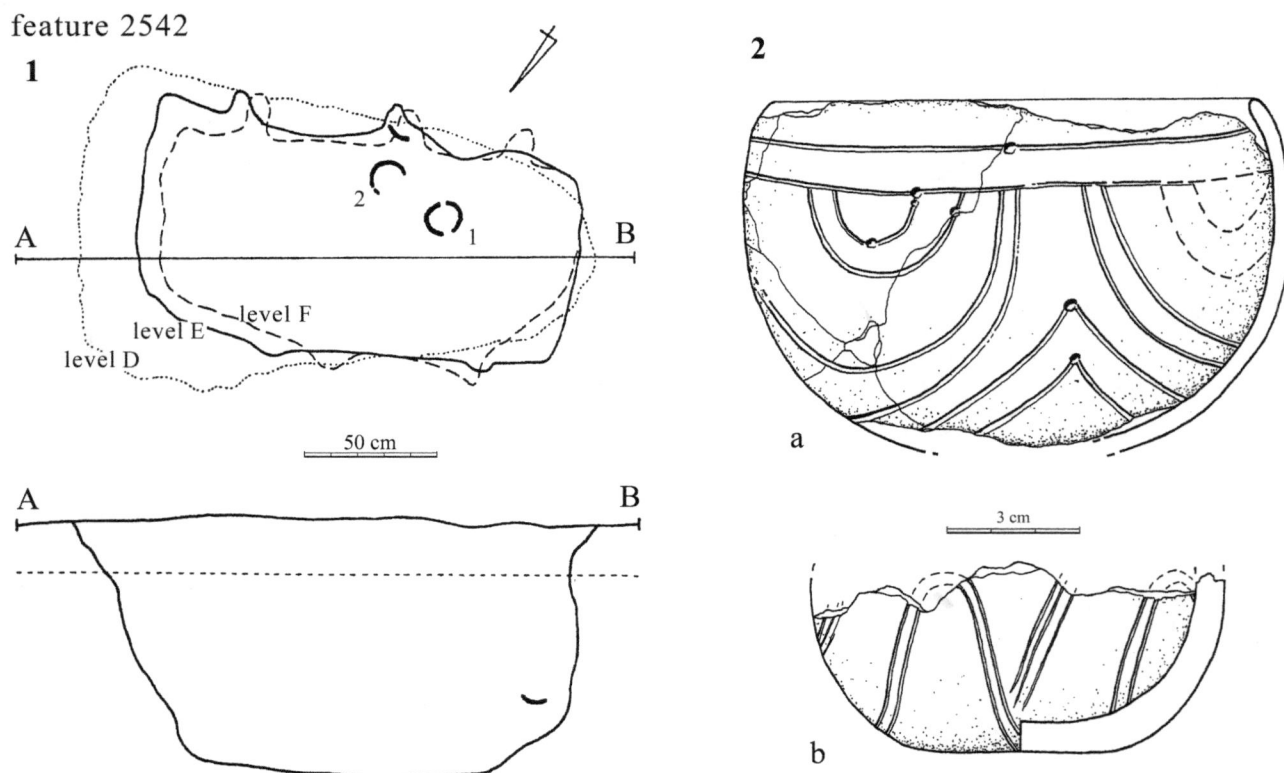

Fig. 21. Aleksandrowice, Site 2. 1 –horizontal outline and cross-section of feature 2542 with location of grave goods; 2 – inventory of grave 2542: a, b – vessels. Drawn by A. Zastawny, A. Czekaj-Zastawny

S–N. The axes of two grave pits from Złotniki ran along the NW–SE line and of the third pit along N–S line. The site at Giebułtów – were all three grave were orientated W–E, was exceptional. Diversity of location of grave pits is visible also on sites with individual burials – in Łoniowa and Olchowa it is the N–S axes, and in w Igołomia-Zofipole the W–E axis.

4.3. Human remains

Among 28 analyzed inhumation graves 15 contained preserved human remains. However, bones from the grave from Giebułtów were destroyed during recovering, while 2 skeletons from Samborzec and one from Igołomia-Zofipole were subsequently lost. In all other case the state of preservation of human remains was not good (some bones are missing due to natural disintegration of action of animals. Only a few bone remains could be subjected to the anthropological analysis (5 skeletons from Samborzec and skull fragments from Szczotkowice). In relation to other graves, Information related to the possible sex or age of the dead is based on descriptions of their discoverers. Analyses of burnt bones from Modlniczka have not been yet completed.

Among skeletons anthropologically determined there are: remains of two females from Samborzec (features 60 and 208; that from feature 60 – age about 50), two children from Samborzec (features 71 and IIIa; one of them about 6 years old), a probable child from Bejsce, three probable males from Giebułtów (graves VI and VII) and Szczotkowice (age 50-60 years). Five skeletons were determined

as of *adultus*: from Samborzec (feature IVa), Giebułtów (graves I and II), and Złotniki (graves I, II, and III).

In all cases the body was place in the grave along the longer axes of the pit (only in grave III in Złotniki we observe a slight deviation). Head of the dead can be directed in various ways. Among graves from Samborzec orientated N–S, one body (woman) was placed with head pointed to N and one (child) to S. Burial in grave II in Złotniki (*adultus*) was orientated to S. In graves with W–E axis the situation is the following: in Samborzec both dead (woman and *adultus*) to E, in Giebułtów to adult persons to W and one to E, in Igołomia-Zofipole to W, and in Złotniki (*adultus*) to E. Positions of heads of dead in burials of the intermediate orientation along NW–SE axis is the following: in Samborzec a child (grave IIIa) is orientated towards W, and in Złotniki an adult person (grave I) towards E.

The observations presented above indicate that bodies were being placed into graves in the following directions: N–S – 3 burials (2 of them definitely of LBK), W–E – 7 burials (2 of them definitely of LBK), NW–SE – 2 burials (one definitely of LBK). Position of the dead in all graves was practically the same – contracted and on the side. The contraction included the whole body: arms bent at elbows, legs bent at hips and knees, feet close to pelvis. Bodies rested either on the left or right side (7 and 4 cases respectively), apparently with no regards to the sex or age of the dead. The only exception can be found in the grave from Igołomia-Zofipole, in which the dead rested on the back, with bent arms and legs spread outwards.

Not a single grave contained human remains purposely damaged or dismembered. Incomplete skeletons are rather results of processes of natural disintegrations or animal interventions. We have also not registered any traces of cutting or other *post-mortem* practices. In three graves traces of ritual covering the body with ochre were registered. Two such cases are from Samborzec. In feature 60 ochre was placed on the head of the dead woman who had in her hands a pot with this coloring substance. In feature 280 (grave III) ochre was spread over the upper part of the dead woman. Their traces were visible also on bead of the necklace. We do not have information about the location of ochre in the grave from Szczotkowice, where all vessels were dyed but beads around the neck or head of the body show no traces of a coloring substance.

As we have said, only human remains from Samborzec were analyzed in details (Gleń-Haduch 1989, 43–59). The author of this analysis discusses in another work (Gleń-Haduch 1995, 115–139) questions related to the state of health of the buried persons. She puts forward a conclusion that the diet of the LBK population was well balanced in the scope of animal and vegetal products, with an adequate amount of the mineral components. The diet was also stable in its nourishment value (no traces of undernourishment). A slight tooth decay related probably to an inadequate hygiene, was visible. In one case we can be observed degenerative changes related to aging or long-time working in the same position. In general, the physical condition of the examined individuals was good.

4.4. Grave inventories

On funerary sites of LBK in its whole extent, burials equipped with grave offerings and those without them are almost equally frequent. Number of artifacts per grave is very diverse – from one to a few dozens.

Among 28 analyzed graves 12 were equipped with artifacts. Artifacts found in the fills of three other grave pits (graves IV and VI from Giebułtów and the cremation grave from Gródek) cannot be interpreted as definite grave goods (they could have been dumped to pits accidentally). The other graves – features 2540 and 2541 from Aleksandrowice, graves IIIa and IVa from Samborzec (Kulczycka-Leciejewiczowa 2008), grave III (feature 1586) from Brzezie, graves I, II, III, and V from Giebułtów, graves I, II, and III from Złotniki – did not contained any artifacts. According to initial information, the cremation graves were equipped with stone adzes. In a few pits single flint objects and potsherds were also found (Czekaj-Zastawny *et al.* in press).

Pottery

Pottery is most common element of grave inventories. In 8 burials 15 whole or almost whole vessels were found (2 vessels from Bejsce have been lost). Among them there are 13 spherical bowls and 2 small amphorae. Fourteen vessels are decorated (12 with engraved and 2 with engraved motifs), one is not decorated.

In the scope of the composition of the pottery paste and its firing, the analyzed vessels are similar to vessels from settlement sites. The paste is well done, usually loamy, with smooth (almost glossy) surfaces. Exceptional are the vessels from feature 2542 from Aleksandrowice, badly preserved due to poor firing of upper parts (the bottom are not fired at all).

The graves were equipped with 1–3 vessels (3 times one vessel, 4 times 2 vessels, and 1 times 3 vessels). In graves with the preserved skeletons the pottery was places close to the head of the dead (in feature 60 from Samborzec in the hands stretched towards the head; Fig. 22). In Olchowa it was concentrated in the NE corner of the grave pit, in Aleksandrowice in the central part of the pit near its southern wall, in Brzezie – in one case in the N part of the pit, in another – in the central and southern parts, in Łoniowa exclusively in the S part. In three graves the pottery was accompanied by other grave goods (Łoniowa, feature 60 from Samborzec, Szczotkowice).

A significant amount of potsherds was recovered from fills the graves – those equipped with offering and those without it. They were found on the level with human remains, and above them. Most of them should be interpreted as accidental additions, although we cannot exclude intentional breaking of vessel during the funeral (Jeunesse 1997). Such a practice was possibly registered in feature 208 from Samborzec, where – 20 cm above the skeleton – fragments of vessels were spread around the head and waist of the dead.

Ornamentations

Ornamentations include beads of various shapes, originally threaded on strings. They were found in 2 graves – in feature 208 from Samborzec (2 "strings"; Fig. 23, 24, 25) and in grave I from Szczotkowice (1 "string"; Fig. 26, 27). In both cases the beads were made of shell and of stone. One of the "strings" from Samborzec was of bivalve shells of various kinds, the other of limestone. In Szczotkowice the "string" was composed of marble beads complemented by big bids of the Spondylus shell.

The beads were of the following shapes: flat almond-like, of the shape of a flat tube, bi-conical, and oval (big forms). The "necklace" of a soft limestone from Samborzec was composed of 31 almond-like beads, perforated in the upper (narrower) part, flat in cross-sections. The "string" around waist had 151 beads of various shells, shaped as flatten tubes with evenly cut ends. In Szczotkowice the "string" was made of 36 beads of a white marble (bi-conical, ends evenly cut) and 3 big beads of the Spondylus shell, concentrated in one part of the ornamentation (the possible composition: bigger-smaller-bigger).

In both graves the "strings" were placed at the upper part of the dead – near the head of neck. The second "string" from Samborzec was originally wrapped around the hips. In Sczotkowice the beads were accompanied by vessels, a clay artifacts, and an animal bone, it Samborzec they were found sole.

Tools

This category includes artifacts of flint, bone, and antler. Only one bone tool was found in the analyzed graves (feature 60 from Samborzec) – an awl made from a fragment of an animal long bone. There is also a rod-like object

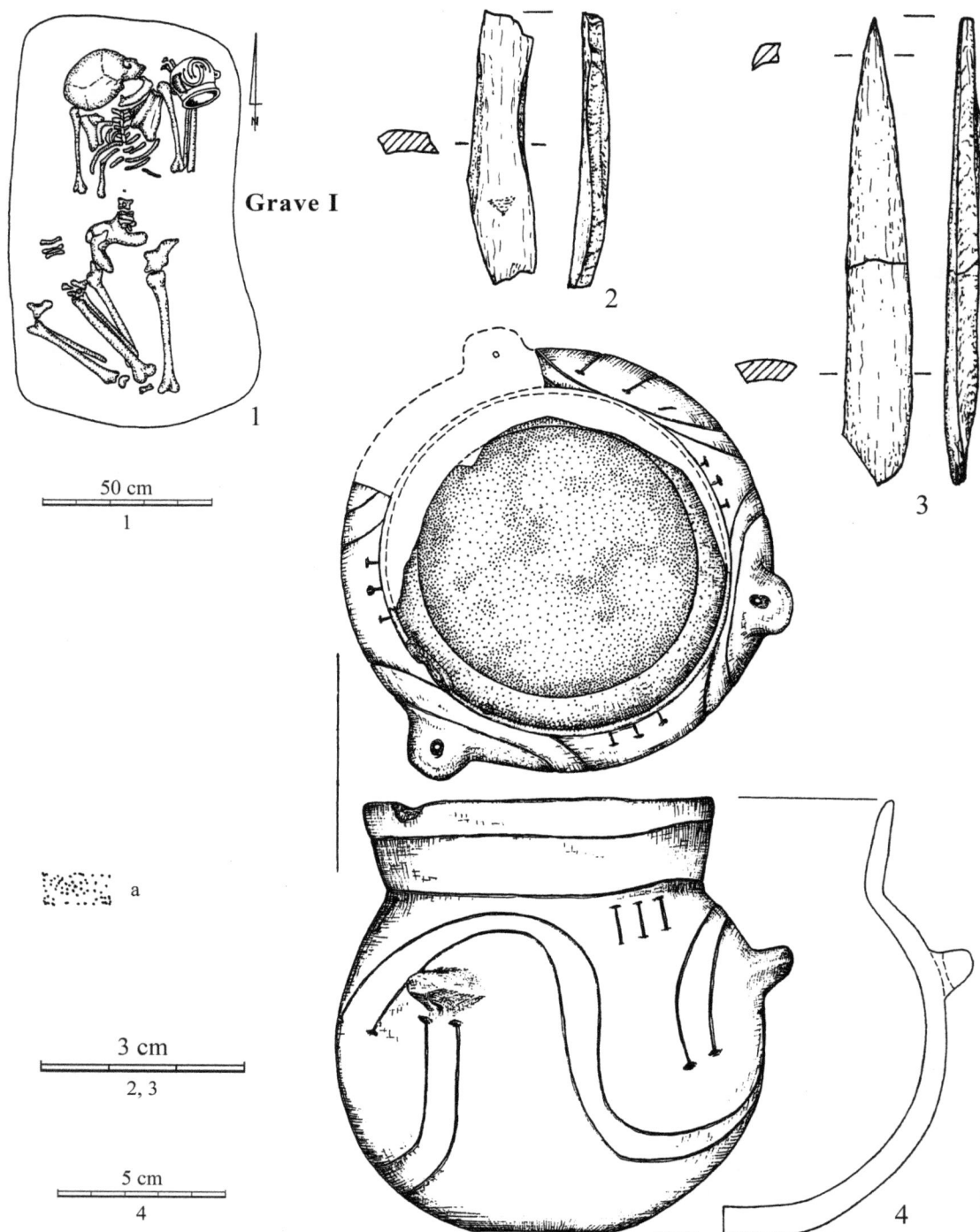

Grave I

50 cm

1

a

3 cm

2, 3

5 cm

4

Fig. 22. Samborzec, Site 1. Grave I (feature 60): 1 – horizontal outline of grave pit with skeleton and grave inventory, 2 – bone tool fragment, 3 – bone tool, 4 – clay vessel with traces of ochre (a). Drawn by E. Osipowa

made of dear antler (from grave IV from Giebułtów). Stone tools were found in two graves. Those from Łoniowa had a specific character. They formed a deposit of 12 elements (originally probably in an organic container), placed in the SE part of the pit on a step on the bottom. An interesting feature of the deposit is its raw material composition. There is: a conical single platform core for blades of the Jurassic flint of the Cracow variety, 6 blades (2 massif) of the same rock, a blade of the chocolate-type flint, a base part of a blade of obsidian, one burin spall of the Jurassic flint of the Cracow variety, and to sickle inserts of the chocolate-type (with a strong sickle-gloss). Moreover, in lower part of the same pit two trapezes of Jurassic flint of the Cracow variety were found. Also the grave from Igołomia-Zofipole contained artifacts of the same rock – a truncated blade with sickle-gloss, a small blade with double truncation, 10 fragments of blades and flakes, and also on obsidian flake.

Grave III

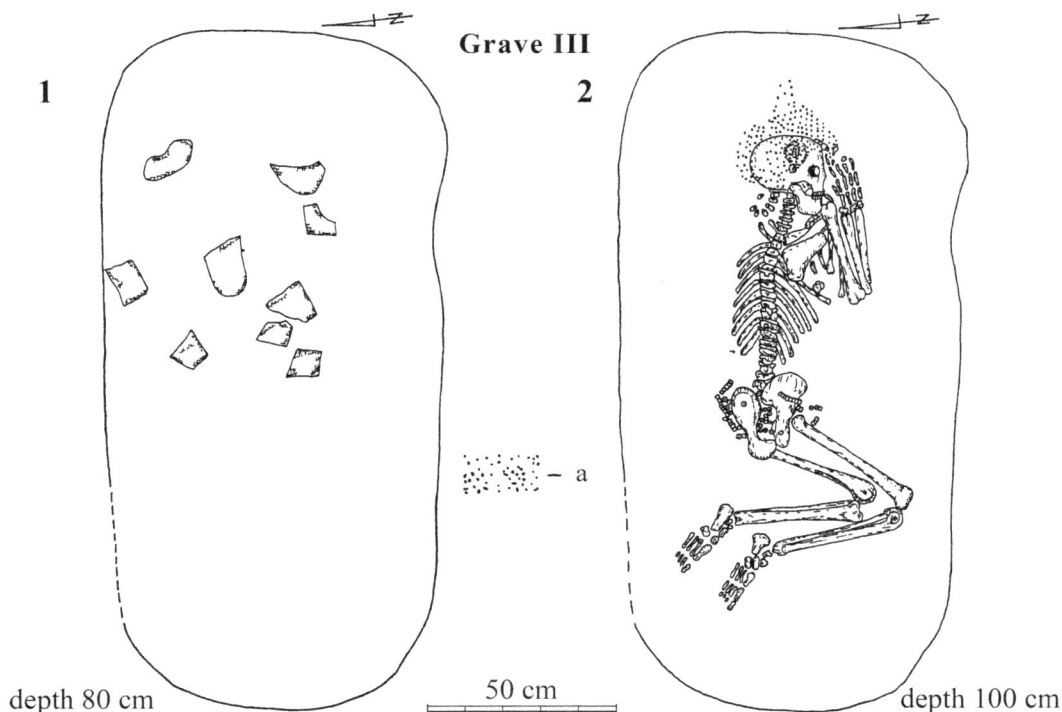

Fig. 23. Samborzec, Site 1. Grave III (feature 208): 1 – outline on the depth of 80 cm, 20 cm above the level with the skeleton, with concentration of potsherds, 2 – horizontal outline of grave pit with skeleton and grave inventory, skull powdered with ochre (a). Drawn by E. Osipowa

The location of the artifacts listed above within grave pits is uncertain. In Samborzec the artifact was found on the skeleton level, possibly close to the waist of the dead. Artifacts from Igołomia-Zofipole were found – according to the field documentation – during cleaning the bones. The artifact of antler from Giebułtów comes generally from the fill of the grave pit.

As we have already mentioned, stone adzes were found in grave in Modlniczka. Moreover, a few pits contained single flint artifacts.

Organic artifacts and food

We can assume that artifacts of organic materials and food were often placed into graves. However, only very small vestiges of these offerings survived till our times. In this respect the grave from Łoniowa with traces of two organic artifacts is exceptional. The container for the deposit of flint artifacts left its traces in the form of a dark smudge of the rectangular outline, with dimensions of 2 x 8 cm, encircling the artifacts. In the deeper part of the pit (in its SE quarter) there was a clay vessel and – close to it – a circular outline of another vessel, probably of wood.

Animal bones interpreted as vestiges food given to graves or symbolic offerings are known from LBK funerary sites outside Poland (Jeunesse 1997, 84–86). In one of the analyzed graves (Szczotkowice) a cervical vertebra of *Bos taurus* (mature animal) was found. Bone fragments and a clam shell are known also from the fill of grave II from Samborzec. In this case we are not sure it they were placed there intentionally. We can also suppose that vessels from graves were originally filled with food. Confirmation of this hypothesis required in a special examination in the future.

Dyes

Ochre was used as a grave offering at least in one case. In feature 60 from Samborzec it was placed in a vessel hold by the dead (woman) in hands (*cf.* Fig. 21). As we have said, in some other inhumation graves ochre was found on bones of the skeleton (*cf.* Fig. 22). Also on the cremation cemetery in Modlniczka there were traces of ochre – on burnt bones and on artifacts.

Other objects

In the analyzed graves there were found single pieces of polishing stones of limestone (grave VII from Giebułtów) and a clay artifact of unknown use (Szczotkowice). It is a rod-like object with an opening on the longer axis.

Male and female grave inventories

Due to a small number of anthropologically determined burials, it is difficult to observe differences between inventories of male and female graves. In relation to the whole LBK milieu we can speak rather about categories of artifacts appearing most often in graves of the specific sex (Jeunesse 1997). The same can be said about the analyzed graves. In burials with preserved skeletal remains (Samborzec) a great variety of grave offerings can be observed. One of the female graves contained a vessel with ochre and a bone tool (feature 60), another with two bead "strings" (feature 208). Both dead were covered by a powdered ochre, so

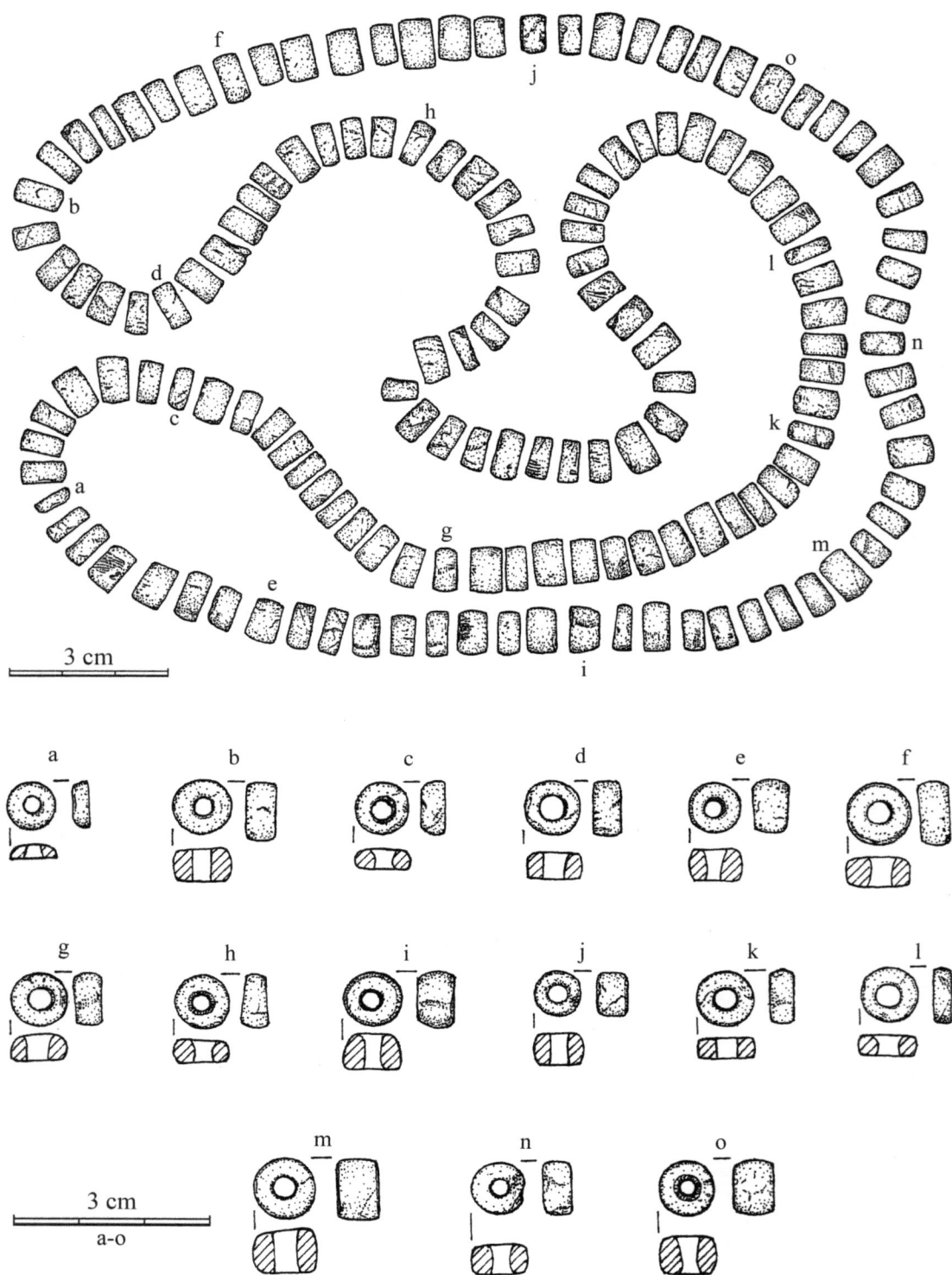

Fig. 24. Samborzec, Site 1. Inventory of grave III (feature 208). "String" of 151 beads of shell: a-o – selection of beads with their outlines and cross-sections. Drawn by E. Osipowa

was a male body from Szczotkowice. The latter grave was exceptionally furnished (if all artifacts recovered by the workers really come from it). The child grave Samborzec (feature 71) contained one grave.

Inventories of cremation graves

In the assumed cremation grave from Gródek nad Bu-

giem (possibly related to LBK) five pottery fragments of the same vessel (decorated by engraved arched lines) were found. The cremations from Modlniczka have not been so-far comprehensively analyzed. According to the field documentation they were furnished with last-form adzes (one or two *per* grave), single flint artifacts and potsherds.

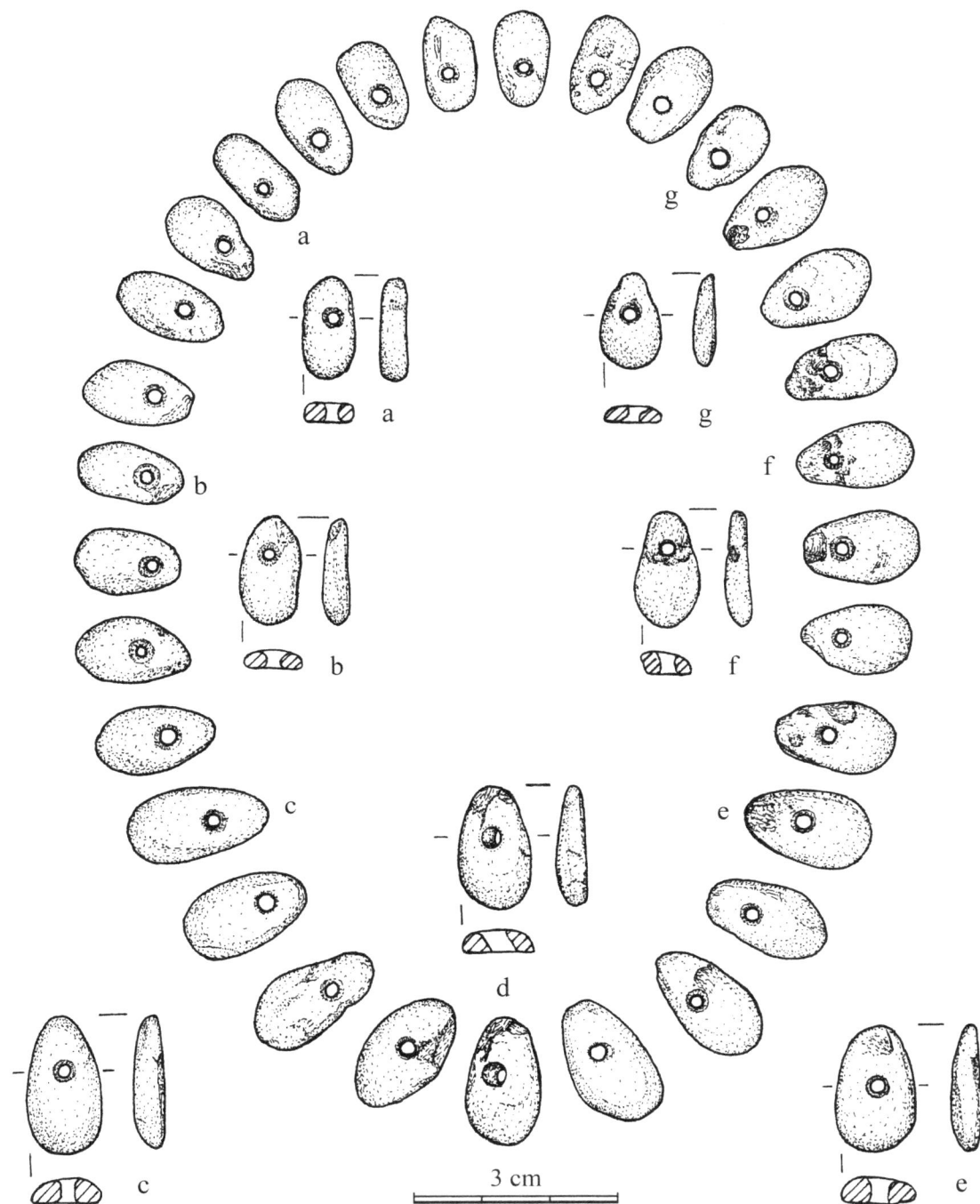

Fig. 25. Samborzec, Site 1. Inventory of grave III (feature 208). Necklace of 31 limestone beads. a-g – selection of beads with their outlines and cross-sections. Drawn by E. Osipowa

4.5. Chronology of the graves

Chronological division of individual phases of the LBK development can be applied only to graves furnished with decorated pottery. In the graves with anon-pottery artifacts an attempt in this direction can be make on the basis of other premises, e.g. stratigraphic relations. Unfurnished graves can be assigning only generally as probably belonging to LBK. Taking into account of all available data we classify the analyzed graves as follows: **Phase LBK I** – probably feature 208 z Samborzec; **Phase LBK II (Music-Note)** – feature 2542 from Aleksandrowice, features 1528, 1543, and 1586 from Brzezie, features 60 and 71 from Samborzec, and grave I from Szczotkowice; **Phase LBK III (Želiezovce)** – grave I (feature 23) from Łoniowa and grave I from Olchowa.

On the area of our interest we have not observed a tendency for furnishing graves of different chronology with specific categories of artifacts.

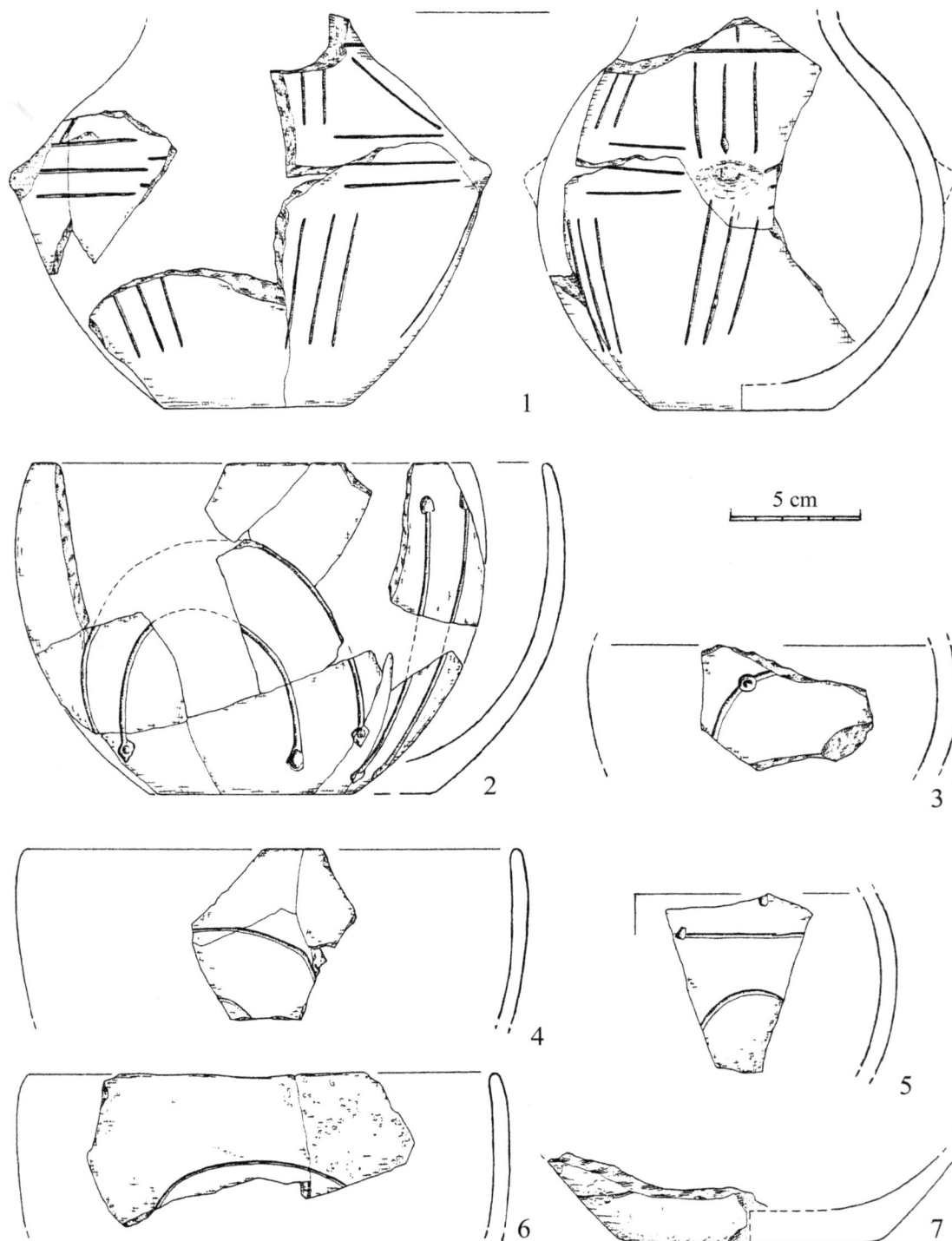

Fig. 26. Szczotkowice, Site 1. Grave inventory: 1, 2 – vessels, 3–7 – small pottery fragments. Drawn by E. Osipowa

4.6. Funerary rite of the Linear Pottery Culture in southeastern Poland on the European background

Burials of the Liner Pottery culture in southeastern Poland are not frequent (27 inhumations and 39 cremations on 13 sites). In comparison with some regions of Central and Western Europe (about 100 funerary sites, including vast burial grounds) they do not give us very much clues for studying funerary customs. Despite it is easy to notice that the Polish finds are typical – in every analyzed element – for LBK in its whole European extent.

Sites with LBK graves have been divided into 3 basic types (Jeunesse 1997, 43–44). Those from southeastern Poland fall mainly to Type 2, i.e. individual graves within settlement sites. Apart from the cemetery at Modlniczka it is difficult to assign any Polish sites to Type 1 (burial grounds proper) or Type 3 (small concentrations of graves linked

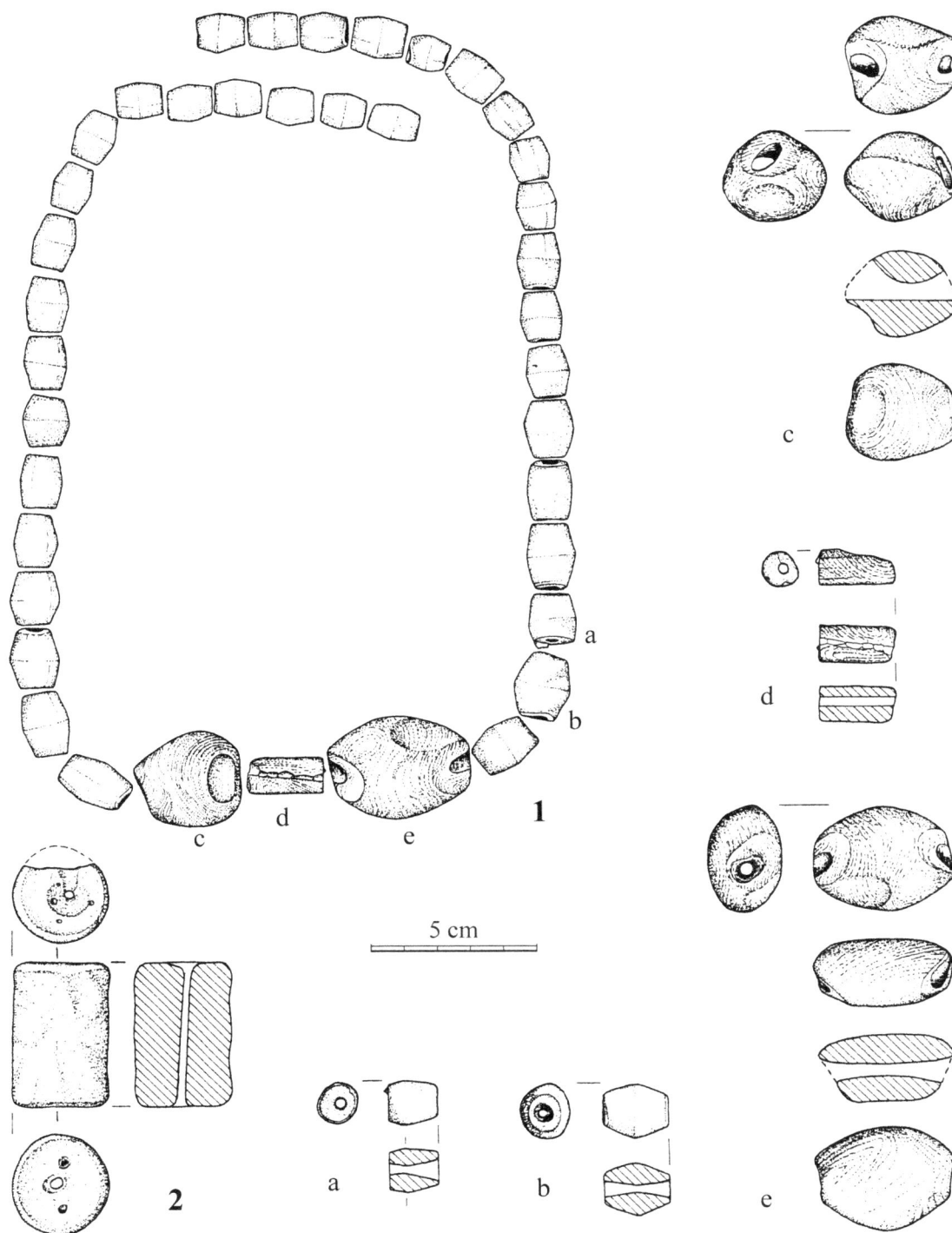

Fig. 27. Szczotkowice, Site 1. Grave inventory: 1 – necklace of 36 marble beads and 3 beads of Spondylus shell in the middle (c-e), a-e – selection of beads with their outlines and cross-sections, 2 – clay artifact. Drawn by E. Osipowa

with settlements). It is related to an inadequate examination of the vicinity of the excavated graves. While burials from Brzezie evidently represent Type 3, the other objects can be linked either with Type 1 or Type 3. Cemeteries of the Linear Pottery Culture appear mainly for the central milieu of LBK (between the Middle Elbe and the upper Veser, the upper and middle Rhine and the upper Danube). Outside these areas (e.g. in Poland and France) small concentrations of

graves and individual graves are more typical (Jeunesse 1997, fig. 5 and list of sites, 147–158). Examples of burials within settlements sites (Type 3) can be found in Olchowa, Łoniowa, and Samborzec.

In LBK inhumation and cremation coexisted. In some regions the latter ritual was as much common as the first, no matter of the developing phase. Ration of burials of both types can be diverse (e.g. in cremation graves constitute

42% of burials and in Nitra about 10%, while in Vedrovice none of 96 graves was a cremation). Importance of the cremation is different on various territories. It was most common in Central Germany (Arnstadt 12 cremations and 10 inhumations; Wandersleben 132 and 179 respectively), in Bavaria (Stephansposching 31 and 10; Aiterhofen 69 and 159), and in Holland (Elsloo 47 and 66). Poland, due to recent discoveries, is not anymore a white spot in this respect. Any far-reaching conclusions are still premature but it seems that in Modlniczka cremation graves may constitute up to 100 % of burials. It will possibly change the opinion that the cremation is rare in the eastern milieu of LBK (Jeunesse 1997). As so-far, in southeastern Poland no site with burials of both rituals is known. Apart from Modlniczka, a cremation grave probably of LBK is known only from Gródek on Bug river. All other graves from this territory are inhumations. Some graves without human remains may be interpreted as symbolic.

All analyzed graves are single burials in purposely dug pits, similar one to another. In most cases they have oval or rectangular outlines and do not show traces of additional constructions. Features of that type are most common on all European LBK funerary sites. Two graves from Aleksandrowice are unusual due to traces of wooden constructions or roofing. They have no analogies in Poland and very few on other territories. The presence of wooden constructions has been confirmed in Mulhouse-Est in Alsace (two graves), Sondershausen in Bavaria (two graves), and in Arnstadt in Central Germany (one grave). They were composed of four vertical forming a square outside the grave and of posts encircling the grave pit (Kahlke 1954, 68; Jeunesse 1997, 60–61). The posts were places on western, southern, and eastern sides. Such constructions are interpreted as "funeral houses" with entrance from the north (Kahlke 1954, 65–71). Feature 2541 from Aleksandrowice – with postholes on three sides – it very similar. Also the orientation of the pit is identical. However, there are no traces of posts encircling the grave outside of its reach. Certain similarities to the described feature can be hound in grave 28 from Sondershausen (Kahlke 1954, 67). Because the construction of the Alexandrowice grave has no analogies in the whole extent of LBK, it is difficult to interpret. We are not sure it the post supported a roof build over the grave or formed a construction of a different type. It is possible that feature 2540 in the same locality, preserved in a very bad state, was originally similar.

Analyses of inhumation graves indicate that their pits were filled with earth taken from their close vicinity, immediately after the burial. Orientation of graves was not very important and no strict rules were applied to it – on Polish territories and elsewhere. In this respect each funeral site has its specificity. Some of them show tendencies to specific orientations (e.g. E–W in Aiterhofen in Bavaria; Nieszery 1995), others do not (e.g. Sondershausen in Central Germany; Behrends 1973, 228). The analyzed graves were orientated in many directions. Nonetheless it is possible to notices that certain orientations were preferable – N–S, E–W, NE–SW, and NW–SE. Only in Giebułtów all graves were directed along the E–W axis. Dead were places in pits along their longer axis, although not necessarily in the same

direction (e.g. in Samborzec graves with the N–S orientation one dead was directed to N, the other to S). All graves (with the exception of that from Igołomia-Zofipole) have one thing in common – the dead rested on a side, with arms bent in elbows, hands directed to the head, legs bent in hips and knees, and feet close to the pelvis. No matter of sex and age, the bodies was placed either on the right side (7 cases) or on the left side (4 cases). On LBK funerary sites outside Poland the left-side crouched position of the dead seems to be most common (Nitra – 59 cases among 73, Aiterhofen – 104 cases among 142, Ensisheim – 32 among 36, Flomborn – all 61 cases). Skeletons on the right side also appear on almost every side, yet less often. However, on some sites this position prevails. For example, in Rutzing in Upper 10 burials (out of 16) were on the right side. In the light of the observation the Igołomia-Zofipole site cannot be considered exceptional.

No human remains bear traces of an intentional damage of defragmentation (although it could have been caused by animals). Such after-death practices can be observed on some LBK sites (e.g. grave 2 in Sondershausen). Instead, in Modlniczka another funerary practice – covering the dead with ochre – has been observed. It was quite common in LBK (Jeunesse 1997, 80) where a powdered was often spread over a dead or around him. Most often it was placed on specific parts of the body, usually the head (as in features 60 and 208 from Samborzec). There are also burials with two concentrations of ochre – near the skull and between the pelvis and knees (as possibly in one of the graves from Szczotkowice). Traces of ochre were also registered in Modlniczka, on same elements of the grave inventories (Czekaj-Zastawny *et al.* in press).

A detailed anthropological analysis, including the determination of sex, age, and state of health of dead, was applied only to the skeletons from Samborzec (Gleń-Haduch 1989, 43–59; 1995, 115–139). In some case only age or sex could be determined. Altogether, the analyses encompassed remains of 2 women, 2 men, 2 children, and 7 persons referred as adults. The examined population was in good health. Causes of death have not been determined. In the future we can also expect interesting results of the analyses of the cremated remains from Modlniczka.

LBK burials in their whole extent can be equally furnished with grave goods (from one to a few dozen objects) or without them. Among 28 analyzed inhumations, 12 contained intentional offerings. They are as follows: Aleksandrowice, feature. 2542: 2 vessels; Brzezie: feature 1528: fragments of 2–3 vessels, feature. 1543: one whole vessel and fragments of 2 other vessels; Łoniowa, feature 23: one vessel, a deposit of 12 flint artifacts, and 2 other flint artifacts; Olchowa, grave I: 3 vessels; Samborzec, feature 60: one vessel, a coloring substance, and a bone artifacts, feature 71: one vessel; feature. 208: 2 "bead strings" (of 151 and 31 beads); Szczotkowice, grave I: 2 vessels, one "bead string" (36 beads or marble and 3 of Spondylus shell), a clay artifact, and animal bones; Bejsce, pit C: 2 vessels; Giebułtów, grave VII: a polishing stone; Igołomia-Zofipole, grave I: 12 artifacts of flint and one of obsidian, 3 pottery fragments. Cremation graves were furnished with mainly with stone shoe-last tools.

Categories of artifacts found in Polish graves are very common on all LBK funerary sites. We have not registered categories typical only for one cemetery or one region, such as bone "armlets" from Nitra, fox jaws from Aiterhofen, bone arrowheads from Schwetzingen or eagle talons from Lingolsheim (Jeunesse 1997). Vessels are most common in inhumation graves and last-form adzes in cremation graves. Altogether, in 6 graves 11 complete or almost complete vessels were found (2 of them – from Bejsce, are lost). They include 7 spherical bowls and 2 small amphorae. Eight vessels are decorated – 6 with engraved motifs and 2 by relief motifs), one has no ornamentation. Individual burials contained 1 to 3 vessels (2 times 1 vessel, 3 times 2 vessels, and 1 time 3 vessels). Grave goods were concentrates in corners of graves pits (Olchowa), usually around the head of the dead (in feature 60 from Samborzec in hands stretched towards the head) or at longer sides of pits (Aleksandrowice). In two cases vessels were accompanied by other objects (feature 60 from Samborzec and grave I from Szczotkowice). Inventories of 3 graves did not include vessels. Among artifacts of other type there are: ornamentations, tools, coloring substance, animal bones, and a polishing slab.

Ornamentations found in the graves are diverse in form and in raw material utilized. The beads, especially those of the Spondylus shell, are very significant. Tools were also common grave goods. Here they were found in three graves – a bone awl in feature 60 from Samborzec, flint artifacts (including 2 sickle inserts) in the grave from Igołomia, and a tool of antler in grave VII from Giebułtów. In one grave (feature 60 from Samborzec) the grave inventory included a coloring substance (powdered ochre in a pot). On LBK cemeteries the most common substances of that kind are ochre and graphite – in particles or powdered (Jeunesse 1997, 80). Ochre was more often used in the latter form, easy to be spread over a body (cf. supra). Analogies to the find from feature 60 from Samborzec (powder ochre in a pot) can be found in graves 2 and 30 from Essenbach (Jeunesse 1997). The grave from Łoniowa is very interesting in many respects. Besides its unusual location (within a house contemporary with the burial) and vestiges of artifacts of organic materials, it is significant by the presence of the deposits of flint artifacts.

It is difficult to define LBK grave goods typical only for men and only for women. Generally, both sexes – no matter of age – were treated equally. We can speak only about categories of artifacts more typical for male graves or female graves, but not about a strict distinction between them (Jeunesse 1997; Czekaj-Zastawny 2003). Analyses of Bavarian cemeteries are especially interested in this respect (Nieszery 1995). Male burials contained stone axes and polished stone picks, flint arrowheads and blades, Spondylus shells with V-shape cuts, bracelets of shell, fox jaws, and animal bones (food offering). Female burials were more often equipped with Spondylus shells with double openings, head sets of shells, stone grinders, and combs of bone or antler. Common for both types of burials were vessels and beads of shell. We are also known examples of female graves equipped by "male artifacts" (e.g. last-form adzes) and male graves with artifacts recognized as "female" (e.g.

Spondylus shells with double openings). A similar situation can be observed in child graves. More often they are equipped as male or female graves. Their inventories can be described as "neutral". Child's graves from southeastern Poland fall into this category. No matter of the sex of the buried child, the graves contain similar artifact, mainly vessels and beads. Also artifacts of other types found in these graves cannot be attributed to a specific sex.

Chronological assignation to specific phases of the LBK development can attempt only to graves equipped with decorated pottery or – sporadically on the basis of stratigraphic relations. Phase I is represented only by one burial (feature 208 from Samborzec). Seven graves are from the Music-Note Phase (feature 2542 from Aleksandrowice, 3 features from Brzezie, feature 60 and – probably – 71 from Samborzec, grave I from Szczotkowice), and two graves from the Želiezovce Phase (Łoniowa and Olchowa). In cases of burials equipped only with not-pottery artifacts a determination of a specific phase is impossible.

In other areas of the LBK extent we observe tendencies to use specific categories or form of artifacts (apart from decorated pottery) in various chronological phases. In southeastern Poland, as well as elsewhere, the chronological development of LBK has its reflection on sepulchral sites. Graves dated to Phase I are known for example from Sondershausen (Central Germany), Vedrovice (Moravia), Flomborn (the middle Rhine), to Phase II from Nitra (Slovakia), Mulhouse-Est (Alsace), Larzicourt (the Paris Basin), Aiterhofen (Bavaria), and to Phase III from Elsloo (the upper Mose), Schwetzingen (the middle Rhine), and Niedermerz (the upper Rhine).

The graves from southeastern Poland are compatible with the model of the funeral rite of the Linear Pottery Culture. They have their local specificities (e.g. lack of certain categories of artifacts) but the elements common for the whole LBK milieu prevail (orientation of grave pits, position of dead, main grave inventories, etc.). The analyzed burials are as much typical as the settlement of this culture in the upper Vistula basin is typical for the LBK settlement on the whole territory of its extent.

5. FINAL REMARKS

An intensive field research on the Linear Pottery Culture in the upper Vistula basin allowed collecting and presenting in this work a great number of evidences. These sources helped to give answers to many detailed questions related to life and death of early farmers. Until now the knowledge of this material outside Poland was negligible, and LBK settlement in the southeastern part of the country was viewed as peripheral and deprived of many elements recognized as typical in other parts of Europe. The work indicates that the settlement region in the upper Vistula basin – in the scope of density and diversity of the settlement, its function, building constructions, and chronological extent – does not falls behind other centers of the culture in question.

Analyzed carried out within our research allowed to draw a new picture of the settlement of the Linear Pottery Culture in the upper Vistula basin. Two elements of this picture are especially important. The first on is related to the increasing number of domestic sites with long post houses. Our evidences suggest that such constructions might have been present on each permanently settled LBK site, and that their small (so-far) number is rather resulted from the state of the research. The second important conclusion is related to the distribution of LBK sites. Collected evidences revealed the presence of the concentrated settlement in areas so-far considered to be deprived of LBK traces, and – within already known groups – settlement more intensive than expected.

A situation related to the funerary evidences is different. A small number of LBK burials on the territory of Poland is rather astonishing. For comparison, 66 graves are known from Poland, while from other territories occupied by LBK – more than. The only Polish cemetery of the culture in question was only recently discovered. It elevated considerably the total number of LBK graves in Poland.

The reason of absence of cemeteries and a general scarcity of LBK is rather surprising. In all other cultural aspects Polish LBK is comparable with its counterparts in other regions. Today, in the period of intensive wide-area excavations, we cannot explain this situation by insufficient state of research. A possible explanation may be a specific way of treatment of dead by LBK people which was not registered in archeological evidences, or perhaps location of burial grounds in remote areas, far away from settlement centers. The latter presumption seems to be more plausible. The only Polish LBK cemetery (Modlniczka) is located in a low wet part of a valley. Such areas are seldom subjected to regular archaeological excavations.

CATALOGUE OF LBK SITES
IN SOUTHEASTERN POLAND (map A)

Identification and location of sites:
Name of a site (and number on the map)
1. Administrative unit appropriate to a given site;
2. River basin
3. Geographical coordinates
4. Geomorphological situation (river basin, location in relation to the land relief)

A. Information on excavated sites:
1. Name(s) of researcher(s) responsible for theexcavation;
2. Date of excavation (years);
3. Bounded research area: excavated and surveyed;

4. Type and number of features;
5. Relative chronology based on archaeological seriation and absolute chronology; number of settlement phases;

B. Information on sites recognized on the basis of surface finds
1. Area of occurrence of portable finds;
2. Taxonomic attribution and – when possible – chronological framework of sites.
C. The most important references.

---

1. Albigowa, site 1
1. Łańcut comm., Łańcut distr., Podkarpackie voiv.
2. Sawa stream basin/Wisłok river basin/San river basin/upper Vistula river basin
3. 50°00'30.8"N, 22°14'13.8"E
4. Valley slope
A
1. K. Moskwa, R. Mazur, W. Mazur
2. 1963
3. 80 m^2
4. Settlement; few(?) features
5. LBK
B
1. Approx. 0.5 ha
2. LBK
C
Czekaj-Zastawny 2008a; Moskwa 1963; Saile *et al.* 2008

2. Albigowa, site 5
1. Łańcut comm., Łańcut distr., Podkarpackie voiv.
2. Sawa stream basin/Wisłok river basin/San river basin/upper Vistula river basin
3. 50°00'40.6"N, 22°14'32.2"E
4. Valley slope
A –
B
1. Approx. 5 ha
2. LBK?
C
Czekaj-Zastawny 2008a

3. Albigowa, site 38
1. Łańcut comm., Łańcut distr., Podkarpackie voiv.
2. Sawa stream basin/Wisłok river basin/San river basin/upper

Vistula river basin
3. 50°01'35.3"N, 22°12'51.2"E
4. Valley border
A
1. S. Kadrow
2. 1987
3. 125 m^2
4. Settlement; 11 features (probably belongs to the 1 long house)
5. LBK, Music Note phase
B
1. Approx. 8 ha
2. LBK
C
Czekaj-Zastawny 2008a; Czopek 1999; Kadrow 1992a; Saile *et al.* 2008

4. Albigowa, site 52
1. Łańcut comm., Łańcut distr., Podkarpackie voiv.
2. Sawa stream basin/Wisłok river basin/San river basin/upper Vistula river basin
3. 50°01'01.8"N, 22°13'04.2"E
4. Valley border
A –
B
1. Approx. 1 ha
2. LBK
C
Czekaj-Zastawny 2008a

5. Albigowa, site 58
1. Łańcut comm., Łańcut distr., Podkarpackie voiv.
2. Sawa stream basin/Wisłok river basin/San river basin/upper Vistula river basin

3. 50°01'23.9"N, 22°14'06.1"E
4. Valley border
A –
B
1. Approx. 100 m²
2. LBK
C
Czekaj-Zastawny 2008a

6. Albigowa, site 60
1. Łańcut comm., Łańcut distr., Podkarpackie voiv.
2. Sawa stream basin/Wisłok river basin/San river basin/upper Vistula river basin
3. 50°00'40.7"N, 22°15'06.9"E
4. Valley slope and border
A –
B
1. Approx. 100 m²
2. LBK
C
Czekaj-Zastawny 2008a

7. Albigowa, site 61
1. Łańcut comm., Łańcut distr., Podkarpackie voiv.
2. Sawa stream basin/Wisłok river basin/San river basin/upper Vistula river basin
3. 50°00'53.8"N, 22°15'03.7"E
4. Valley slope and border
A –
B
1. Approx. 100 m²
2. LBK
C
Czekaj-Zastawny 2008a

8. Aleksandrowice, site 2
1. Zabierzów comm., Kraków distr., Małopolskie voiv.
2. Brzoskwinia stream basin/upper Vistula river basin
3. 50°04'54.7"N, 19°45'52.6"E
4. Valley slope
A
1. The Cracow Team for Archaeological Supervision of Motorway Construction, Institute of Archaeology and Ethnology Polish Academy of Sciences, Museum of Archaeology Cracow, Jagiellonian University (Krakowski Zespół do Badań Autostrad, Instutut Archeologii i Etnologii Polskiej Akademii Nauk, Muzeum Archeologiczne w Krakowie, Uniwersytet Jagielloński)
2. 1997–1998
3. 38500 m²
4. Settlement; 6 features (and probably much more destroyed by younger settlement), 3 human graves
5. LBK, Music Note phase
B
1. Approx. 8 ha
2. LBK
C
Czekaj-Zastawny 2000a; 2008a

9. Alojzów, site 3
1. Werbkowice comm., Hrubieszów distr., Lubelskie voiv.
2. Huczwa river basin/Bug river basin/Vistula river basin
3. 50°45'10.8"N, 23°49'14.5"E
4. Valley slope
A –

B
1. Approx. 0.5 ha
2. LBK
C
Czekaj-Zastawny 2008a

10. Andruszkowice, site 4
1. Samborzec comm., Sandomierz distr., Świętokrzyskie voiv.
2. Koprzywianka stream basin/upper Vistula river basin
3. 50°40'11.6"N, 21°41'51.9"E
4. Border zone of upland
A –
B
1. Approx. 100 m²
2. LBK
C
Czekaj-Zastawny 2008a; Kowalewska-Marszałek 1992

11. Andruszkowice, site 6
1. Samborzec comm., Sandomierz distr., Świętokrzyskie voiv.
2. Koprzywianka stream basin/upper Vistula river basin
3. 50°40'10.5"N, 21°42'18"E
4. Border zone of upland
A –
B
1. Approx. 5 ha
2. LBK, Želiezovce phase (through ŽIIb)
C
Czekaj-Zastawny 2008a; Kowalewska-Marszałek 1992

12. Andruszkowice, site 7
1. Samborzec comm., Sandomierz distr., Świętokrzyskie voiv.
2. Koprzywianka stream basin/upper Vistula river basin
3. 50°40'16"N, 21°42'28.9"E
4. Border zone of upland/valley slope and border
A –
B
1. Approx. 100 m²
2. LBK, Ia (*Gniechowice*) phase
C
Czekaj-Zastawny 2008a; Kowalewska-Marszałek 1992

13. Babica, site 2
1. Czudec comm., Strzyżów distr., Podkarpackie voiv.
2. Wisłok river basin/San river basin/upper Vistula river basin
3. 49°56'07.2"N, 21°53'59.1"E
4. Valley border
A –
B
1. Approx. 100 m²
2. LBK?
C
Czekaj-Zastawny 2008a; Sulimirski 1961

14. Baranów, site 15
1. Skalbimierz comm., Kazimierza Wielka distr., Świętokrzyskie voiv.
2. Nidzica river basin/upper Vistula river basin
3. 50°17'35.5"N, 20°21'13.4"E
4. Valley border
A –
B
1. Approx. 100 m²
2. LBK?

C

Czekaj-Zastawny 2008a

15. Barbarka, site 1
1. Skała comm., Kraków distr., Małopolskie voiv.
2. Dłubnia river basin/upper Vistula river basin
3. 50°15'42.9"N, 19°53'33.3"E
4. Outside valleys

A –

B
1. Approx. 2.5 ha
2. LBK

C

Czekaj-Zastawny 2008a

16. Barbarka, site 4
1. Skała comm., Kraków distr., Małopolskie voiv.
2. Dłubnia river basin/upper Vistula river basin
3. 50°15'55.1"N, 19°53'57.8"E
4. Valley border

A –

B
1. Approx. 100 m^2
2. LBK?

C

Czekaj-Zastawny 2008a

17. Batowice, site 4/III
1. Zielonki comm., Kraków distr., Małopolskie voiv.
2. Dłubnia river basin/upper Vistula river basin
3. 50°06'44.7"N, 20°01'11.9"E
4. Low terrace

A –

B
1. Approx. 6 ha
2. LBK?

C

Czekaj-Zastawny 2008a; Kruk 1969

18. Bazów, site 4
1. Łoniów comm., Sandomierz distr., Świętokrzyskie voiv.
2. Koprzywianka stream basin/upper Vistula river basin
3. 50°35'11.2"N, 21°48'34.1"E
4. Border zone of upland

A –

B
1. Approx. 100 m^2
2. LBK

C

Czekaj-Zastawny 2008a; Kowalewska-Marszałek 1992

19. Beszowa, site 1
1. Łubnice comm., Staszów distr., Świętokrzyskie voiv.
2. Wschodnia stream basin/upper Vistula river basin
3. 50°25'27.4"N, 21°06'56.2"E
4. Border zone of upland

A –

B
1. Approx. 100 m^2
2. LBK

C

Czekaj-Zastawny 2008a

20. Beszyce Górne, site 24
1. Koprzywnica comm., Sandomierz distr., Świętokrzyskie voiv.
2. Koprzywianka stream basin/upper Vistula river basin
3. 50°35'49.9"N, 21°30'27.1"E
4. Valley low terrace

A –

B
1. Approx. 100 m^2
2. LBK

C

Czekaj-Zastawny 2008a; Kowalewska-Marszałek 1992

21. Będziemyśl, site 16
1. Sędziszów Małopolski comm., Ropczyce-Sędziszów distr., Podkarpackie voiv.
2. Wisłoka river basin/Vistula river basin
3. 50°03'22.9"N, 21°46'21.1"E
4. Valley slope and border

A –

B
1. Approx. 100 m^2
2. LBK

C

Czekaj-Zastawny 2008a

22. Będziemyśl, site 20
1. Sędziszów Małopolski comm., Ropczyce-Sędziszów distr., Podkarpackie voiv.
2. Wisłoka river basin/Vistula river basin
3. 50°03'15.1"N, 21°46'44.9"E
4. Valley slope and border

A –

B
1. Approx. 100 m^2
2. LBK

C

Czekaj-Zastawny 2008a

23. Będzienica, site 9
1. Iwierzyce comm., Ropczyce-Sędziszów distr., Podkarpackie voiv.
2. Wielopolka stream basin/Wisłoka river basin/upper Vistula river basin
3. 49°59'44.3"N, 21°46'41.6"E
4. Valley border

A –

B
1. Approx. 100 m^2
2. LBK

C

Czekaj-Zastawny 2008a

24. Białoborze, site 7
1. Stopnica comm., Busko-Zdrój distr., Świętokrzyskie voiv.
2. Wschodnia river basin/upper Vistula river basin
3. 50°26'52.2"N, 20°57'51.7"E
4. Valley slope

A –

B
1. Approx. 5 ha
2. LBK

C

Czekaj-Zastawny 2008a

25. Biały Kościół, site 2
1. Wielka Wieś comm., Kraków distr., Małopolskie voiv.
2. Prądnik river basin/upper Vistula river basin
3. 50°10'26.7"N, 19°50'41"E

4. "Nad Dziurawcem" Cave

A

1. S. Czarnowski
2. 1899–1900
3. Cave sediments completely explorated
4. Cave camp
5. LBK

B

1. –
2. LBK

C

Czekaj-Zastawny 2008a; Rook 1980

26. Biały Kościół, site 10
1. Wielka Wieś comm., Kraków distr., Małopolskie voiv.
2. Prądnik river basin/upper Vistula river basin
3. 50°10'00.2"N, 19°50'07"E
4. Outside valleys

A –

B

1. Approx. 0.5 ha
2. LBK?

C

Czekaj-Zastawny 2008a; Lech *et al.* 1984

27. Biechów, site 5
1. Pacanów comm., Busko Zdrój distr., Świętokrzyskie voiv.
2. Strumień river basin/upper Vistula river basin
3. 50°22'41.1"N, 20°59'30.3"E
4. Valley low terrace/valley slope and border

A –

B

1. Approx. 100 m²
2. LBK

C

Czekaj-Zastawny 2008a

28. Biechów, site 13
1. Pacanów comm., Busko Zdrój distr., Świętokrzyskie voiv.
2. Strumień river basin/upper Vistula river basin
3. 50°22'25"N, 20°59'46.2"E
4. Valley floor

A –

B

1. Approx. 100 m²
2. LBK

C

Czekaj-Zastawny 2008a

29. Biechów, site 16
1. Pacanów comm., Busko Zdrój distr., Świętokrzyskie voiv.
2. Strumień river basin/upper Vistula river basin
3. 50°22'40.2"N, 21°00'06.3"E
4. Border zone of upland

A –

B

1. Approx. 100 m²
2. LBK

C

Czekaj-Zastawny 2008a

30. Bieliny, site 5
1. Ulanów comm., Nisko distr., Podkarpackie voiv.
2. San river basin/upper Vistula river basin
3. 50°26'46.2"N, 22°17'09.8"E
4. Valley low terrace/valley border

A –

B

1. Approx. 100 m²
2. LBK

C

Czekaj-Zastawny 2008a

31. Biesiadki, site 2
1. Gnojnik comm., Brzesko distr., Małopolskie voiv.
2. Dunajec river basin/upper Vistula river basin
3. 49°53'42.8"N, 20°39'20.6"E
4. Valley slope

A –

B

1. Approx. 100 m²
2. LBK

C

Czekaj-Zastawny 2008a

32. Biesiadki, site 11
1. Gnojnik comm., Brzesko distr., Małopolskie voiv.
2. Dunajec river basin/upper Vistula river basin
3. 49°53'49.5"N, 20°39'22.5"E
4. Valley border

A –

B

1. Approx. 100 m²
2. LBK

C

Czekaj-Zastawny 2008a

33. Biesiadki, site 12
1. Gnojnik comm., Brzesko distr., Małopolskie voiv.
2. Dunajec river basin/upper Vistula river basin
3. 49°53'46.2"N, 20°39'32.8"E
4. Valley border

A –

B

1. Approx. 100 m²
2. LBK

C

Czekaj-Zastawny 2008a

34. Biesiadki, site 13
1. Gnojnik comm., Brzesko distr., Małopolskie voiv.
2. Dunajec river basin/upper Vistula river basin
3. 49°53'36.2"N, 20°39'46.1"E
4. Valley border

A –

B

1. Approx. 100 m²
2. LBK

C

Czekaj-Zastawny 2008a

35. Biesiadki, site 16
1. Gnojnik comm., Brzesko distr., Małopolskie voiv.
2. Dunajec river basin/upper Vistula river basin
3. 49°53'31.2"N, 20°39'33.1"E
4. Valley border

A –

B

1. Approx. 100 m²
2. LBK

C

Czekaj-Zastawny 2008a

36. Biesiadki, site 65
  1. Gnojnik comm., Brzesko distr., Małopolskie voiv.
  2. Dunajec river basin/upper Vistula river basin
  3. 49°54'32.8"N, 20°40'02.9"E
  4. Valley border
A –
B
  1. Approx. 1 ha
  2. LBK
C
  Valde-Nowak 2007

37. Bilczów, site 3
  1. Wiślica comm., Busko-Zdrój distr., Świętokrzyskie voiv.
  2. Nida river basin/upper Vistula river basin
  3. 50°23'29.8"N, 20°44'16.6"E
  4. Valley slope
A –
B
  1. Approx. 100 m²
  2. LBK?
C
  Czekaj-Zastawny 2008a

38. Biskupice, site 3
  1. Biskupice comm., Wieliczka distr., Małopolskie voiv.
  2. Raba river basin/upper Vistula river basin
  3. 49°57'41.6"N, 20°07'53.7"E
  4. Outside valleys
A
  1. J. Rydzewski
  2. 1966
  3. ?
  4. Settlement or camp;
  5. LBK
B
  1. Approx. 5 ha
  2. LBK
C
  Czekaj-Zastawny 2008a; Szybowicz 1980

39. Biskupice, site 18
  1. Biskupice comm., Wieliczka distr., Małopolskie voiv.
  2. Raba river basin/upper Vistula river basin
  3. 49°57'31.4"N, 20°07'41.4"E
  4. Outside valleys
A –
B
  1. Approx. 1 ha
  2. LBK
C
  Czekaj-Zastawny 2008a

40. Biskupice, site 1
  1. Iwanowice comm., Kraków distr., Małopolskie voiv.
  2. Dłubnia river basin/upper Vistula river basin
  3. 50°13'54.6"N, 19°59'00"E
  4. Valley upper terrace
A –
B
  1. Approx. 100 m²
  2. LBK?
C
  Czekaj-Zastawny 2008a

41. Biskupice, site 2
  1. Iwanowice comm., Kraków distr., Małopolskie voiv.
  2. Dłubnia river basin/upper Vistula river basin
  3. 50°13'54.7"N, 19°59'15.3"E
  4. Outside valleys
A –
B
  1. Approx. 100 m²
  2. LBK?
C
  Czekaj-Zastawny 2008a

42. Biskupice, site 9
  1. Iwanowice comm., Kraków distr., Małopolskie voiv.
  2. Dłubnia river basin/upper Vistula river basin
  3. 50°14'07"N, 19°59'03.1"E
  4. Valley upper terrace
A –
B
  1. Approx. 0.5 ha
  2. LBK
C
  Czekaj-Zastawny 2008a

43. Biskupice, site 10
  1. Iwanowice comm., Kraków distr., Małopolskie voiv.
  2. Dłubnia river basin/upper Vistula river basin
  3. 50°14'13.7"N, 19°59'14.5"E
  4. Border zone of upland
A –
B
  1. Approx. 1.5 ha
  2. LBK
C
  Czekaj-Zastawny 2008a

44. Biskupice, site 4
  1. Koszyce comm., Proszowice distr., Małopolskie voiv.
  2. Szreniawa river basin/upper Vistula river basin
  3. 50°10'37.1"N, 20°31'07"E
  4. Valley upper terrace
A –
B
  1. Approx. 100 m²
  2. LBK
C
  Czekaj-Zastawny 2008a; Rydzewski 1972

45. Biskupice, site 7
  1. Pacanów comm., Busko Zdrój distr., Świętokrzyskie voiv.
  2. Strumień river basin/upper Vistula river basin
  3. 50°24'41.3"N, 21°07'17.7"E
  4. Valley slope
A –
B
  1. Approx. 100 m²
  2. LBK
C
  Czekaj-Zastawny 2008a

46. Biórków Wielki, site 16
  1. Koniusza comm., Proszowice distr., Małopolskie voiv.
  2. Szreniawa river basin/upper Vistula river basin
  3. 50°10'03.1"N, 20°10'08.1"E
  4. Valley slope
A –

B

1. Approx. 100 m²
2. LBK?

C

Czekaj-Zastawny 2008a

47. Błogocice, site 1

1. Radziemice comm., Proszowice distr., Małopolskie voiv.
2. Szreniawa river basin/upper Vistula river basin
3. 50°14'28.7"N, 20°13'38"E
4. Outside valleys

A –

B

1. Approx. 50 m²
2. LBK?

C

Czekaj-Zastawny 2008a

48. Błonie, site 2

1. Koprzywnica comm., Sandomierz distr., Świętokrzyskie voiv.
2. Upper Vistula river basin
3. 50°35'19.9"N, 21°37'03"E
4. Valley slope

A –

B

1. Approx. 100 m²
2. LBK

C

Czekaj-Zastawny 2008a; Kowalewska-Marszałek 1992

49. Bobin, site 1

1. Proszowice comm., Proszowice distr., Małopolskie voiv.
2. Szreniawa river basin/upper Vistula river basin
3. 50°10'26.1"N, 20°26'36.8"E
4. Valley low terrace

A –

B

1. Approx. 100 m²
2. LBK

C

Czekaj-Zastawny 2008a; Rydzewski 1972

50. Bobin, site 4

1. Proszowice comm., Proszowice distr., Małopolskie voiv.
2. Szreniawa river basin/upper Vistula river basin
3. 50°10'14.8"N, 20°26'41.7"E
4. Valley low terrace

A –

B

1. Approx. 100 m²
2. LBK

C

Czekaj-Zastawny 2008a; Rydzewski 1972

51. Bochnia, site 82

1. Bochnia comm., Bochnia distr., Małopolskie voiv.
2. Raba river basin/upper Vistula river basin
3. 49°59'21.1"N, 20°24'51.9"E
4. Valley slope

A –

B

1. Approx. 0.5 ha
2. LBK?

C

Czekaj-Zastawny 2008a

52. Bodaczów, site 34

1. Szczebrzeszyn comm., Zamość distr., Lubelskie voiv.
2. Wieprz river basin/Bug river basin/Vistula river basin
3. 50°43'09.6"N, 23°01'54.3"E
4. Valley slope

A –

B

1. Approx. 100 m²
2. LBK

C

Czekaj-Zastawny 2008a

53. Bodzanów, site 5

1. Biskupice comm., Wieliczka distr., Małopolskie voiv.
2. Raba river basin/upper Vistula river basin
3. 49°59'27.4"N, 20°08'33.7"E
4. Outside valleys

A –

B

1. Approx. 5 ha
2. LBK

C

Czekaj-Zastawny 2008a

54. Boguchwała, site 1

1. Boguchwała comm., Rzeszów distr., Podkarpackie voiv.
2. Wisłok river basin/San river basin/upper Vistula river basin
3. 49°59'14.7"N, 21°54'56.6"E
4. Valley low terrace

A –

B

1. Approx. 1 ha
2. LBK, Music Note phase, Želiezovce phase; imports of Bükk culture

C

Czekaj-Zastawny 2008a; Moskwa 1961

55. Boguchwała, site 2

1. Boguchwała comm., Rzeszów distr., Podkarpackie voiv.
2. Wisłok river basin/San river basin/upper Vistula river basin
3. 49°58'32.2"N, 21°54'56.5"E
4. Valley low terrace

A

1. A. Żaki, G. Leńczyk; A Dzieduszycka-Machnikowa
2. 1947, 1953, 1956
3. 200 m²
4. Settlement; 25 features (3 elongated pits belongs to long houses in it)
5. LBK, Music Note phase, Želiezovce phase (through ŽIIb); imports of Bükk culture

B

1. Approx. 5 ha
2. LBK

C

Czekaj-Zastawny 2008a; Dzieduszycka-Machnikowa 1960; Saile *et al.* 2008; Żaki 1948

56. Bolechowice, site 1

1. Zabierzów comm., Kraków distr., Małopolskie voiv.
2. Rudawa stream basin/upper Vistula river basin
3. 50°09'04.9"N, 19°48'49.4"E
4. "Bezimienna" Cave

A

1. G. Ossowski
2. 1879
3. ?

4. Cave camp

5. LBK

B

1. –

2. LBK

C

Czekaj-Zastawny 2008a; Ossowski 1880; Rook 1980

57. Bolechowice, site 3

1. Zabierzów comm., Kraków distr., Małopolskie voiv.

2. Rudawa river basin/upper Vistula river basin

3. 50°09'29.2"N, 19°49'07.6"E

4. Valley slope

A –

B

1. Approx. 0.5 ha

2. LBK

C

Czekaj-Zastawny 2008a

58. Bolechowice, site 9

1. Zabierzów comm., Kraków distr., Małopolskie voiv.

2. Rudawa river basin/upper Vistula river basin

3. 50°08'40.9"N, 19°47'55.7"E

4. Valley border

A

1. A Breitenfellner, E. Rook

2. 1987-88

3. 150 m^2

4. Settlement; 50 features (the most belongs to two long houses)

5. LBK, Music Note phase

B

1. Approx. 5 ha

2. LBK

C

Breitenfellner & Rook 1991; Czekaj-Zastawny 2008a

59. Bolechowice, site 25

1. Zabierzów comm., Kraków distr., Małopolskie voiv.

2. Rudawa stream basin/upper Vistula river basin

3. 50°08'42.6"N, 19°48'50.6"E

4. Valley slope

A –

B

1. Approx. 0.5 ha

2. LBK

C

Czekaj-Zastawny 2008a

60. Bolesław, site 1

1. Bolesław comm., Dąbrowa distr., Małopolskie voiv.

2. Upper Vistula river basin

3. 50°16'31"N, 20°53'21.7"E

4. Valley border

A –

B

1. Approx. 100 m^2

2. LBK?

C

Czekaj-Zastawny 2008a

61. Borek Nowy, site 3

1. Błażowa comm., Rzeszów distr., Podkarpackie voiv.

2. Wisłok river basin/San river basin/upper Vistula river basin

3. 49°55'24.5"N, 22°04'56.5"E

4. Valley slope

A –

B

1. Approx. 100 m^2

2. LBK

C

Czekaj-Zastawny 2008a

62. Bosutów, site 11/I

1. Zielonki comm., Kraków distr., Małopolskie voiv.

2. Dłubnia river basin/upper Vistula river basin

3. 50°07'32.2"N, 19°58'59.8"E

4. Outside valleys

A –

B

1. Approx. 0.5 ha

2. LBK?

C

Czekaj-Zastawny 2008a; Kruk 1969

63. Brodzica, site 23

1. Hrubieszów comm., Hrubieszów distr., Lubelskie voiv.

2. Huczwa river basin/Bug river basin/Vistula river basin

3. 50°47'57.3"N, 23°50'52.2"E

4. Valley border

A –

B

1. Approx. 0.5 ha

2. LBK

C

Czekaj-Zastawny 2008a

64. Broniszowice, site X

1. Bodzechów comm., Ostrowiec Świetokrzyski distr., Świętokrzyskie voiv.

2. Opatówka stream basin/upper Vistula river basin

3. 50°52'21.2"N, 21°19'55.2"E

4. Valley border

A –

B

1. Approx. 5 ha

2. LBK

C

Bąbel 1975; Czekaj-Zastawny 2008a; Kowalewska-Marszałek 1992

65. Broniszowice, site XI

1. Bodzechów comm., Ostrowiec Świetokrzyski distr., Świętokrzyskie voiv.

2. Opatówka stream basin/upper Vistula river basin

3. 50°52'19.6"N, 21°19'28.9"E

4. Valley border

A –

B

1. Approx. 100 m^2

2. LBK?

C

Bąbel 1975; Czekaj-Zastawny 2008a; Kowalewska-Marszałek 1992

66. Brończyce, site 1

1. Bejsce comm., Kazimierza Wielka distr., Świętokrzyskie voiv.

2. Nidzica river basin/upper Vistula river basin

3. 50°13'15.7"N, 20°35'57.2"E

4. Valley low terrace

A –
B

1. Approx. 100 m^2
2. LBK, Želiezovce phase

C

Czekaj-Zastawny 2008a

67. Brończyce, site 1

1. Słomniki comm., Kraków distr., Małopolskie voiv.
2. Szreniawa river basin/upper Vistula river basin
3. 50°13'48.4"N, 20°06'53.9"E
4. Border zone of upland

A –
B

1. Approx. 15 ha
2. LBK, Želiezovce phase

C

Czekaj-Zastawny 2008a; Kruk 1970

68. Brończyce, site 5

1. Słomniki comm., Kraków distr., Małopolskie voiv.
2. Szreniawa river basin/upper Vistula river basin
3. 50°13'43.1"N, 20°07'32.6"E
4. Valley low terrace

A –
B

1. Approx. 5 ha
2. LBK

C

Czekaj-Zastawny 2008a; Kruk 1970

69. Brończyce, site 6

1. Słomniki comm., Kraków distr., Małopolskie voiv.
2. Szreniawa river basin/upper Vistula river basin
3. 50°13'53.1"N, 20°07'51.8"E
4. Valley low terrace

A –
B

1. Approx. 5 ha
2. LBK

C

Czekaj-Zastawny 2008a; Kruk 1970

70. Bródek, site 2

1. Łabunie comm., Zamość distr., Lubelskie voiv.
2. Wieprz river basin/Bug river basin/Vistula river basin
3. 50°40'06.1"N, 23°24'11.4"E
4. Valley slope

A –
B

1. Approx. 100 m^2
2. LBK

C

Czekaj-Zastawny 2008a

71. Brzezie, site 17

1. Kłaj comm., Wieliczka distr., Małopolskie voiv.
2. Tusznica stream basin/Raba river basin/upper Vistula river basin
3. 49°59'45.5"N, 20°13'12.4"E
4. Valley low terrace

A

1. A. Czekaj-Zastawny (The Cracow Team for Archaeological Supervision of Motorway Construction, Institute of Archaeology and Ethnology Polish Academy of Sciences, Museum of Archaeology Cracow, Jagiellonian University)

2. 2000-2007
3. 6.5 ha
4. Settlement; 1447 features (26 long houses and 3 human graves in it)
5. LBK, Music Note phase; imports of Tisadob-Kapušany and Bükk culture

6230 ± 100 BP, 6155 ± 100 BP, 6410 ± 100 BP, 6330 ± 100 BP, 6215 ± 80 BP, 6180 ± 80 BP, 6130 ± 80 BP, 5830 ± 80 BP, 5780 ± 70 BP, 6140 ± 80 BP, 5840 ± 70 BP, 5720 ± 80 BP, 5640 ± 80 BP, 6190 ± 70 BP, 5660 ± 80 BP, 6260 ± 80 BP

B

1. Approx. 10 ha
2. LBK

C

Czekaj-Zastawny 2008a; 2008b; Czekaj-Zastawny & Zastawny 2006; Czekaj-Zastawny *et al.* 2007

72. Brzezie, site 40

1. Kłaj comm., Wieliczka distr., Małopolskie voiv.
2. Tusznica stream basin/Raba river basin/upper Vistula river basin
3. 49°59'37.1"N, 20°13'53.4"E
4. Valley slope

A

1. The Cracow Team for Archaeological Supervision of Motorway Construction, Institute of Archaeology and Ethnology Polish Academy of Sciences, Museum of Archaeology Cracow, Jagiellonian University) – P. Włodarczak, A. Golański, E. Schellner
2. 2004-2005
3. 25047 m^2
4. Settlement; 720 features (at list 5 long houses in it)
5. LBK, Želiezovce phase

B

1. Approx. 1 ha
2. LBK

C

Czekaj-Zastawny 2008a; Włodarczak 2006

73. Brzezinka, site 6

1. Zabierzów comm., Kraków distr., Małopolskie voiv.
2. Rudawa stream basin/upper Vistula river basin
3. 50°08'03.9"N, 19°44'46.4"E
4. Valley border/valley upper terrace

A –
B

1. Approx. 5 ha
2. LBK, Music Note phase, Želiezovce phase

C

Czekaj-Zastawny 2008a

74. Brzoskwinia, site 14

1. Rudawa comm., Kraków distr., Małopolskie voiv.
2. Rudawa stream basin/upper Vistula river basin
3. 50°05'47.7"N, 19°43'26.4"E
4. Valley slope

A –
B

1. Approx. 100 m^2
2. LBK

C

Data from AZP card

75. Budy Łańcuckie, site 5

1. Białobrzegi comm., Łańcut distr., Podkarpackie voiv.

2. Wisłok river basin/San river basin/upper Vistula river basin
3. 50°07'09.4"N, 22°24'55.4"E
4. Valley low terrace

A –

B

1. Approx. 100 m²
2. LBK

C

Czekaj-Zastawny 2008a

76. Budy Łańcuckie, site 9A
1. Białobrzegi comm., Łańcut distr., Podkarpackie voiv.
2. Wisłok river basin/San river basin/upper Vistula river basin
3. 50°06'56.9"N, 22°24'38.4"E
4. Valley low terrace

A –

B

1. Approx. 100 m²
2. LBK?

C

Czekaj-Zastawny 2008a

77. Chałupki, site 2
1. Przeworsk comm., Przeworsk distr., Podkarpackie voiv.
2. Mleczka stream basin/Wisłok river basin/San river basin/upper Vistula river basin
3. 50°04'57.2"N, 22°31'25.4"E
4. Valley slope

A –

B

1. Approx. 100 m²
2. LBK

C

Czekaj-Zastawny 2008a

78. Chełm, site 1
1. Bochnia comm., Bochnia distr., Małpolskie voiv.
2. Raba river basin/upper Vistula river basin
3. 49°58'31.4"N, 20°18'42.4"E
4. Valley low terrace

A

1. M. Cabalska
2. 1966-67
3. 150 m²
4. Settlement trace; no features, 2 pottery fragments
5. LBK

B

1. Approx. 100 m²
2. LBK

C

Cabalska 1969; 1975; Czekaj-Zastawny 2008a; Sochacki 1969

79. Chorągwica, site 7
1. Wieliczka comm., Wieliczka distr., Małpolskie voiv.
2. Raba river basin/upper Vistula river basin
3. 49°57'46.6"N, 20°05'38.4"E
4. Outside valleys

A –

B

1. Approx. 100 m²
2. LBK

C

Czekaj-Zastawny 2008a

80. Chroberz, site 5
1. Złota comm., Pińczów distr., Świętokrzyskie voiv.

2. Nida river basin/upper Vistula river basin
3. 50°25'04.8"N, 20°33'43.4"E
4. Valley low terrace

A –

B

1. Approx. 100 m²
2. LBK?

C

Czekaj-Zastawny 2008a

81. Chruszczyna, site 2
1. Kazimierza Wielka comm., Kazimierza Wielka distr., Świętokrzyskie voiv.
2. Nidzica river basin/upper Vistula river basin
3. 50°14'11"N, 20°29'04.4"E
4. Valley slope

A –

B

1. Approx. 0.5 ha
2. LBK?

C

Czekaj-Zastawny 2008a; Rydzewski 1973

82. Chruszczyna, site 3
1. Kazimierza Wielka comm., Kazimierza Wielka distr., Świętokrzyskie voiv.
2. Nidzica river basin/upper Vistula river basin
3. 50°14'04.3"N, 20°29'01.4"E
4. Valley slope

A –

B

1. Approx. 0.5 ha
2. LBK?

C

Czekaj-Zastawny 2008a; Rydzewski 1973

83. Cianowice, site 16
1. Skała comm., Kraków distr., Małpolskie voiv.
2. Prądnik river basin/upper Vistula river basin
3. 50°10'38.4"N, 19°52'34"E
4. Valley slope

A –

B

1. Approx. 100 m²
2. LBK?

C

Czekaj-Zastawny 2008a

84. Ciborowice, site 1
1. Proszowice comm., Proszowice distr., Małpolskie voiv.
2. Szreniawa river basin/upper Vistula river basin
3. 50°11'09.1"N, 20°21'34"E
4. Valley low terrace

A –

B

1. Approx. 5 ha
2. LBK

C

Czekaj-Zastawny 2008a; Rydzewski 1972

85. Czajęcice, site 3
1. Proszowice comm., Proszowice distr., Małpolskie voiv.
2. Szreniawa river basin/upper Vistula river basin
3. 50°10'59.4"N, 20°27'48.4"E
4. Border zone of upland

A –

B

1. Approx. 100 m²
2. LBK?

C

Czekaj-Zastawny 2008a; Rydzewski 1972

86. Czaple Małe, site 18
1. Gołcza comm., Miechów distr., Małpolskie voiv.
2. Dłubnia river basin/upper Vistula river basin
3. 50°17'44.4"N, 19°56'55.4"E
4. Outside valleys

A –

B

1. Approx. 100 m²
2. LBK

C

Czekaj-Zastawny 2008a

87. Czarna, site 2
1. Czarna comm., Łańcut distr., Podkarpackie voiv.
2. Wisłok river basin/San river basin/upper Vistula river basin
3. 50°06'20.2"N, 22°10'38.4"E
4. Valley low terrace

A –

B

1. Approx. 100 m²
2. LBK?

C

Czekaj-Zastawny 2008a

88. Czchów, site 10
1. Czchów comm., Brzesko distr., Małpolskie voiv.
2. Dunajec basin/upper Vistula river basin
3. 49°50'06.1"N, 20°38'19.4"E
4. Outside valleys

A

1. P. Valde-Nowak, P. Madej
2. 1997, 1999
3. 235 m²
4. Settlement trace; no features, few pottery fragments

B

1. Approx. 100 m²
2. LBK

C

Czekaj-Zastawny 2008a; Kruk 1970; Madej & Valde-Nowak 1997-1998; 2001; Valde-Nowak & Madej 1997

89. Czechy, site 1
1. Słomniki comm., Kraków distr., Małpolskie voiv.
2. Szreniawa river basin/upper Vistula river basin
3. 50°13'34.5"N, 20°09'35.4"E
4. Valley low terrace

A –

B

1. Approx. 100 m²
2. LBK

C

Czekaj-Zastawny 2008a; Kruk 1970

90. Czechy, site 3
1. Słomniki comm., Kraków distr., Małpolskie voiv.
2. Szreniawa river basin/upper Vistula river basin
3. 50°12'58.6"N, 20°10'42.4"E
4. Valley low terrace

A –

B

1. Approx. 0.5 ha
2. LBK

C

Czekaj-Zastawny 2008a

91. Czechy, site 15
1. Słomniki comm., Kraków distr., Małpolskie voiv.
2. Szreniawa river basin/upper Vistula river basin
3. 50°13'14.4"N, 20°10'13.4"E
4. Valley low terrace

A –

B

1. Approx. 0.5 ha
2. LBK

C

Czekaj-Zastawny 2008a

92. Czerwona Góra, site III
1. Sadowie comm., Opatów distr., Świętokrzyskie voiv.
2. Opatówka stream basin/upper Vistula river basin
3. 50°50'29.6"N, 21°18'08.4"E
4. Valley border

A –

B

1. Approx. 100 m²
2. LBK?

C

Bąbel 1975; Czekaj-Zastawny 2008a; Kowalewska-Marszałek 1992

93. Czerwona Góra, site VI
1. Sadowie comm., Opatów distr., Świętokrzyskie voiv.
2. Opatówka stream basin/upper Vistula river basin
3. 50°50'59.7"N, 21°18'05.4"E
4. Valley border

A –

B

1. Approx. 100 m²
2. LBK

C

Bąbel 1975; Czekaj-Zastawny 2008a; Kowalewska-Marszałek 1992

94. Czerwona Góra, site VII
1. Sadowie comm., Opatów distr., Świętokrzyskie voiv.
2. Opatówka stream basin/upper Vistula river basin
3. 50°51'05.9"N, 21°18'59.4"E
4. Valley border

A –

B

1. Approx. 3 ha
2. LBK

C

Bąbel 1975; Czekaj-Zastawny 2008a; Kowalewska-Marszałek 1992

95. Czułówek, site 12
1. Czernichów comm., Kraków distr., Małpolskie voiv.
2. Upper Vistula river basin
3. 50°02'24.2"N, 19°39'49.4"E
4. Outside valleys

A –

B

1. Approx. 100 m²
2. LBK?

C

Czekaj-Zastawny 2008a

96. Czyżów, site 16
1. Stopnica comm., Busko Zdrój distr., Świętokrzyskie voiv.
2. Wschodnia river basin/upper Vistula river basin
3. 50°28'56.7"N, 20°59'25.4"E
4. Valley border

A –

B
1. Approx. 0.5 hectere
2. LBK

C
Czekaj-Zastawny 2008a

97. Ćmielów, site 2
1. Ćmielów comm., Ostrowiec Świętokrzyski distr., Świętokrzyskie voiv.
2. Kamienna stream basin/upper Vistula river basin
3. 50°53'27.1"N, 21°29'31"E
4. Valley slope

A
1. Muzeum Okręgowe w Sandomierzu
2. 1985
3. 50 m^2
4. Settlement or camp; no features, 100 pottery fragments
5. LBK, Ia (*Gniechowice*) phase, Music Note phase

B
1. Approx. 5 ha
2. LBK

C
Czekaj-Zastawny 2008a; Kowalewska-Marszałek 1992; Ścibior 1993

98. Ćmielów, site 3
1. Ćmielów comm., Ostrowiec Świętokrzyski distr., Świętokrzyskie voiv.
2. Kamienna stream basin/upper Vistula river basin
3. 50°52'27.2"N, 21°29'18"E
4. Border zone of upland

A –

B
1. Approx. 5 ha
2. LBK

C
Czekaj-Zastawny 2008a; Kowalewska-Marszałek 1992; Ścibior 1986

99. Damice, site 2
1. Iwanowice comm., Kraków distr., Małopolskie voiv.
2. Dłubnia river basin/upper Vistula river basin
3. 50°12'21"N, 19°57'52.4"E
4. Valley slope

A –

B
1. Approx. 100 m^2
2. LBK?

C
Czekaj-Zastawny 2008a

100. Damice, site 3
1. Iwanowice comm., Kraków distr., Małopolskie voiv.
2. Dłubnia river basin/upper Vistula river basin
3. 50°12'05.1"N, 19°57'34.3"E
4. Valley border

A –

B
1. Approx. 0.5 ha
2. LBK?

C
Czekaj-Zastawny 2008a

101. Damice, site 6
1. Iwanowice comm., Kraków distr., Małopolskie voiv.
2. Dłubnia river basin/upper Vistula river basin
3. 50°12'09.6"N, 19°56'48.3"E
4. Border zone of upland

A –

B
1. Approx. 0.5 ha
2. LBK?

C
Czekaj-Zastawny 2008a

102. Dąbie, site 2
1. Włoszczowa comm., Włoszczowa distr., Świętokrzyskie voiv.
2. Biała Nida stream basin/Nida river basin/upper Vistula river basin
3. 50°43'52"N, 20°02'44.2"E
4. Valley slope

A –

B
1. Approx. 0.5 ha
2. LBK

C
Czekaj-Zastawny 2008a

103. Dąbrowa, site 3
1. Kłaj comm., Wieliczka distr., Małopolskie voiv.
2. Tusznica stream basin/Raba river basin/upper Vistula river basin
3. 50°00'09.8"N, 20°14'27.7"E
4. Valley border/border zone of upland

A
1. J. Rydlewski
2. 1996
3. 50 m^2
4. Settlement; no features, few hundred pottery fragments
5. LBK

B
1. Approx. 5 ha
2. LBK

C
Czekaj-Zastawny 2008a; Zastawny 2008

104. Dąbrowa, site 11
1. Kłaj comm., Wieliczka distr., Małopolskie voiv.
2. Tusznica stream basin/Raba river basin/upper Vistula river basin
3. 49°59'58.1"N, 20°15'40.6"E
4. Valley border

A –

B
1. Approx. 1 ha
2. LBK

C
Czekaj-Zastawny 2008a

105. Dąbrowa, site 22
1. Świlcza comm., Rzeszów distr., Małopolskie voiv.
2. Wisłok river basin/San river basin/upper Vistula river basin
3. 50°04'08.7"N, 21°48'36.6"

4. Valley slope and border

A –

B

   1. Approx. 100 m^2

   2. LBK

C

   Czekaj-Zastawny 2008a

106. Dobranowice, site 6

   1. Wieliczka comm., Wieliczka distr., Małopolskie voiv.

   2. Raba river basin/upper Vistula river basin

   3. 49°56'46.1"N, 20°07'19.3"E

   4. Outside valleys

A –

B

   1. Approx. 100 m^2

   2. LBK

C

   Czekaj-Zastawny 2008a; Szybowicz 1980

107. Dobużek Kolonia, site 1

   1. Łaszczów comm., Tomaszów Lubelski distr., Lubelskie voiv.

   2. Huczwa stream basin/Bug river basin/upper Vistula river basin

   3. 50°33'16.5"N, 23°43'46.3"E

   4. Valley slope and border

A –

B

   1. Approx. 0.5 ha

   2. LBK?

C

   Czekaj-Zastawny 2008a

108. Drzenkowice, site 3

   1. Ćmielów comm., Ostrowiec Świętokrzyski distr., Świętokrzyskie voiv.

   2. Opatówka stream basin/upper Vistula river basin

   3. 50°51'51.3"N, 21°27'33.4"E

   4. Valley border

A –

B

   1. Approx. 1 ha

   2. LBK

C

   Czekaj-Zastawny 2008a; Kowalski 1975; Kowalewska-Marszałek 1992

109. Dwikozy, site 68

   1. Dwikozy comm., Sandomierz distr., Świętokrzyskie voiv.

   2. Upper Vistula river basin

   3. 50°44'02"N, 21°49'44.1"E

   4. Valley border

A –

B

   1. Approx. 1 ha

   2. LBK

C

   Czekaj-Zastawny 2008a; Kowalewska-Marszałek 1992

110. Dwikozy, site 72

   1. Dwikozy comm., Sandomierz distr., Świętokrzyskie voiv.

   2. Upper Vistula river basin

   3. 50°43'23.2"N, 21°46'27.2"E

   4. Valley border

A –

B

   1. Approx. 1 ha

   2. LBK

C

   Czekaj-Zastawny 2008a; Kowalewska-Marszałek 1992

111. Dwikozy, site 78

   1. Dwikozy comm., Sandomierz distr., Świętokrzyskie voiv.

   2. Upper Vistula river basin

   3. 50°43'40.8"N, 21°46'29.9"E

   4. Border zone of upland/ valley border

A –

B

   1. Approx. 100 m^2

   2. LBK

C

   Czekaj-Zastawny 2008a; Kowalewska-Marszałek 1992

112. Dwikozy, site 92

   1. Dwikozy comm., Sandomierz distr., Świętokrzyskie voiv.

   2. Upper Vistula river basin

   3. 50°43'50.8"N, 21°45'15.3"E

   4. Border zone of upland/ valley border

A –

B

   1. Approx. 1 ha

   2. LBK

C

   Czekaj-Zastawny 2008a; Kowalewska-Marszałek 1992

113. Działoszyce, site 5

   1. Działoszyce comm., Pińczów distr., Świętokrzyskie voiv.

   2. Nidzica river basin/upper Vistula river basin

   3. 50°21'27.4"N, 20°20'29.7"E

   4. Valley low terrace

A –

B

   1. Approx. 100 m^2

   2. LBK

C

   Czekaj-Zastawny 2008a; Liguzińska-Kruk 1981

114. Dziekanowice, site 1

   1. Działoszyce comm., Pińczów distr., Świętokrzyskie voiv.

   2. Nidzica river basin/upper Vistula river basin

   3. 50°21'05.2"N, 20°21'09.6"E

   4. Valley low terrace

A

   1. J. Machnik, S. Milisauskas, J. Kruk

   2. 1967

   3. 175 m^2

   4. Settlement or camp; no features, 23 pottery fragments

   5. LBK, Music Note phase

B

   1. Approx. 1 ha

   2. LBK

C

   Czekaj-Zastawny 2008a; Jaśkowiak & Milisauskas 2001

115. Dziekanowice, site 9/II

   1. Zielonki comm., Kraków distr., Małopolskie voiv.

   2. Dłubnia river basin/upper Vistula river basin

   3. 50°07'06.8"N, 20°01'24"E

   4. Valley low terrace

A –

B

1. Approx. 0.5 ha
2. LBK

C

Czekaj-Zastawny 2008a; Kruk 1969

116. Dziemierzyce, site 9/II
1. Racławice comm., Miechów distr., Małopolskie voiv.
2. Szreniawa river basin/upper Vistula river basin
3. 50°17'52"N, 20°12'15.4"E
4. Outside valleys

A –

B

1. Approx. 100 m^2
2. LBK

C

Czekaj-Zastawny 2008a

117. Dzierążnia, site 1
1. Działoszyce comm., Pińczów distr., Świętokrzyskie voiv.
2. Nidzica river basin/upper Vistula river basin
3. 50°22'53.4"N, 20°25'06.7"E
4. Valley slope

A –

B

1. Approx. 100 m^2
2. LBK

C

Czekaj-Zastawny 2008a; Liguzińska-Kruk 1982

118. Dziesławice, site 1
1. Stopnica comm., Busko Zdrój distr., Świętokrzyskie voiv.
2. Wschodnia river basin/upper Vistula river basin
3. 50°28'12.3"N, 20°58'22"E
4. Valley slope

A –

B

1. Approx. 1 ha
2. LBK

C

Czekaj-Zastawny 2008a

119. Dziewięcioły, site 3
1. Miechów comm., Miechów distr., Małopolskie voiv.
2. Szreniawa river basin/upper Vistula river basin
3. 50°18'03.1"N, 20°11'12.3"E
4. Outside valleys

A –

B

1. Approx. 100 m^2
2. LBK?

C

Czekaj-Zastawny 2008a

120. Faliszowice, site 1
1. Zakliczyn comm., Tarnów distr., Małopolskie voiv.
2. Dunajec river basin/upper Vistula river basin
3. 49°51'41.7"N, 20°43'31.8"E
4. Border zone of upland

A –

B

1. Approx. 100 m^2
2. LBK

C

Czekaj-Zastawny 2008a

121. Falniów, site 4
1. Miechów comm., Miechów distr., Małopolskie voiv.
2. Szreniawa river basin/upper Vistula river basin
3. 50°21'41.9"N, 19°58'06.8"E
4. Valley border

A –

B

1. Approx. 100 m^2
2. LBK?

C

Czekaj-Zastawny 2008a

122. Falniów, site 10
1. Miechów comm., Miechów distr., Małopolskie voiv.
2. Szreniawa river basin/upper Vistula river basin
3. 50°21'32.6"N, 19°57'04.2"E
4. Outside valleys

A –

B

1. Approx. 100 m^2
2. LBK?

C

Czekaj-Zastawny 2008a

123. Fałkowice, site 4
1. Gdów comm., Wieliczka distr., Małopolskie voiv.
2. Raba river basin/upper Vistula river basin
3. 49°53'57"N, 20°09'48.4"E
4. Valley upper terrace

A –

B

1. Approx. 100 m^2
2. LBK

C

Czekaj-Zastawny 2008a

124. Fredropol, site 2
1. Fredropol comm., Przemyśl distr., Podkarpackie voiv.
2. San river basin/upper Vistula river basin
3. 49°41'39.6"N, 22°44'16"E
4. Valley slope

A

1. T. Aksamit
2. 1966
3. 200 m^2
4. Settlement; 2 features (1 elongated pit in it)
5. LBK, Music Note phase, Želiezovce phase, imports of
   Bükk culture

B

1. Approx. 0.5 ha
2. LBK, Music Note phase, Želiezovce phase

C

Aksamit 1968; Czekaj-Zastawny 2008a; Czopek 1999; Saile
et al. 2008

125. Garbacz-Skała, site IV
1. Waśniów comm., Ostrowiec distr., Świętokrzyskie voiv.
2. Opatówka river basin/upper Vistula river basin
3. 50°51'37.7"N, 21°15'57"E
4. Valley slope

A –

B

1. Approx. 100 m^2
2. LBK?

C

Bąbel 1975; Czekaj-Zastawny 2008a; Kowalewska-Marszałek

1992

126. Garbów Stary, site 2
1. Dwikozy comm., Sandomierz distr., Świętokrzyskie voiv.
2. Upper Vistula river basin
3. 50°45'49.7"N, 21°48'14.6"E
4. Valley border
A –
B
    1. Approx. 100 m²
    2. LBK
C
    Czekaj-Zastawny 2008a; Kowalewska-Marszałek 1992

127. Gdów, site 8
1. Gdów comm., Wieliczka distr., Małopolskie voiv.
2. Raba river basin/upper Vistula river basin
3. 49°54'56"N, 20°12'07.7"E
4. Valley border/outside valleys
A –
B
    1. Approx. 100 m²
    2. LBK
C
    Czekaj-Zastawny 2008a

128. Gdów, site 20
1. Gdów comm., Wieliczka distr., Małopolskie voiv.
2. Raba river basin/upper Vistula river basin
3. 49°54'58.9"N, 20°12'30.3"E
4. Valley border/outside valleys
A –
B
    1. Approx. 100 m²
    2. LBK
C
    Czekaj-Zastawny 2008a

129. Gdów, site 23
1. Gdów comm., Wieliczka distr., Małopolskie voiv.
2. Raba river basin/upper Vistula river basin
3. 49°54'52.1"N, 20°11'45.9"E
4. Valley border
A –
B
    1. Approx. 100 m²
    2. LBK
C
    Czekaj-Zastawny 2008a

130. Gdów, site 24
1. Gdów comm., Wieliczka distr., Małopolskie voiv.
2. Raba river basin/upper Vistula river basin
3. 49°54'07.8"N, 20°12'07.3"E
4. Valley border
A –
B
    1. Approx. 100 m²
    2. LBK
C
    Czekaj-Zastawny 2008a

131. Gdów, site 27
1. Gdów comm., Wieliczka distr., Małopolskie voiv.
2. Raba river basin/upper Vistula river basin
3. 49°54'34.8"N, 20°12'56.2"E

4. Valley slope
A –
B
    1. Approx. 100 m²
    2. LBK
C
    Czekaj-Zastawny 2008a

132. Gdów, site 28
1. Gdów comm., Wieliczka distr., Małopolskie voiv.
2. Raba river basin/upper Vistula river basin
3. 49°54'24.4"N, 20°12'59.2"E
4. Valley slope and border
A –
B
    1. Approx. 100 m²
    2. LBK
C
    Czekaj-Zastawny 2008a

133. Giebułtów, site 1
1. Wielka Wieś comm., Kraków distr., Małopolskie voiv.
2. Prądnik river basin/upper Vistula river basin
3. 50°08'41.6"N, 19°53'02.4"E
4. Border zone of upland
A
    1. J. Żurowski
    2. 1926
    3. 200 m²
    4. Settlement; 12 features (7 human graves probably LBK in it)
    5. LBK, Music Note phase
B
    1. Approx. 15 ha
    2. LBK, Music Note phase
C
    Czekaj-Zastawny 2008a; Dzieduszycka 1959; Reyman 1939

134. Gierczyce, site 1
1. Wojciechowice comm., Opatów distr., Świętokrzyskie voiv.
2. Opatówka stream basin/upper Vistula river basin
3. 50°47'23.2"N, 21°32'32"E
4. Valley slope
A –
B
    1. Approx. 100 m²
    2. LBK
C
    Czekaj-Zastawny 2008a; Kowalewska-Marszałek 1992

135. Gliniska, site 2
1. Tyszowice comm., Tomaszów Lub. distr., Lubelskie voiv.
2. Huczwa river basin/Bug river basin/Vistula river basin
3. 50°40'17.8"N, 23°42'51.7"E
4. Valley upper terrace
A –
B
    1. Approx. 100 m²
    2. LBK
C
    Czekaj-Zastawny 2008a

136. Gnatowice, site 1
1. Koniusza comm., Proszowice distr., Małopolskie voiv.
2. Szreniawa river basin/upper Vistula river basin
3. 50°11'52.8"N, 20°10'52.6"E

4. Valley border

A –

B

1. Approx. 5 ha
2. LBK

C

Czekaj-Zastawny 2008a; Kruk 1970

137. Gnatowice, site 3

1. Koniusza comm., Proszowice distr., Małopolskie voiv.
2. Szreniawa river basin/upper Vistula river basin
3. 50°11'49.5"N, 20°10'19.4"E
4. Valley upper terrace

A –

B

1. Approx. 1 ha
2. LBK

C

Czekaj-Zastawny 2008a; Kruk 1970

138. Gnatowice, site 8

1. Koniusza comm., Proszowice distr., Małopolskie voiv.
2. Szreniawa river basin/upper Vistula river basin
3. 50°12'00.1"N, 20°09'52.2"E
4. Border zone of upland

A –

B

1. Approx. 100 m^2
2. LBK

C

Czekaj-Zastawny 2008a

139. Gniazdowice, site 1

1. Proszowice comm., Proszowice distr., Małopolskie voiv.
2. Szreniawa river basin/upper Vistula river basin
3. 50°12'31.9"N, 20°15'29.8"E
4. Border zone of upland

A –

B

1. Approx. 15 ha
2. LBK

C

Czekaj-Zastawny 2008a; Kruk 1970

140. Gniazdowice, site 6

1. Proszowice comm., Proszowice distr., Małopolskie voiv.
2. Szreniawa river basin/upper Vistula river basin
3. 50°12'45.5"N, 20°15'17.2"E
4. Valley slope

A –

B

1. Approx. 100 m^2
2. LBK

C

Czekaj-Zastawny 2008a

141. Gnieszowice, site 50

1. Koprzywnica comm., Sandomierz distr., Świętokrzyskie voiv.
2. Koprzywianka stream basin/upper Vistula river basin
3. 50°36'05.6"N, 21°32'49.3"E
4. Border zone of upland

A –

B

1. Approx. 100 m^2
2. LBK

C

Czekaj-Zastawny 2008a; Kowalewska-Marszałek 1992

142. Gnieszowice, site 51

1. Koprzywnica comm., Sandomierz distr., Świętokrzyskie voiv.
2. Koprzywianka stream basin/upper Vistula river basin
3. 50°36'06.3"N, 21°33'26"E
4. Border zone of upland

A –

B

1. Approx. 100 m^2
2. LBK

C

Czekaj-Zastawny 2008a; Kowalewska-Marszałek 1992

143. Gnojnik, site 4

1. Gnojnik comm., Brzesko distr., Małopolskie voiv.
2. Upper Vistula river basin
3. 49°53'12.6"N, 20°36'17.8"E
4. Valley border

A –

B

1. Approx. 1 ha
2. LBK

C

Czekaj-Zastawny 2008a

144. Gołębiów, site 31

1. Lipnik comm., Opatów distr., Świętokrzyskie voiv.
2. Opatówka stream basin/upper Vistula river basin
3. 50°43'11.7"N, 21°31'56"E
4. Valley border

A –

B

1. Approx. 100 m^2
2. LBK

C

Czekaj-Zastawny 2008a; Kowalewska-Marszałek 1992

145. Gołyszyn, site 3

1. Skała comm., Kraków distr., Małopolskie voiv.
2. Dłubnia river basin/upper Vistula river basin
3. 50°16'13"N, 19°54'58.4"E
4. Outside valleys

A –

B

1. Approx. 0.5 ha
2. LBK?

C

Czekaj-Zastawny 2008a

146. Gołyszyn, site 5

1. Skała comm., Kraków distr., Małopolskie voiv.
2. Dłubnia river basin/upper Vistula river basin
3. 50°16'33.6"N, 19°54'54.7"E
4. Valley slope

A –

B

1. Approx. 0.5 ha
2. LBK?

C

Czekaj-Zastawny 2008a

147. Gołyszyn, site 20

1. Skała comm., Kraków distr., Małopolskie voiv.

2. Dłubnia river basin/upper Vistula river basin
3. 50°16'49.3"N, 19°55'06.8"E
4. Border zone of upland
A –
B
1. Approx. 4 ha
2. LBK?
C
Czekaj-Zastawny 2008a

148. Gołębiów, site 31
1. Lipnik comm., Opatów distr., Świętokrzyskie voiv.
2. Opatówka stream basin/upper Vistula river basin
3. 50°43'11.7"N, 21°31'56"E
4. Valley border
A –
B
1. Approx. 100 m²
2. LBK
C
Czekaj-Zastawny 2008a; Kowalewska-Marszałek 1992

149. Gorysławice, site 1
1. Wiślica comm., Busko Zdrój distr., Świętokrzyskie voiv.
2. Nida river basin/upper Vistula river basin
3. 50°21'09.2"N, 20°40'48.7"E
4. Valley low terrace
A
1. W. Bender, W. Szymański
2. 1960
3. ?
4. Camp?; no features, few pottery fragments
5. LBK
B
1. Approx. 5 ha
2. LBK
C
Czekaj-Zastawny 2008a

150. Gorzyczany, site I
1. Samborzec comm., Samborzec distr., Świętokrzyskie voiv.
2. Upper Vistula river basin
3. 50°38'25.5"N, 21°36'29.7"E
4. Valley border
A
1. D. Rauhut
2. 1957
3. ?
4. Settlement trace; no features, 3 pottery fragments
5. LBK
B
1. Approx. 100 m²
2. LBK
C
Balcer 1975; Czekaj-Zastawny 2008a;
Kowalewska-Marszałek 1992; Podkowińska 1959; Rauhut 1970

151. Gosprzydowa, site 6
1. Gnojnik comm., Brzesko distr., Małopolskie voiv.
2. Upper Vistula river basin
3. 49°52'04"N, 20°35'04.2"E
4. Valley border
A –
B
1. Approx. 100 m²

2. LBK
C
Czekaj-Zastawny 2008a

152. Goszyce, site 16
1. Kocmyrzów-Luborzyca comm., Kraków distr., Małopolskie voiv.
2. Szreniawa river basin/upper Vistula river basin
3. 50°11'04.6"N, 20°08'08.1"E
4. Valley slope
A –
B
1. Approx. 100 m²
2. LBK
C
Czekaj-Zastawny 2008a

153. Gozdów, site 1
1. Werbkowice comm., Hrubieszów distr., Lubelskie voiv.
2. Huczwa stream basin/Bug river basin/Vistula river basin
3. 50°46'11.6"N, 23°48'04.7"E
4. Valley slope
A –
B
1. Approx. 0.5 ha
2. LBK
C
Czekaj-Zastawny 2008a

154. Goźlice, site 11
1. Klimontów comm., Sandomierz distr., Świętokrzyskie voiv.
2. Upper Vistula river basin
3. 50°41'47.4"N, 21°29'02.1"E
4. Valley slope
A –
B
1. Approx. 100 m²
2. LBK?
C
Czekaj-Zastawny 2008a; Kowalewska-Marszałek 1992

155. Goźlice, site 60
1. Klimontów comm., Sandomierz distr., Świętokrzyskie voiv.
2. Upper Vistula river basin
3. 50°42'04.6"N, 21°28'33.6"E
4. Valley slope
A –
B
1. Approx. 0.5 ha
2. LBK
C
Czekaj-Zastawny 2008a; Kowalewska-Marszałek 1992

156. Górka Jaklińska, site 3
1. Koniusza comm., Proszowice distr., Małopolskie voiv.
2. Szreniawa river basin/upper Vistula river basin
3. 50°10'04.9"N, 20°15'53.3"E
4. Valley border
A –
B
1. Approx. 100 m²
2. LBK
C
Czekaj-Zastawny 2008a

157. Górka Stogniowska, site 1
 1. Proszowice comm., Proszowice distr., Małopolskie voiv.
 2. Szreniawa river basin/upper Vistula river basin
 3. 50°11'44.5"N, 20°19'43.4"E
 4. Valley low terrace
A
 1. P. Kaczanowski
 2. 1980
 3. 120 m^2
 4. Camp or settlement trace; no features, 6 pottery fragments
 5. LBK, Music Note phase
B
 1. Approx. 100 m^2
 2. LBK
C
 Czekaj-Zastawny 2008a; Kaczanowski *et al.* 1984

158. Górka Stogniowska, site 5
 1. Proszowice comm., Proszowice distr., Małopolskie voiv.
 2. Szreniawa river basin/upper Vistula river basin
 3. 50°11'23.5"N, 20°20'05.5"E
 4. Valley low terrace
A –
B
 1. Approx. 100 m^2
 2. LBK
C
 Czekaj-Zastawny 2008a; Rydzewski 1972

159. Grabina, site 4
 1. Klimontów comm., Sandomierz distr., Świętokrzyskie voiv.
 2. Upper Vistula river basin
 3. 50°41'50.6"N, 21°26'55.7"E
 4. Valley slope and border
A –
B
 1. Approx. 100 m^2
 2. LBK
C
 Czekaj-Zastawny 2008a; Kowalewska-Marszałek 1992

160. Grabina, site 17
 1. Klimontów comm., Sandomierz distr., Świętokrzyskie voiv.
 2. Upper Vistula river basin
 3. 50°41'27.6"N, 21°27'51.6"E
 4. Valley border
A –
B
 1. Approx. 100 m^2
 2. LBK
C
 Czekaj-Zastawny 2008a; Kowalewska-Marszałek 1992

161. Gródek, site 6
 1. Hrubieszów comm., Hrubieszów distr., Lubelskie voiv.
 2. Bug river basin/Vistula river basin
 3. 50°47'41.7"N, 23°57'05.7"E
 4. Valley upper terrace
A
 1. J. Kowalczyk, T. Liana, T. Piętka
 2. 1953, 1957, 1961
 3. 420 m^2
 4. Settlement; 15 features
 5. LBK; Ia (*Gniechowice*) phase, Music Note phase
B
 1. Approx. 1 ha

 2. LBK
C
 Czekaj-Zastawny 2008a; Kempisty 1962; Liana & Piętka
 1958; Uzarowiczowa 1964

162. Gruszów, site 11
 1. Pałecznica comm., Proszowice distr., Małopolskie voiv.
 2. Upper Vistula river basin
 3. 50°15'55.4"N, 20°16'17.7"E
 4. Valley border
A –
B
 1. Approx. 100 m^2
 2. LBK?
C
 Czekaj-Zastawny 2008a

163. Grzegorzowice, site 3
 1. Iwanowice comm., Kraków distr., Małopolskie voiv.
 2. Dłubnia river basin/upper Vistula river basin
 3. 50°15'54"N, 19°58'01.2"E
 4. Outside valleys
A –
B
 1. Approx. 1 ha
 2. LBK?
C
 Czekaj-Zastawny 2008a

164. Grzegorzowice, site 6
 1. Iwanowice comm., Kraków distr., Małopolskie voiv.
 2. Dłubnia river basin/upper Vistula river basin
 3. 50°15'21.8"N, 19°58'02.2"E
 4. Border zone of upland
A –
B
 1. Approx. 1.5 ha
 2. LBK?
C
 Czekaj-Zastawny 2008a

165. Grzęska, site 4
 1. Przeworsk comm., Przeworsk distr., Podkarpackie voiv.
 2. Mleczka stream basin/Sawa river basin/upper Vistula river basin
 3. 50°04'19.4"N, 22°27'27.5"E
 4. Valley low terrace
A –
B
 1. Approx. 1 ha
 2. LBK
C
 Czekaj-Zastawny 2008a

166. Grzęska, site 15
 1. Przeworsk comm., Przeworsk distr., Podkarpackie voiv.
 2. Mleczka stream basin/Sawa river basin/upper Vistula river basin
 3. 50°04'57.2"N, 22°27'48.8"E
 4. Valley low terrace
A –
B
 1. Approx. 0.5 ha
 2. LBK?
C
 Czekaj-Zastawny 2008a

167. Grzęska, site 24
1. Przeworsk comm., Przeworsk distr., Podkarpackie voiv.
2. Mleczka stream basin/Sawa river basin/upper Vistula river basin
3. 50°04'45.7"N, 22°26'41.8"E
4. Valley low terrace

A –

B
1. Approx. 0.5 ha
2. LBK?

C
Czekaj-Zastawny 2008a

168. Gwoździec, site 2
1. Zakliczyn comm., Tarnów distr., Małopolskie voiv.
2. Dunajec river basin/upper Vistula river basin
3. 49°53'08"N, 20°46'40.5"E
4. Valley slope

A
1. A Kukułka
2. 1996-98, 2000
3. 500 m^2
4. Settlement; 33 features (few features belongs to one long house in it)
5. LBK, Ia (*Gniechowice*) phase, Ib (*Zofipole*) phase, Music Note phase; imports of Tisadob-Kapušany group

B
1. Approx. 1 ha
2. LBK

C
Czekaj-Zastawny 2008a; Kukułka 1997; 1998; 2001

169. Hołdowiec, site 1
1. Kazimierza Wielka comm., Kazimierza Wielka distr., Świętokrzyskie voiv.
2. Nidzica river basin/upper Vistula river basin
3. 50°17'01.8"N, 20°29'41.2"E
4. Valley low terrace

A –

B
1. Approx. 100 m^2
2. LBK

C
Czekaj-Zastawny 2008a

170. Hruszowice, site 3
1. Stubno comm., Przemyśl distr., Podkarpackie voiv.
2. San river basin/upper Vistula river basin
3. 49°55'59.5"N, 22°59'32.1"E
4. Valley border

A –

B
1. Approx. 100 m^2
2. LBK

C
Czekaj-Zastawny 2008a

171. Igołomia, site 1
1. Igołomia-Wawrzeńczyce comm., Kraków distr., Małopolskie voiv.
2. Upper Vistula river basin
3. 50°05'08.6"N, 20°15'18.8"E
4. Valley low terrace

A
1. S. Nosek, L. Gajewski
2. 1953-56

3. 1275 m^2
4. Settlement or camp; few features (?), a few dozens pottery fragments
5. LBK, Music Note phase

B
1. Approx. 15 ha
2. LBK

C
Czekaj-Zastawny 2008a; Gajewski 1957, 1959, 1963a; Nosek 1955

172. Igołomia, site 4
1. Igołomia-Wawrzeńczyce comm., Kraków distr., Małopolskie voiv.
2. Upper Vistula river basin
3. 50°05'27.4"N, 20°15'05.6"E
4. Valley low terrace

A
1. B Baczyńska, T. Rodak, A Zastawny
2. 1996-97, 2002-03
3. 200 m^2
4. Settlement; 7 features
5. LBK, Želiezovce phase

B
1. Approx. 5 ha
2. LBK

C
Czekaj-Zastawny 2008a; Zastawny 1997; 2002; 2003

173. Igołomia, site 5
1. Igołomia-Wawrzeńczyce comm., Kraków distr., Małopolskie voiv.
2. Upper Vistula river basin
3. 50°05'15.7"N, 20°14'47.6"E
4. Valley low terrace

A –

B
1. Approx. 100 m^2
2. LBK

C
Czekaj-Zastawny 2008a

174. Igołomia, site 17
1. Igołomia-Wawrzeńczyce comm., Kraków distr., Małopolskie voiv.
2. Upper Vistula river basin
3. 50°05'35.9"N, 20°14'50.5"E
4. Valley slope

A –

B
1. Approx. 100 m^2
2. LBK

C
Czekaj-Zastawny 2008a

175. Ilkowice, site 1
1. Słaboszów comm., Miechów distr., Małopolskie voiv.
2. Niddzica river basin/upper Vistula river basin
3. 50°23'21.2"N, 20°13'50.4"E
4. Valley slope

A –

B
1. Approx. 1 ha
2. LBK

C
Czekaj-Zastawny 2008a; Żurowski 1926

176. Iwanowice Dworskie, site 5
  1. Iwanowice comm., Kraków distr., Małopolskie voiv.
  2. Dłubnia river basin/upper Vistula river basin
  3. 50°13'21.7"N, 19°58'53.3"E
  4. Valley low terrace
A –
B
  1. Approx. 0.5 ha
  2. LBK
C
  Czekaj-Zastawny 2008a; Kruk 1969

177. Iwanowice Dworskie, site 6
  1. Iwanowice comm., Kraków distr., Małopolskie voiv.
  2. Dłubnia river basin/upper Vistula river basin
  3. 50°13'05.5"N, 19°58'57"E
  4. Valley low terrace
A
  1. J. Kruk, J. & A. Machnikowie
  2. 1962-69
  3. 1,3 ha
  4. Settlement; 6 features (1 elongated pit in it)
  5. LBK, Music Note phase, Želiezovce phase
B
  1. Approx. 5 ha
  2. LBK
C
  Czekaj-Zastawny 2008a; Kadrow 1991; Kruk 1969; Lorenc 1998; Machnikowie & Kaczanowski 1987; Nowosad 1998

178. Iwanowice Dworskie, site 20
  1. Iwanowice comm., Kraków distr., Małopolskie voiv.
  2. Dłubnia river basin/upper Vistula river basin
  3. 50°13'15.8"N, 19°59'12.6"E
  4. Valley low terrace
A –
B
  1. Approx. 3 ha
  2. LBK
C
  Czekaj-Zastawny 2008a; Kruk 1969

179. Iwanowice Włościańskie, site 1
  1. Iwanowice comm., Kraków distr., Małopolskie voiv.
  2. Dłubnia river basin/upper Vistula river basin
  3. 50°13'09.6"N, 19°58'02.1"E
  4. Border zone of upland
A
  1. L. Kozłowski, J. & A. Machnikowie,
  2. 1911, 1978
  3. 460 m^2
  4. Settlement or camp; 3 features (1 elongated pit in it)
  5. LBK, Music Note phase, Želiezovce phase
B
  1. Approx. 15 ha
  2. LBK
C
  Czekaj-Zastawny 2008a; Machnikowie & Kaczanowski 1987; Nawrocka 1998

180. Iwanowice Włościańskie, site 16
  1. Iwanowice comm., Kraków distr., Małopolskie voiv.
  2. Dłubnia river basin/upper Vistula river basin
  3. 50°13'41.6"N, 19°56'25.7"E
  4. Valley low terrace/border zone of upland/valley border
A –

B
  1. Approx. 100 m^2
  2. LBK
C
  Czekaj-Zastawny 2008a; Kruk 1969

181. Iwierzyce, site 15
  1. Iwierzyce comm., Ropczyce-Sedziszów distr., Podkarpackie voiv.
  2. Wielopolka stream basin/Wisłoka river basin/upper Vistula river basin
  3. 50°01'47.7"N, 21°45'46.5"E
  4. Valley slope and border
A –
B
  1. Approx. 0.5 ha
  2. LBK
C
  Czekaj-Zastawny 2008a

182. Jachimowice, site 2
  1. Samborzec comm., Sandomierz distr., Świętokrzyskie voiv.
  2. Koprzywianka stream basin/upper Vistula river basin
  3. 50°37'08.3"N, 21°32'43.9"E
  4. Outside valleys
A –
B
  1. Approx. 100 m^2
  2. LBK
C
  Czekaj-Zastawny 2008a; Kowalewska-Marszałek 1992

183. Jadowniki Mokre, site 3
  1. Wietrzychowice comm., Tarnów distr., Małopolskie voiv.
  2. Kisielina stream basin/upper Vistula river basin
  3. 50°10'06"N, 20°44'51.9"E
  4. Valley border
A –
B
  1. Approx. 1 ha
  2. LBK
C
  Czekaj-Zastawny 2008a; Madyda *et al.* 1971

184. Jaksice, site 2
  1. Miechów comm., Miechów distr., Małopolskie voiv.
  2. Szreniawa river basin/upper Vistula river basin
  3. 50°19'20.6"N, 20°00'35.4"E
  4. Valley slope
A –
B
  1. Approx. 5 ha
  2. LBK
C
  Czekaj-Zastawny 2008a; Kruk 1970

185. Jaksice, site 3
  1. Miechów comm., Miechów distr., Małopolskie voiv.
  2. Szreniawa river basin/upper Vistula river basin
  3. 50°19'46.8"N, 20°00'01.9"E
  4. Valley slope
A –
B
  1. Approx. 15 ha
  2. LBK

C

Czekaj-Zastawny 2008a; Kruk 1970

186. Jaksice, site 4
1. Miechów comm., Miechów distr., Małopolskie voiv.
2. Szreniawa river basin/upper Vistula river basin
3. 50°19'18.1"N, 20°00'21.5"E
4. Valley border
A –
B
   1. Approx. 0.5 ha
   2. LBK
C

Czekaj-Zastawny 2008a; Kruk 1970

187. Jaksice, site 6
1. Miechów comm., Miechów distr., Małopolskie voiv.
2. Szreniawa river basin/upper Vistula river basin
3. 50°19'43"N, 20°00'32.6"E
4. Valley border
A –
B
   1. Approx. 0.5 ha
   2. LBK
C

Czekaj-Zastawny 2008a; Kruk 1970

188. Jakubowice, site 1
1. Proszowice comm., Proszowice distr., Małopolskie voiv.
2. Szreniawa river basin/upper Vistula river basin
3. 50°11'09.9"N, 20°19'13.8"E
4. Valley floor and valley low terrace
A –
B
   1. Approx. 100 m^2
   2. LBK
C

Czekaj-Zastawny 2008a; Rydzewski 1972

189. Jakubowice, site 7
1. Proszowice comm., Proszowice distr., Małopolskie voiv.
2. Szreniawa river basin/upper Vistula river basin
3. 50°10'52.2"N, 20°19'11.7"E
4. Valley low terrace
A –
B
   1. Approx. 100 m^2
   2. LBK
C

Czekaj-Zastawny 2008a

190. Jakubowice, site 13
1. Proszowice comm., Proszowice distr., Małopolskie voiv.
2. Szreniawa river basin/upper Vistula river basin
3. 50°10'58.8"N, 20°20'11.7"E
4. Valley floor and valley low terrace
A –
B
   1. Approx. 1 ha
   2. LBK
C

Czekaj-Zastawny 2008a

191. Jakubowice, site 3
1. Słaboszów comm., Miechów distr., Małopolskie voiv.
2. Nidzica river basin/upper Vistula river basin

3. 50°10'46.5"N, 20°19'56"E
4. Valley upper terrace
A –
B
   1. Approx. 100 m^2
   2. LBK?
C

Czekaj-Zastawny 2008a; Liguzińska-Kruk 1982

192. Jałowęsy, site 2
1. Opatów comm., Opatów distr., Świętokrzyskie voiv.
2. Opatówka stream basin/upper Vistula river basin
3. 50°48'29.7"N, 21°22'06.9"E
4. Valley slope
A –
B
   1. Approx. 0.5 ha
   2. LBK
C

Czekaj-Zastawny 2008a; Kowalewska-Marszałek 1992

193. Januszowice, site 8
1. Słomniki comm., Kraków distr., Małopolskie voiv.
2. Szreniawa river basin/upper Vistula river basin
3. 50°16'02.2"N, 20°02'52.5"E
4. Valley low terrace
A –
B
   1. Approx. 100 m^2
   2. LBK
C

Czekaj-Zastawny 2008a; Kruk 1970

194. Januszowice, site 12
1. Słomniki comm., Kraków distr., Małopolskie voiv.
2. Szreniawa river basin/upper Vistula river basin
3. 50°15'24.1"N, 20°03'20.8"E
4. Valley upper terrace
A –
B
   1. Approx. 100 m^2
   2. LBK
C

Czekaj-Zastawny 2008a; Kruk 1970

195. Januszowice, site 14
1. Słomniki comm., Kraków distr., Małopolskie voiv.
2. Szreniawa river basin/upper Vistula river basin
3. 50°16'07.3"N, 20°03'06.4"E
4. Valley upper terrace
A –
B
   1. Approx. 100 m^2
   2. LBK
C

Czekaj-Zastawny 2008a

196. Januszowice, site 15
1. Słomniki comm., Kraków distr., Małopolskie voiv.
2. Szreniawa river basin/upper Vistula river basin
3. 50°15'45.4"N, 20°03'13.2"E
4. Valley upper terrace
A –
B
   1. Approx. 100 m^2
   2. LBK

C

Czekaj-Zastawny 2008a; Kruk 1970

197. Jasienica, site 3
1. Łoniów comm., Sandomierz distr., Świętokrzyskie voiv.
2. Upper Vistula river basin
3. 50°32'48.8"N, 21°33'00.4"E
4. Border zone of upland

A –

B

1. Approx. 1 ha
2. LBK

C

Czekaj-Zastawny 2008a; Kowalewska-Marszałek 1992

198. Jastrzębiec, site 14
1. Stopnica comm., Busko Zdrój distr., Świętokrzyskie voiv.
2. Wschodnia stream basin/upper Vistula river basin
3. 50°29'04.4"N, 20°56'19.7"E
4. Valley slope

A –

B

1. Approx. 100 m^2
2. LBK

C

Czekaj-Zastawny 2008a

199. Jazdowiczki, site 3
1. Proszowice comm., Proszowice distr., Małopolskie voiv.
2. Szreniawa river basin/upper Vistula river basin
3. 50°11'49.6"N, 20°15'36.5"E
4. Valley slope and valley low terrace

A –

B

1. Approx. 0.5 ha
2. LBK

C

Czekaj-Zastawny 2008a

200. Jazdowiczki, site 4
1. Proszowice comm., Proszowice distr., Małopolskie voiv.
2. Szreniawa river basin/upper Vistula river basin
3. 50°12'01.4"N, 20°15'48.9"E
4. Valley low terrace

A –

B

1. Approx. 0.5 ha
2. LBK

C

Czekaj-Zastawny 2008a; Kruk 1970

201. Jerzmanowice, site 18
1. Jerzmanowice-Przeginia comm., Kraków distr., Małopolskie voiv.
2. Prądnik river basin/upper Vistula river basin
3. 50°13'00.8"N, 19°46'29.8"E
4. Valley slope and valley low terrace

A –

B

1. Approx. 100 m^2
2. LBK?

C

Czekaj-Zastawny 2008a

202. Jeziory, site 6
1. Łoniów comm., Sandomierz distr., Świętokrzyskie voiv.

2. Upper Vistula river basin
3. 50°34'25.3"N, 21°28'08.3"E
4. Valley border

A –

B

1. Approx. 100 m^2
2. LBK

C

Czekaj-Zastawny 2008a; Kowalewska-Marszałek 1992

203. Jeziory, site 8
1. Łoniów comm., Sandomierz distr., Świętokrzyskie voiv.
2. Upper Vistula river basin
3. 50°34'47.7"N, 21°27'38.5"E
4. Valley border

A –

B

1. Approx. 100 m^2
2. LBK

C

Czekaj-Zastawny 2008a; Kowalewska-Marszałek 1992

204. Jurkowice, site 1
1. Opatów comm., Opatów distr., Świętokrzyskie voiv.
2. Opatówka stream basin/upper Vistula river basin
3. 50°47'31.9"N, 21°22'26.9"E
4. Valley slope

A

1. W. Antoniewicz, Z. Podkowińska
2. 1924
3. 100 m^2
4. Camp; 6 features
5. LBK, Želiezovce phase

B

1. Approx. 0.5 ha
2. LBK

C

Czekaj-Zastawny 2008a; Kowalewska-Marszałek 1992; Podkowińska 1959

205. Jurkowice, site 14
1. Opatów comm., Opatów distr., Świętokrzyskie voiv.
2. Opatówka stream basin/upper Vistula river basin
3. 50°47'42.3"N, 21°22'51.1"E
4. Valley slope

A –

B

1. Approx. 100 m^2
2. LBK

C

Czekaj-Zastawny 2008a; Kowalewska-Marszałek 1992

206. Jurkowice, site 29
1. Opatów comm., Opatów distr., Świętokrzyskie voiv.
2. Opatówka stream basin/upper Vistula river basin
3. 50°47'23.2"N, 21°22'47.7"E
4. Valley slope

A –

B

1. Approx. 100 m^2
2. LBK

C

Czekaj-Zastawny 2008a; Kowalewska-Marszałek 1992

207. Jurków, site 5
1. Czchów comm., Brzesko distr., Małopolskie voiv.

2. Dunajec river basin/upper Vistula river basin
3. 49°50'54"N, 20°41'25.3"E
4. Valley low terrace

A

1. P. Valde-Nowak, P. Madej
2. 1998
3. 150 m^2
4. Settlement or camp; no features, 12 pottery fragments
5. LBK

B

1. Approx. 0.5 ha
2. LBK

C

Czekaj-Zastawny 2008a; Valde-Nowak & Madej 1998

208. Jurków, site 1

1. Wiślica comm., Busko Zdrój distr., Świętokrzyskie voiv.
2. Nida river basin/upper Vistula river basin
3. 50°21'23"N, 20°38'10.6"E
4. Valley low terrace and border zone of upland

A

1. J. Gurba, L. Graba-Łęcka-Paderewska
2. 1951-53, 1963
3. Rescue excavation by the route
4. ?; any information about the features, 13 pottery fragments
5. LBK, Music Note phase

B

1. Approx. 100 m^2
2. LBK

C

Czekaj-Zastawny 2008a; Graba-Łęcka-Paderewska 1963;
Gurba 1953

209. Jurków, site 2

1. Wiślica comm., Busko Zdrój distr., Świętokrzyskie voiv.
2. Nida river basin/upper Vistula river basin
3. 50°21'13.6"N, 20°38'20"E
4. Valley upper terrace

A

1. J. Gurba, L. Graba-Łęcka-Paderewska
2. 1951-53, 1963
3. Rescue excavation by the route
4. ?; any information about the features, 13 pottery fragments
5. LBK, Music Note phase

B

1. Approx. 0.5 ha
2. LBK

C

Czekaj-Zastawny 2008a; Graba-Łęcka-Paderewska 1963;
Gurba 1953

210. Jurków, site 15

1. Wiślica comm., Busko Zdrój distr., Świętokrzyskie voiv.
2. Nida river basin/upper Vistula river basin
3. 50°21'38"N, 20°38'36.7"E
4. Valley upper terrace

A –

B

1. Approx. 1 ha
2. LBK

C

Czekaj-Zastawny 2008a

211. Jurków, site 25

1. Wiślica comm., Busko Zdrój distr., Świętokrzyskie voiv.
2. Nida river basin/upper Vistula river basin

3. 50°20'51.6"N, 20°38'18.1"E
4. Valley low terrace

A –

B

1. Approx. 100 m^2
2. LBK

C

Czekaj-Zastawny 2008a

212. Jurków, site 37

1. Wiślica comm., Busko Zdrój distr., Świętokrzyskie voiv.
2. Nida river basin/upper Vistula river basin
3. 50°21'35.1"N, 20°38'24.4"E
4. Valley upper terrace and border zone of upland

A –

B

1. Approx. 100 m^2
2. LBK

C

Czekaj-Zastawny 2008a

213. Jurków, site 51

1. Wiślica comm., Busko Zdrój distr., Świętokrzyskie voiv.
2. Nida river basin/upper Vistula river basin
3. 50°20'53.3"N, 20°39'18.9"E
4. Border zone of upland

A –

B

1. Approx. 100 m^2
2. LBK

C

Czekaj-Zastawny 2008a

214. Kaczowice, site 6

1. Radziemice comm., Proszowice distr., Małopolskie voiv.
2. Szreniawa river basin/upper Vistula river basin
3. 50°16'41.3"N, 20°14'01.5"E
4. Valley low terrace

A –

B

1. Approx. 0.5 ha
2. LBK

C

Czekaj-Zastawny 2008a

215. Kaczowice, site 13

1. Radziemice comm., Proszowice distr., Małopolskie voiv.
2. Szreniawa river basin/upper Vistula river basin
3. 50°17'02.6"N, 20°13'58.8"E
4. Valley upper terrace

A –

B

1. Approx. 0.5 ha
2. LBK

C

Czekaj-Zastawny 2008a

216. Kalina, site 2

1. Miechów comm., Miechów distr., Małopolskie voiv.
2. Nidzica river basin/upper Vistula river basin
3. 50°21'38.2"N, 20°06'16.6"E
4. Outside valleys

A –

B

1. Approx. 15 ha
2. LBK

C

Czekaj-Zastawny 2008a

217. Kalina, site 3
1. Miechów comm., Miechów distr., Małopolskie voiv.
2. Nidzica river basin/upper Vistula river basin
3. 50°21'52.4"N, 20°05'55"E
4. Outside valleys

A –
B
1. Approx. 5 ha
2. LBK?
C

Czekaj-Zastawny 2008a

218. Kalina, site 4
1. Miechów comm., Miechów distr., Małopolskie voiv.
2. Nidzica river basin/upper Vistula river basin
3. 50°22'10.7"N, 20°06'40.9"E
4. Valley slope and border/outside valleys

A –
B
1. Approx. 15 ha
2. LBK
C

Czekaj-Zastawny 2008a

219. Kalina, site 20
1. Miechów comm., Miechów distr., Małopolskie voiv.
2. Nidzica river basin/upper Vistula river basin
3. 50°22'37.7"N, 20°07'28.5"E
4. Outside valleys

A –
B
1. Approx. 100 m^2
2. LBK
C

Czekaj-Zastawny 2008a

220. Kalina Wielka, site 5
1. Słaboszów comm., Miechów distr., Małopolskie voiv.
2. Nidzica river basin/upper Vistula river basin
3. 50°22'58.8"N, 20°08'46.9"E
4. Valley slope and border/outside valleys

A –
B
1. Approx. 0.5 ha
2. LBK
C

Czekaj-Zastawny 2008a

221. Kalina Wielka, site 13
1. Słaboszów comm., Miechów distr., Małopolskie voiv.
2. Nidzica river basin/upper Vistula river basin
3. 50°22'32.3"N, 20°09'39.8"E
4. Outside valleys

A –
B
1. Approx. 0.5 ha
2. LBK
C

Czekaj-Zastawny 2008a

222. Kamienica, site 5
1. Gołcza comm., Miechów distr., Małopolskie voiv.
2. Szreniawa river basin/upper Vistula river basin

3. 50°20'53.3"N, 19°53'01"E
4. Outside valleys
A –
B
1. Approx. 0.5 ha
2. LBK?
C

Czekaj-Zastawny 2008a

223. Kamień Łukawski, site 4
1. Dwikozy comm., Sandomierz distr., Świętokrzyskie voiv.
2. Upper Vistula river basin
3. 50°41'17.1"N, 21°47'14.4"E
4. Border zone of upland
A –
B
1. Approx. 0.5 ha
2. LBK
C

Czekaj-Zastawny 2008a

224. Kamyszów, site 9
1. Kazimierza Wielka comm., Kazimierza Wielka distr., Świętokrzyskie voiv.
2. Nidzica river basin/upper Vistula river basin
3. 50°18'29.6"N, 20°28'42.1"E
4. Valley low terrace
A –
B
1. Approx. 100 m^2
2. LBK
C

Czekaj-Zastawny 2008a

225. Kamyszów, site 1
1. Kazimierza Wielka comm., Kazimierza Wielka distr., Świętokrzyskie voiv.
2. Nidzica river basin/upper Vistula river basin
3. 50°18'07.7"N, 20°28'54.4"E
4. Valley border
A –
B
1. Approx. 100 m^2
2. LBK
C

Czekaj-Zastawny 2008a

226. Karwów, site 13
1. Opatów comm., Opatów distr., Świętokrzyskie voiv.
2. Opatówka stream basin/upper Vistula river basin
3. 50°46'23.4"N, 21°28'08.9"E
4. Valley slope
A –
B
1. Approx. 100 m^2
2. LBK
C

Czekaj-Zastawny 2008a; Kowalewska-Marszałek 1992

227. Kaszów, site 7
1. Liszki comm., Kraków distr., Małopolskie voiv.
2. Sanka stream basin/upper Vistula river basin
3. 50°02'05.8"N, 19°43'14.7"E
4. Valley slope
A –

B
1. Approx. 100 m²
2. LBK

C
Czekaj-Zastawny 2008a

228. Kazimierza Mała, site 1
1. Kazimierza Wielka comm., Kazimierza Wielka distr.,
   Świętokrzyskie voiv.
2. Nidzica river basin/upper Vistula river basin
3. 50°15'33.3"N, 20°31'49.1"E
4. Valley border

A
1. K. Tunia
2. 1998-2006
3. 800 m²
4. Settlement; ca. 20-25 features (probably 1 long house in it?)
5. LBK, Ib (*Zofipole*) phase, Music Note phase

B
1. Approx. 1 ha
2. LBK

C
Information from K. Tunia

229. Kępa, site 2
1. Słomniki comm., Kraków distr., Małopolskie voiv.
2. Szreniawa river basin/upper Vistula river basin
3. 50°13'38.8"N, 20°08'00.5"E
4. Valley low terrace

A –
B
1. Approx. 0.5 ha
2. LBK, Želiezovce phase

C
Czekaj-Zastawny 2008a; Kruk 1970

230. Kępa, site 5
1. Słomniki comm., Kraków distr., Małopolskie voiv.
2. Szreniawa river basin/upper Vistula river basin
3. 50°13'13.9"N, 20°07'59.9"E
4. Valley low terrace

A –
B
1. Approx. 100 m²
2. LBK?

C
Czekaj-Zastawny 2008a

231. Kępie Zaleszańskie, site 4
1. Zaleszany comm., Stalowa Wola distr., Podkarpackie voiv.
2. Łęg stream basin/upper Vistula river basin
3. 50°38'38.4"N, 21°52'53.5"E
4. Valley border

A –
B
1. Approx. 1 ha
2. LBK

C
Czekaj-Zastawny 2008a

232. Kępie Zaleszańskie, site 12
1. Zaleszany comm., Stalowa Wola distr., Podkarpackie voiv.
2. Łęg stream basin/upper Vistula river basin
3. 50°38'25.3"N, 21°49'07.4"E
4. Valley border

A –

233. Kielanówka, site 2
1. Boguchwała comm., Rzeszów distr., Podkarpackie voiv.
2. Wisłok river basin/upper Vistula river basin
3. 50°01'32"N, 21°55'21.9"E
4. Valley slope

A –
B
1. Approx. 100 m²
2. LBK

C
Czekaj-Zastawny 2008a

234. Kielnarowa, site 3
1. Tyczyn comm., Rzeszów distr., Podkarpackie voiv.
2. Wisłok river basin/upper Vistula river basin
3. 49°56'38.1"N, 22°04'33.6"E
4. Outside valleys

A –
B
1. Approx. 100 m²
2. LBK

C
Czekaj-Zastawny 2008a

235. Kijany, site 1
1. Bejsce comm., Kazimierza Wielka distr., Świętokrzyskie
   voiv.
2. Nidzica river basin/upper Vistula river basin
3. 50°12'52.4"N, 20°37'06"E
4. Valley low terrace

A –
B
1. Approx. 100 m²
2. LBK

C
Czekaj-Zastawny 2008a

236. Kijany, site 5
1. Bejsce comm., Kazimierza Wielka distr., Świętokrzyskie
   voiv.
2. Nidzica river basin/upper Vistula river basin
3. 50°12'49.8"N, 20°37'43.1"E
4. Valley low terrace

A –
B
1. Approx. 15 ha
2. LBK?

C
Czekaj-Zastawny 2008a

237. Klępie Górne, site 25
1. Stopnica comm., Busko Zdrój distr., Świętokrzyskie voiv.
2. Wschodnia stream basin/upper Vistula river basin
3. 50°25'19"N, 21°00'52"E
4. Valley slope

A –
B
1. Approx. 100 m²
2. LBK?

C

Czekaj-Zastawny 2008a

238. Klonów, site 3
1. Racławice comm., Miechów distr., Małopolskie voiv.
2. Szreniawa river basin/upper Vistula river basin
3. 50°19'57.7"N, 20°10'48.6"E
4. Valley slope and border zone of upland

A –
B

1. Approx. 5 ha
2. LBK

C

Czekaj-Zastawny 2008a

239. Klonów, site 5
1. Racławice comm., Miechów distr., Małopolskie voiv.
2. Szreniawa river basin/upper Vistula river basin
3. 50°20'23.7"N, 20°10'39.5"E
4. Outside valleys

A –
B

1. Approx. 0.5 ha
2. LBK?

C

Czekaj-Zastawny 2008a

240. Klonów, site 15
1. Racławice comm., Miechów distr., Małopolskie voiv.
2. Szreniawa river basin/upper Vistula river basin
3. 50°20'01.2"N, 20°11'02.4"E
4. Valley border

A –
B

1. Approx. 5 ha
2. LBK, Želiezovce phase

C

Czekaj-Zastawny 2008a

241. Klonów, site 25
1. Racławice comm., Miechów distr., Małopolskie voiv.
2. Szreniawa river basin/upper Vistula river basin
3. 50°20'14.4"N, 20°11'28.7"E
4. Outside valleys

A –
B

1. Approx. 0.5 ha
2. LBK

C

Czekaj-Zastawny 2008a

242. Klonów, site 31
1. Racławice comm., Miechów distr., Małopolskie voiv.
2. Szreniawa river basin/upper Vistula river basin
3. 50°20'18"N, 20°10'40.9"E
4. Valley slope

A –
B

1. Approx. 100 m^2
2. LBK

C

Czekaj-Zastawny 2008a

243. Kłaj, site 1
1. Kłaj comm., Wieliczka distr., Małopolskie voiv.
2. Raba river basin/upper Vistula river basin

3. 49°59'11.3"N, 20°18'28.8"E
4. Valley low terrace

A –
B

1. Approx. 5 ha
2. LBK

C

Czekaj-Zastawny 2008a; Szybowicz 1980

244. Kłokowice, site 36
1. Fredropol comm., Przemyśl distr., Podkarpackie voiv.
2. Wiar stream basin/San river basin/upper Vistula river basin
3. 49°39'57.4"N, 22°45'39.6"E
4. Valley slope

A –
B

1. Approx. 0.5 ha
2. LBK

C

Czekaj-Zastawny 2008a

245. Kłokowice, site 39
1. Fredropol comm., Przemyśl distr., Podkarpackie voiv.
2. Wiar stream basin/San river basin/upper Vistula river basin
3. 49°39'28.9"N, 22°46'23.7"E
4. Valley slope

A –
B

1. Approx. 100 m^2
2. LBK?

C

Czekaj-Zastawny 2008a

246. Kobylany, site 1
1. Zabierzów comm., Kraków distr., Małopolskie voiv.
2. Kobylanka stream basin/Rudawa stream basin/upper Vistula river basin
3. 50°09'29.7"N, 19°45'54.9"E
4. "Pod Słupami" Cave

A

1. G. Ossowski
2. 1879
3. Cave sediments completely explorated
4. Cave camp
5. LBK, Želiezovce phase

B

1. –
2. LBK

C

Czekaj-Zastawny 2008a; Rook 1980

247. Kobylany, site 2
1. Zabierzów comm., Kraków distr., Małopolskie voiv.
2. Kobylanka stream basin/Rudawa stream basin/upper Vistula river basin
3. 50°09'44.2"N, 19°46'00"E
4. "Zdaminowa" Cave

A

1. G. Ossowski
2. 1879
3. Cave sediments completely explorated
4. Cave camp
5. LBK

B

1. –
2. LBK

67

C

Czekaj-Zastawny 2008a; Rook 1980

248. Kobylniki, site 2
1. Skalbimierz comm., Kazimierza Wielka distr., Świętokrzyskie voiv.
2. Nidzica river basin/upper Vistula river basin
3. 50°19'11.7"N, 20°27'33.4"E
4. Valley low terrace

A –
B
1. Approx. 100 m²
2. LBK
C
Czekaj-Zastawny 2008a

249. Kobylniki, site 2
1. Skalbimierz comm., Kazimierza Wielka distr., Świętokrzyskie voiv.
2. Nidzica river basin/upper Vistula river basin
3. 50°19'32"N, 20°27'25.1"E
4. Valley upper terrace

A –
B
1. Approx. 100 m²
2. LBK
C
Czekaj-Zastawny 2008a

250. Kochów, site 3
1. Opatów comm., Opatów distr., Świętokrzyskie voiv.
2. Opatówka river basin/upper Vistula river basin
3. 50°46'27.8"N, 21°22'35.7"E
4. Valley slope

A –
B
1. Approx. 100 m²
2. LBK?
C
Czekaj-Zastawny 2008a; Kowalewska-Marszałek 1992

251. Kocmyrzów, site 8
1. Kocmyrzów-Luborzyca comm., Kraków distr., Małopolskie voiv.
2. Upper Vistula river basin
3. 50°07'42.5"N, 20°08'39.2"E
4. Valley slope

A –
B
1. Approx. 100 m²
2. LBK?
C
Czekaj-Zastawny 2008a

252. Kołaczkowice, site 20
1. Busko Zdrój comm., Busko Zdrój distr., Świętokrzyskie voiv.
2. Wschodnia stream basin/upper Vistula river basin
3. 50°29'33.7"N, 20°51'34.8"E
4. Valley slope

A –
B
1. Approx. 100 m²
2. LBK?
C
Czekaj-Zastawny 2008a

253. Koniecmosty, site 2
1. Wiślica comm., Busko Zdrój distr., Świętokrzyskie voiv.
2. Nida river basin/upper Vistula river basin
3. 50°20'22.6"N, 20°39'56.4"E
4. Valley slope

A –
B
1. Approx. 100 m²
2. LBK
C
Czekaj-Zastawny 2008a

254. Koniecmosty, site 15
1. Wiślica comm., Busko Zdrój distr., Świętokrzyskie voiv.
2. Nida river basin/upper Vistula river basin
3. 50°20'09.1"N, 20°39'57.6"E
4. Valley slope

A –
B
1. Approx. 1 ha
2. LBK
C
Czekaj-Zastawny 2008a

255. Kończyce, site 14/II
1. Michałowice comm., Kraków distr., Małopolskie voiv.
2. Dłubnia river basin/upper Vistula river basin
3. 50°07'29.1"N, 20°01'16.6"E
4. Valley low terrace

A –
B
1. Approx. 0.5 ha
2. LBK
C
Czekaj-Zastawny 2008a; Kruk 1969

256. Kończyce, site 15/I
1. Michałowice comm., Kraków distr., Małopolskie voiv.
2. Dłubnia river basin/upper Vistula river basin
3. 50°07'42.4"N, 20°01'36.3"E
4. Border zone of upland

A –
B
1. Approx. 6 ha
2. LBK
C
Czekaj-Zastawny 2008a; Kruk 1969

257. Koprzywnica, site 3
1. Koprzywnica comm., Sandomierz distr., Świętokrzyskie voiv.
2. Koprzywianka stream basin/upper Vistula river basin
3. 50°35'39.5"N, 21°34'29"E
4. Valley border

A –
B
1. Approx. 100 m²
2. LBK
C
Czekaj-Zastawny 2008a; Kowalewska-Marszałek 1992

258. Koprzywnica, site 64
1. Koprzywnica comm., Sandomierz distr., Świętokrzyskie voiv.
2. Koprzywianka stream basin/upper Vistula river basin
3. 50°35'28.7"N, 21°33'12.6"E

4. Border zone of upland

A –

B

1. Approx. 1.5 ha
2. LBK

C

Czekaj-Zastawny 2008a; Kowalewska-Marszałek 1992

259. Kormanice, site 1

1. Fredropol comm., Przemyśl distr., Podkarpackie voiv.
2. Wiar stream basin/San river basin/upper Vistula river basin
3. 49°41'49.8"N, 22°45'01.2"E
4. Valley slope and border

A

1. T. Aksamit; M. Proksa
2. 1966-67, 1969, 1971, 1973; 1977-78
3. 10850 m²
4. Settlement; 2471 features (at list few long houses in it)
5. LBK, Music Note phase, Želiezovce phase; imports of Bükk culture

B

1. Approx. 15 ha
2. LBK

C

Aksamit 1966; 1971; Czekaj-Zastawny 2008a; Czopek 1999

260. Korniaktów, site 5

1. Białobrzegi comm., Łańcut distr., Podkarpackie voiv.
2. Wisłok river basin/San river basin/upper Vistula river basin
3. 50°07'19.7"N, 22°22'48.9"E
4. Valley slope and border/valley low terrace

A –

B

1. Approx. 100 m²
2. LBK

C

Czekaj-Zastawny 2008a

261. Kosin, site 32

1. Annopol comm., Kraśnik distr., Lubelskie voiv.
2. Upper Vistula river basin
3. 50°49'08.7"N, 21°54'46.9"E
4. Valley border

A –

B

1. Approx. 100 m²
2. LBK

C

Czekaj-Zastawny 2008a

262. Kosina, site 35

1. Łańcut comm., Łańcut distr., Podkarpackie voiv.
2. Wisłok river basin/San river basin/upper Vistula river basin
3. 50°03'59.8"N, 22°20'41"E
4. Valley low terrace

A

1. S. Kadrow, S. Czopek
2. 1986
3. 100 m²
4. Camp or settlement trace; no features, 7 pottery fragments
5. LBK, Music Note phase

B

1. Approx. 1 ha
2. LBK

C

Czekaj-Zastawny 2008a; Kadrow 1992b; Saile *et al.* 2008

263. Kosina, site 42

1. Łańcut comm., Łańcut distr., Podkarpackie voiv.
2. Wisłok river basin/San river basin/upper Vistula river basin
3. 50°03'13.9"N, 22°20'10.4"E
4. Valley slope

A –

B

1. Approx. 100 m²
2. LBK?

C

Czekaj-Zastawny 2008a

264. Kosina, site 42

1. Łańcut comm., Łańcut distr., Podkarpackie voiv.
2. Wisłok river basin/San river basin/upper Vistula river basin
3. 50°03'55.4"N, 22°19'36.2"E
4. Valley slope

A –

B

1. Approx. 100 m²
2. LBK

C

Czekaj-Zastawny 2008a

265. Kosmów, site 1

1. Hrubieszów comm., Hrubieszów distr., Lubelskie voiv.
2. Bug river basin/Vistula river basin
3. 50°43'48.2"N, 24°00'41.8"E
4. Valley low terrace

A –

B

1. Approx. 0.5 ha
2. LBK

C

Czekaj-Zastawny 2008a

266. Kosmów, site 6

1. Hrubieszów comm., Hrubieszów distr., Lubelskie voiv.
2. Bug river basin/Vistula river basin
3. 50°43'00"N, 23°59'50.9"E
4. Valley slope and border

A –

B

1. Approx. 100 m²
2. LBK

C

Czekaj-Zastawny 2008a

267. Kosowice, site IX

1. Bodzechów comm., Ostrowiec Świętokrzyski distr., Świętokrzyskie voiv.
2. Opatówka stream basin/upper Vistula river basin
3. 50°53'11.3"N, 21°17'06.2"E
4. Valley border

A –

B

1. Approx. 200 m²
2. LBK

C

Bąbel 1975; Czekaj-Zastawny 2008a; Kowalewska-Marszałek 1992

268. Kościejów, site 34

1. Racławice comm., Miechów distr., Małopolskie voiv.
2. Nidzica river basin/upper Vistula river basin
3. 50°20'04.4"N, 20°16'20.9"E

4. Valley slope and border/outside valleys

A –

B

   1. Approx. 0.5 ha

   2. LBK

C

Czekaj-Zastawny 2008a

269. Kotorów, site 14

   1. Werbkowice comm., Hrubieszów distr., Lubelskie voiv.

   2. Huczwa stream basin/Bug river basin/Vistula river basin

   3. 50°43'08.5"N, 23°43'30.3"E

   4. Valley slope

A –

B

   1. Approx. 100 m^2

   2. LBK

C

Czekaj-Zastawny 2008a

270. Kowala, site 1

   1. Proszowice comm., Proszowice distr., Małopolskie voiv.

   2. Szreniawa river basin/upper Vistula river basin

   3. 50°10'38.6"N, 20°21'20.3"E

   4. Valley low terrace

A

   1. J. & A. Kraussowie

   2. 1966

   3. 80 m^2

   4. Settlement or camp; 1 feature

   5. LBK, Music Note phase

B

   1. Approx. 5 ha

   2. LBK

C

Czekaj-Zastawny 2008a; Krauss 1970; Rydzewski 1972

271. Kowala, site 7

   1. Proszowice comm., Proszowice distr., Małopolskie voiv.

   2. Szreniawa river basin/upper Vistula river basin

   3. 50°10'23.6"N, 20°21'17.5"E

   4. Border zone of upland

A –

B

   1. Approx. 100 m^2

   2. LBK

C

Czekaj-Zastawny 2008a

272. Kowala, site 8

   1. Proszowice comm., Proszowice distr., Małopolskie voiv.

   2. Szreniawa river basin/upper Vistula river basin

   3. 50°10'31.4"N, 20°21'56.5"E

   4. Valley low terrace and valley slope

A –

B

   1. Approx. 100 m^2

   2. LBK

C

Czekaj-Zastawny 2008a

273. Kraczkowa, site 1

   1. Łańcut comm., Łańcut distr., Podkarpackie voiv.

   2. Wisłok river basin/San river basin/upper Vistula river basin

   3. 50°02'10"N, 22°10'56.6"E

   4. Valley slope and border

A

   1. T. Aksamit; P. Mitura

   2. 1966; 1998

   3. 500 m^2

   4. Settlement; ca. 52 features (1-2 long houses in it)

   5. LBK, Music Note phase, Želiezovce phase; imports of
      Szilmeg group and Bükk culture

B

   1. Approx. 5 ha

   2. LBK

C

Aksamit 1964a; Czekaj-Zastawny 2008a; Czopek 1999;
Proksa 1984; Saile *et al.* 2008

274. Kraczkowa, site 22

   1. Łańcut comm., Łańcut distr., Podkarpackie voiv.

   2. Wisłok river basin/San river basin/upper Vistula river basin

   3. 50°02'00.8"N, 22°08'58.4"E

   4. Valley slope

A –

B

   1. Approx. 1 ha

   2. LBK

C

Czekaj-Zastawny 2008a

275. Kraków-Bieżanów, site 27

   1. Kraków comm., Kraków distr., Małopolskie voiv.

   2. Malinówka stream basin/upper Vistula river basin

   3. 50°00'17.5"N, 20°01'30.8"E

   4. Valley slope

A

   1. The Cracow Team for Archaeological Supervision of
      Motorway Construction, Institute of Archaeology and
      Ethnology Polish Academy of Sciences, Museum of
      Archaeology Cracow, Jagiellonian University

   2. 1998-99

   3. 3 ha and 6500 m^2

   4. Settlement trace

   5. LBK

B

   1. Approx. 100 m^2

   2. LBK?

C

Czekaj-Zastawny 2008a; Kadrow 2003

276. Kraków-Bieżanów, site 29

   1. Kraków comm., Kraków distr., Małopolskie voiv.

   2. Upper Vistula river basin

   3. 50°00'01.5"N, 20°01'28.9"E

   4. Valley border

A –

B

   1. Approx. 0.5 ha

   2. LBK

C

Czekaj-Zastawny 2008a

277. Kraków-Bronowice Małe, site 5

   1. Kraków comm., Kraków distr., Małopolskie voiv.

   2. Upper Vistula river basin

   3. 50°04'46.9"N, 19°52'59.5"E

   4. Valley slope

A –

B

   1. Approx. 100 m^2

2. LBK

C

Czekaj-Zastawny 2008a

278. Kraków-Chełm, site 1
1. Kraków comm., Kraków distr., Małopolskie voiv.
2. Rudawa stream basin/upper Vistula river basin
3. 50°03'49.1"N, 19°51'05.4"E
4. Outside valleys

A –

B

1. Approx. 1 ha
2. LBK

C

Czekaj-Zastawny 2008a

279. Kraków-Chełm, site 2
1. Kraków comm., Kraków distr., Małopolskie voiv.
2. Rudawa stream basin/upper Vistula river basin
3. 50°04'07.6"N, 19°51'26.7"E
4. Outside valleys

A –

B

1. Approx. 1 ha
2. LBK

C

Czekaj-Zastawny 2008a

280. Kraków-Chełm, site 4
1. Kraków comm., Kraków distr., Małopolskie voiv.
2. Rudawa stream basin/upper Vistula river basin
3. 50°03'55.9"N, 19°52'08.4"E
4. Outside valleys

A –

B

1. Approx. 1 ha
2. LBK

C

Czekaj-Zastawny 2008a

281. Kraków-Górka Narodowa, site 9
1. Kraków comm., Kraków distr., Małopolskie voiv.
2. Prądnik stream basin/upper Vistula river basin
3. 50°06'12.5"N, 19°57'13.3"E
4. Outside valleys

A

1. A Dagnan-Ginter, A. Tyniec- Kępińska, P. Olejarczyk
2. 1998-2000, 2007-2008
3. 22939 m^2
4. Settlement; few dozen features (at list 2 long huoses in it)
5. LBK, Music Note phase, Želiezovce phase

B

1. Approx. 25 ha
2. LBK

C

Czekaj-Zastawny 2008a; Lech *et al.* 1984; information from P. Olejarczyk

282. Kraków-Mistrzejowice, site 127
1. Kraków comm., Kraków distr., Małopolskie voiv.
2. Dłubnia river basin/upper Vistula river basin
3. 50°05'35.1"N, 20°01'21.4"E
4. Valley low terrace

A

1. I. Mianowska
2. 2007-08

3. 7200 m^2
4. Settlement; several dozen features (1 ling house in it)
5. LBK, Music Note phase, Želiezovce phase

B

1. Approx. 15 ha
2. LBK

C

Information from I. Mianowska

283. Kraków-Nowa Huta-Bieńczyce, site 11
1. Kraków comm., Kraków distr., Małopolskie voiv.
2. Dłubnia river basin/upper Vistula river basin
3. 50°04'53.8"N, 20°02'08.6"E
4. Valley low terrace

A –

B

1. Approx. 100 m^2
2. LBK

C

Czekaj-Zastawny 2008a

284. Kraków-Nowa Huta-Branice, site 76
1. Kraków comm., Kraków distr., Małopolskie voiv.
2. Upper Vistula river basin
3. 50°04'05.5"N, 20°07'59.1"E
4. Valley low terrace

A

1. M. Godłowska, J. Rydzewski
2. 1981, 1984
3. 5000 m^2
4. Camp; 3 features
5. LBK, Music Note phase

B

1. Approx. 0.5 ha
2. LBK

C

Czekaj-Zastawny 2008a; Godłowska 1986

285. Kraków-Nowa Huta-Cło, site 7, 58, 65
1. Kraków comm., Kraków distr., Małopolskie voiv.
2. Upper Vistula river basin
3. 50°04'57.6"N, 20°11'01.8"E
4. Valley low terrace

A

1. M. Cabalska, S. Buratyński, R. Zając
2. 1950, 1954, 1968-69
3. Approx. 5000 m^2
4. Camp?; no features, 7 pottery fragments
5. LBK, Music Note phase, Želiezovce phase

B

1. Approx. 15 ha
2. LBK

C

Czekaj-Zastawny 2008a; Godłowska 1976

286. Kraków-Nowa Huta-Krzesławice, site 41
1. Kraków comm., Kraków distr., Małopolskie voiv.
2. Dłubnia river basin/upper Vistula river basin
3. 50°04'55"N, 20°04'03.2"E
4. Valley low terrace

A

1. S. Buratyński, M. Kaczanowska
2. 1957, 1979-87
3. 1700 m^2
4. Settlement; 18 features (probably 1 long house in it)
5. LBK, Music Note phase, Želiezovce (through IIb); imports

of Tisadob-Kapušany group and Bükk culture

B

1. Approx. 1 ha
2. LBK

C

Buratyński 1968; Czekaj-Zastawny 2008a; Godłowska 1976; Kaczanowska 1988

287. Kraków-Nowa Huta-Mistrzejowice, site 14

1. Kraków comm., Kraków distr., Małopolskie voiv.
2. Dłubnia river basin/upper Vistula river basin
3. 50°05'57.5"N, 20°01'34.3"E
4. Valley low terrace

A –

B

1. Approx. 2.5 ha
2. LBK

C

Czekaj-Zastawny 2008a; Kruk 1969

288. Kraków-Nowa Huta-Mogiła, site 1

1. Kraków comm., Kraków distr., Małopolskie voiv.
2. Dłubnia river basin/upper Vistula river basin
3. 50°03'32.2"N, 20°03'38.2"E
4. Valley low terrace

A –

B

1. Approx. 5 ha
2. LBK

C

Czekaj-Zastawny 2008a; Godłowska 1976

289. Kraków-Nowa Huta-Mogiła, site 48

1. Kraków comm., Kraków distr., Małopolskie voiv.
2. Dłubnia river basin/upper Vistula river basin
3. 50°04'00.1"N, 20°04'39.2"E
4. Valley low terrace

A

1. S. Buratyński
2. 1960-61
3. 45000 m^2
4. Settlement trace; no features, few pottery fragments
5. LBK

B

1. Approx. 1 ha
2. LBK

C

Czekaj-Zastawny 2008a; Godłowska 1976

290. Kraków-Nowa Huta-Mogiła, site 53, 55

1. Kraków comm., Kraków distr., Małopolskie voiv.
2. Dłubnia river basin/upper Vistula river basin
3. 50°04'21.7"N, 20°04'13.9"E
4. Valley low terrace

A

1. L. Kozłowski, M. Drewko, R. Hahulska-Ledwos, A. Kogus, R. Zając
2. 1912-13, 1963-65
3. 46000 m^2
4. Settlement; few features (?)
5. LBK, Želiezovce phase (through IIb)

B

1. Approx. 5 ha
2. LBK

C

Czekaj-Zastawny 2008a; Godłowska 1976

291. Kraków-Nowa Huta-Mogiła, site 51, 62

1. Kraków comm., Kraków distr., Małopolskie voiv.
2. Dłubnia river basin/upper Vistula river basin
3. 50°04'00.7"N, 20°04'59.8"E
4. Valley low terrace

A

1. S. Buratyński, M. Godłowska, M. Kaczanowska, G. Kałka-Tobołowa, R. Zając,
2. 1961, 1966-70
3. 31200 m^2
4. Settlement; 80 features (traces of 19 households in it)
5. LBK, Ia (*Gniechowice*) phase, Ib (*Zofipole*) phase, Music Note phase, Želiezovce phase (through ŽIIb); imports of Tisadob-Kapušany group and Bükk culture

B

1. Approx. 6.5 ha
2. LBK

C

Czekaj-Zastawny 2008a; Godłowska 1966; 1976; 1991; 1992

292. Kraków-Nowa Huta-Bieńczyce (os. Sportowe), site 15

1. Kraków comm., Kraków distr., Małopolskie voiv.
2. Dłubnia river basin/upper Vistula river basin
3. 50°04'54.2"N, 20°02'37.4"E
4. Valley low terrace

A

1. R. Hahulska-Ledwos
2. 1952
3. 550 m^2
4. Settlement; 10 features (traces of 1 households in it)
5. LBK, Music Note phase, Želiezovce phase

B

1. Approx. 5.5 ha
2. LBK

C

Czekaj-Zastawny 2008a; Godłowska 1976; Hachulska-Ledwos 1963

293. Kraków-Nowa Huta-Bieńczyce (os. Szkolne), site 12

1. Kraków comm., Kraków distr., Małopolskie voiv.
2. Dłubnia river basin/upper Vistula river basin
3. 50°04'42"N, 20°02'48.4"E
4. Valley low terrace

A

1. R. Hahulska-Ledwos
2. 1952
3. 500 m^2 (?)
4. Settlement; approx. 41 features
5. LBK, Music Note phase

B

1. Approx. 1 ha
2. LBK

C

Czekaj-Zastawny 2008a; Godłowska 1976; Hachulska-Ledwos 1963

294. Kraków-Nowa Huta-Pleszów, site 17-20

1. Kraków comm., Kraków distr., Małopolskie voiv.
2. Dłubnia river basin/upper Vistula river basin
3. 50°04'25.2"N, 20°06'15.6"E
4. Valley low terrace

A

1. S. Buratyński, M. Godłowska, M. Kaczanowska, A Rachwaniec, E. Rook
2. 1952-63, 1965-73, 1981
3. 2.5 ha

4. Settlement; 17 features (probably traces of 1-3 long houses in it) and more features destroyed by younger cultures
5. LBK, Ia (*Gniechowice*) phase, Ib (*Zofipole*) phase, Music Note phase, Želiezovce phase (through ŽIIb); imports of Tisadob-Kapušany group and Bükk culture
5905 ± 40 BP, 5910 ± 40 BP, 5985 ± 50 BP, 6075 ± 40 BP, 6255 ± 40 BP, 6050 ± 40 BP

B

1. Approx. 5 ha
2. LBK

C

Czekaj-Zastawny 2008a; Godłowska 1976; Godłowska *et al.* 1985; Kozłowski 1969; Kulczycka-Leciejewiczowa 1969

295. Kraków-Nowa Huta-Wyciąże, site 5
1. Kraków comm., Kraków distr., Małopolskie voiv.
2. Upper Vistula river basin
3. 50°04'25.9"N, 20°09'28.3"E
4. Valley low terrace

A

1. S. Buratyński, K. Bielenin
2. 1950-52
3. 2,8 ha
4. Settlement; 30 features (probably traces few long houses in it)
5. LBK, Music Note phase, Želiezovce phase; imports of Barca I group and Bükk culture

B

1. Approx. 15 ha
2. LBK

C

Czekaj-Zastawny 2008a; Godłowska 1976; Kozłowski 1968

296. Kraków-Nowa Huta-Zesławice, site 63
1. Kraków comm., Kraków distr., Małopolskie voiv.
2. Dłubnia river basin/upper Vistula river basin
3. 50°06'10.1"N, 20°03'14.9"E
4. Valley low terrace

A

1. A Kogus
2. 1967
3. ?
4. Settlement trace; no features, 1 pottery fragment
5. LBK

B

1. Approx. 100 m²
2. LBK

C

Czekaj-Zastawny 2008a; Godłowska 1976

297. Kraków-Olszanica, site 1
1. Kraków comm., Kraków distr., Małopolskie voiv.
2. Rudawa river basin/upper Vistula river basin
3. 50°03'41.3"N, 19°50'04.9"E
4. Outside valleys

A –

B

1. Approx. 0.5 ha
2. LBK

C

Czekaj-Zastawny 2008a; Cabalska 1960

298. Kraków-Olszanica, site 4
1. Kraków comm., Kraków distr., Małopolskie voiv.
2. Rudawa river basin/upper Vistula river basin
3. 50°04'15"N, 19°50'06.3"E

4. Valley border

A

1. S. Buratyński, A. Żaki; S. Milisauskas, J. Kruk
2. 1951, 1967-73
3. 1.5 ha
4. Settlement; 92 features (19 long houses in it)
5. LBK, Music Note phase, Želiezovce phase; imports of Bükk culture
6700 ± 220 BP, 6430 ± 75 BP, 6300 ± 400 BP, 6150 ± 210 BP, 6095 ± 350 BP, 6020 ± 220 BP, 6000 ± 340 BP, 5800 ± 210 BP, 5025 ± 260 BP

B

1. Approx. 15 ha
2. LBK

C

Czekaj-Zastawny 2008a; Kozłowski & Kulczycka 1961; Milisauskas 1986; 1989

299. Kraków-Olszanica, site 11
1. Kraków comm., Kraków distr., Małopolskie voiv.
2. Rudawa river basin/upper Vistula river basin
3. 50°04'46.2"N, 19°49'54.7"E
4. Outside valleys

A –

B

1. Approx. 1 ha
2. LBK

C

Czekaj-Zastawny 2008a; Milisauskas 1986

300. Kraków-Przegorzały, site 4
1. Kraków comm., Kraków distr., Małopolskie voiv.
2. Upper Vistula river basin
3. 50°02'56.7"N, 19°52'27.7"E
4. Valley upper terrace

A –

B

1. Approx. 100 m²
2. LBK?

C

Czekaj-Zastawny 2008a

301. Kraków-Pychowice, site 5
1. Kraków comm., Kraków distr., Małopolskie voiv.
2. Upper Vistula river basin
3. 50°02'06.7"N, 19°53'45.9"E
4. Valley slope and border

A

1. E. Zaitz
2. 1976
3. ?
4. Settlement trace; no features, 3 pottery fragments
5. LBK

B

1. Approx. 100 m²
2. LBK

C

Czekaj-Zastawny 2008a

302. Kraków-Skotniki, site 10
1. Kraków comm., Kraków distr., Małopolskie voiv.
2. Upper Vistula river basin
3. 50°01'03.1"N, 19°52'08.9"E
4. Valley slope

A –

B

1. Approx. 100 m²
2. LBK

C

Czekaj-Zastawny 2008a

303. Kraków-Stare Miasto, site 1

1. Kraków comm., Kraków distr., Małopolskie voiv.
2. Upper Vistula river basin
3. 50°03'30"N, 19°56'27"E
4. Valley low terrace

A –

B

1. Approx. 100 m²
2. LBK?

C

Czekaj-Zastawny 2008a

304. Kraków-Wawel, site 1

1. Kraków comm., Kraków distr., Małopolskie voiv.
2. Upper Vistula river basin
3. 50°03'14.6"N, 19°56'09.8"E
4. Valley upper terrace

A –

B

1. Approx. 100 m²
2. LBK?

C

Czekaj-Zastawny 2008a

305. Kraków-Witkowice, site 10

1. Kraków comm., Kraków distr., Małopolskie voiv.
2. Prądnik river basin/upper Vistula river basin
3. 50°06'01.6"N, 19°56'22.9"E
4. Valley border and floor

A

1. J. Rydlewski
2. 1996-97
3. ?
4. Settlement?
5. LBK

B

1. Approx. 5 ha
2. LBK

C

Czekaj-Zastawny 2008a

306. Kraków-Zwierzyniec, site 1

1. Kraków comm., Kraków distr., Małopolskie voiv.
2. Rudawa river basin/upper Vistula river basin
3. 50°03'11.3"N, 19°53'19.5"E
4. Valley border/valley upper terrace

A –

B

1. Approx. 100 m²
2. LBK

C

Czekaj-Zastawny 2008a; Chmielewski & Madeyska 1976

307. Kraków-Zwierzyniec, site 15

1. Kraków comm., Kraków distr., Małopolskie voiv.
2. Rudawa river basin/upper Vistula river basin
3. 50°03'26.7"N, 19°53'41.5"E
4. Valley low terrace

A –

B

1. Approx. 100 m²
2. LBK?

C

Czekaj-Zastawny 2008a; Jamka 1963

308. Krakuszowice, site 5

1. Gdów comm., Wieliczka distr., Małopolskie voiv.
2. Raba river basin/upper Vistula river basin
3. 49°56'52.3"N, 20°14'17.5"E
4. Outside valleys

A –

B

1. Approx. 100 m²
2. LBK

C

Czekaj-Zastawny 2008a

309. Krobielice, site 16

1. Klimontów comm., Sandomierz distr., Świętokrzyskie voiv.
2. Koprzywianka stream basin/upper Vistula river basin
3. 50°40'39"N, 21°31'35.1"E
4. Valley slope

A –

B

1. Approx. 100 m²
2. LBK

C

Czekaj-Zastawny 2008a; Kowalewska-Marszałek 1992

310. Krowia Góra, site 10

1. Koprzywnica comm., Sandomierz distr., Świętokrzyskie voiv.
2. Koprzywianka stream basin/upper Vistula river basin
3. 50°34'01.1"N, 21°33'27.9"E
4. Valley border

A –

B

1. Approx. 1 ha
2. LBK

C

Czekaj-Zastawny 2008a; Kowalewska-Marszałek 1992

311. Kryłów, site 13

1. Mircze comm., Hrubieszów distr., Lubelskie voiv.
2. Bug river basin/Vistula river basin
3. 50°41'27.1"N, 24°03'39"E
4. Valley slope

A –

B

1. Approx. 0.5 ha
2. LBK

C

Czekaj-Zastawny 2008a

312. Krzczonowice, site 1

1. Ćmielów comm., Ostrowiec Świętokrzyski distr., Świętokrzyskie voiv.
2. Kamienna stream basin/upper Vistula river basin
3. 50°51'18.4"N, 21°29'37.3"E
4. Valley border

A –

B

1. Approx. 1 ha
2. LBK

C

Czekaj-Zastawny 2008a; Kowalewska-Marszałek 1992;
Kowalski 1975

313. Krzczonowice, site 7
1. Ćmielów comm., Ostrowiec Świętokrzyski distr.,
Świętokrzyskie voiv.
2. Kamienna stream basin/upper Vistula river basin
3. 50°51'33.7"N, 21°30'14.2"E
4. Valley border

A –
B

1. Approx. 100 m²
2. LBK

C

Czekaj-Zastawny 2008a; Kowalewska-Marszałek 1992;
Kowalski 1975

314. Krzemienica, site 6
1. Czarna comm., Łańcut distr., Podkarpackie voiv.
2. Wisłok river basin/San river basin/upper Vistula river basin
3. 50°04'21.8"N, 22°11'00.7"E
4. Valley slope and border

A –
B

1. Approx. 0.5 ha
2. LBK

C

Czekaj-Zastawny 2008a

315. Książ Wielki, site 13
1. Książ Wielki comm., Miechów distr., Małopolskie voiv.
2. Nidzica river basin/upper Vistula river basin
3. 50°27'05.3"N, 20°09'01.9"E
4. Valley slope

A –
B

1. Approx. 100 m²
2. LBK

C

Czekaj-Zastawny 2008a

316. Książ Wielki, site 16
1. Książ Wielki comm., Miechów distr., Małopolskie voiv.
2. Nidzica river basin/upper Vistula river basin
3. 50°26'19"N, 20°08'25"E
4. Valley slope

A –
B

1. Approx. 100 m²
2. LBK

C

Czekaj-Zastawny 2008a

317. Książnice, site 25
1. Gdów comm., Wieliczka distr., Małopolskie voiv.
2. Raba river basin/upper Vistula river basin
3. 49°56'43.6"N, 20°16'28.8"E
4. Valley border

A –
B

1. Approx. 100 m²
2. LBK

C

Czekaj-Zastawny 2008a

318. Książnice, site 13
1. Gdów comm., Wielicka distr., Małopolskie voiv.
2. Raba river basin/upper Vistula river basin
3. 49°57'33.2"N, 20°18'14.6"E
4. Valley low terrace

A –
B

1. Approx. 3 ha
2. LBK

C

Czekaj-Zastawny 2008a

319. Książnice, site 16
1. Gdów comm., Wielicka distr., Małopolskie voiv.
2. Raba river basin/upper Vistula river basin
3. 49°57'23.3"N, 20°17'35.7"E
4. Valley upper terrace/valley border

A –
B

1. Approx. 100 m²
2. LBK?

C

Czekaj-Zastawny 2008a

320. Książnice Małe, site 4
1. Koszyce comm., Proszowice distr., Małopolskie voiv.
2. Szreniawa river basin/upper Vistula river basin
3. 50°10'21.6"N, 20°32'12.2"E
4. Valley low terrace

A –
B

1. Approx. 0.5 ha
2. LBK

C

Czekaj-Zastawny 2008a; Rydzewski 1972

321. Książnice Małe, site 6
1. Koszyce comm., Proszowice distr., Małopolskie voiv.
2. Szreniawa river basin/upper Vistula river basin
3. 50°10'38.6"N, 20°31'40.5"E
4. Valley low terrace

A –
B

1. Approx. 0.5 ha
2. LBK

C

Czekaj-Zastawny 2008a; Rydzewski 1972

322. Książnice Wielkie, site 1
1. Koszyce comm., Proszowice distr., Małopolskie voiv.
2. Szreniawa river basin/upper Vistula river basin
3. 50°09'39.4"N, 20°31'46.6"E
4. Border zone of upland

A –
B

1. Approx. 0.5 ha
2. LBK

C

Czekaj-Zastawny 2008a; Rydzewski 1972

323. Książnice Wielkie, site 5
1. Koszyce comm., Proszowice distr., Małopolskie voiv.
2. Szreniawa river basin/upper Vistula river basin
3. 50°09'24.8"N, 20°33'11.8"E
4. Border zone of upland

A –

B

1. Approx. 0.5 ha
2. LBK

C

Czekaj-Zastawny 2008a; Rydzewski 1972

324. Książnice Wielkie, site 11

1. Koszyce comm., Proszowice distr., Małopolskie voiv.
2. Szreniawa river basin/upper Vistula river basin
3. 50°10'11.5"N, 20°31'52.5"E
4. Valley floor

A –

B

1. Approx. 0.5 ha
2. LBK

C

Czekaj-Zastawny 2008a; Rydzewski 1972

325. Książnice Wielkie, site 12

1. Koszyce comm., Proszowice distr., Małopolskie voiv.
2. Szreniawa river basin/upper Vistula river basin
3. 50°10'02.6"N, 20°32'34.2"E
4. Valley floor

A –

B

1. Approx. 100 m^2
2. LBK

C

Czekaj-Zastawny 2008a; Rydzewski 1972

326. Książnice Wielkie, site 15

1. Koszyce comm., Proszowice distr., Małopolskie voiv.
2. Szreniawa river basin/upper Vistula river basin
3. 50°10'15.4"N, 20°30'54.5"E
4. Valley low terrace

A –

B

1. Approx. 0.5 ha
2. LBK

C

Czekaj-Zastawny 2008a; Rydzewski 1972

327. Książnice Wielkie, site 16

1. Koszyce comm., Proszowice distr., Małopolskie voiv.
2. Szreniawa river basin/upper Vistula river basin
3. 50°09'44.1"N, 20°31'04.8"E
4. Valley low terrace

A –

B

1. Approx. 100 m^2
2. LBK

C

Czekaj-Zastawny 2008a; Rydzewski 1972

328. Książnice Wielkie, site 17

1. Koszyce comm., Proszowice distr., Małopolskie voiv.
2. Szreniawa river basin/upper Vistula river basin
3. 50°10'00.1"N, 20°30'33"E
4. Valley low terrace

A –

B

1. Approx. 15 ha
2. LBK

C

Czekaj-Zastawny 2008a; Rydzewski 1972

329. Książniczki, site 16/II

1. Koszyce comm., Proszowice distr., Małopolskie voiv.
2. Dłubnia river basin/upper Vistula river basin
3. 50°07'45"N, 20°00'53.6"E
4. Valley low terrace

A –

B

1. Approx. 0.5 ha
2. LBK

C

Czekaj-Zastawny 2008a; Kruk 1969

330. Książniczki, site 17/II

1. Koszyce comm., Proszowice distr., Małopolskie voiv.
2. Dłubnia river basin/upper Vistula river basin
3. 50°08'07.4"N, 20°00'42"E
4. Border zone of upland

A –

B

1. Approx. 4.5 ha
2. LBK

C

Czekaj-Zastawny 2008a; Kruk 1969

331. Laski Dworskie, site 1

1. Gołcza comm., Kraków distr., Małopolskie voiv.
2. Dłubnia river basin/upper Vistula river basin
3. 50°16'17.2"N, 19°55'41.7"E
4. Valley upper terrace

A –

B

1. Approx. 0.5 ha
2. LBK?

C

Czekaj-Zastawny 2008a

332. Lichobórz, site 22

1. Hrubieszów comm., Hrubieszów distr., Lubelskie voiv.
2. Bug river basin/upper Vistula river basin
3. 50°39'03.6"N, 23°32'53.1"E
4. Valley slope

A –

B

1. Approx. 100 m^2
2. LBK

C

Czekaj-Zastawny 2008a

333. Lipnik, site 21

1. Lipnik comm., Opatów distr., Świętokrzyskie voiv.
2. Opatówka stream basin/upper Vistula river basin
3. 50°44'19.1"N, 21°28'51.7"E
4. Valley border

A –

B

1. Approx. 1 ha
2. LBK

C

Czekaj-Zastawny 2008a; Kowalewska-Marszałek 1992

334. Lipnik, site 22

1. Lipnik comm., Opatów distr., Świętokrzyskie voiv.
2. Opatówka stream basin/upper Vistula river basin
3. 50°44'50.5"N, 21°28'40.3"E
4. Valley slope

A –

B

1. Approx. 100 m^2
2. LBK

C

Czekaj-Zastawny 2008a; Kowalewska-Marszałek 1992

335. Lipowa, site 4

1. Opatów comm., Opatów distr., Świętokrzyskie voiv.
2. Opatówka stream basin/upper Vistula river basin
3. 50°49'26.3"N, 21°26'39.5"E
4. Valley slope

A –

B

1. Approx. 0.5 ha
2. LBK?

C

Czekaj-Zastawny 2008a; Kowalewska-Marszałek 1992; Kowalski 1975

336. Lipsko-Kosobudy, site 12

1. Zamość comm., Zamość distr., Lubelskie voiv.
2. Wieprz river basin/upper Vistula river basin
3. 50°39'10.9"N, 23°13'46.2"E
4. Valley slope

A –

B

1. Approx. 100 m^2
2. LBK?

C

Czekaj-Zastawny 2008a

337. Lipsko-Polesie, site 11

1. Zamość comm., Zamość distr., Lubelskie voiv.
2. Wieprz river basin/upper Vistula river basin
3. 50°38'37.9"N, 23°12'56.7"E
4. Valley slope

A –

B

1. Approx. 0.5 ha
2. LBK

C

Czekaj-Zastawny 2008a

338. Lubomierz, site 3

1. Łapanów comm., Bochnia distr., Małopolskie voiv.
2. Raba river basin/upper Vistula river basin
3. 49°51'23.2"N, 20°14'47.7"E
4. Outside valleys

A –

B

1. Approx. 5 ha
2. LBK

C

Czekaj-Zastawny 2008a

339. Łańcut, site 2

1. Łańcut comm., Łańcut distr., Podkarpackie voiv.
2. Sawa stream basin/Wisłok river basin/San river basin/upper Vistula river basin
3. 50°03'54"N, 22°12'28.8"E
4. Valley border

A

1. K. Moskwa; A Krauss
2. 1956; 1966
3. ?
4. Settlement; ?

5. LBK

B

1. Approx. 5 ha
2. LBK

C

Czekaj-Zastawny 2008a

340. Łańcut, site 3

1. Łańcut comm., Łańcut distr., Podkarpackie voiv.
2. Sawa stream basin/Wisłok river basin/San river basin/upper Vistula river basin
3. 50°04'40.1"N, 22°12'10.9"E
4. Valley upper terrace

A

1. A. Gruszczyńska
2. 1982-90
3. 2850 m^2
4. Settlement; ca. 240 features (ca. 14 long houses in it)
5. LBK, Music Note phase, Želiezovce phase; imports of Bükk culture

B

1. Approx. 15 ha
2. LBK

C

Czekaj-Zastawny 2008a; Czopek 1999; Gruszczyńska 1991; 1992; Saile *et al.* 2008

341. Łapczyca, site 23

1. Bochnia comm., Bochnia distr., Małopolskie voiv.
2. Raba river basin/upper Vistula river basin
3. 49°56'50"N, 20°21'49.5"E
4. Valley border

A –

B

1. Approx. 0.5 ha
2. LBK

C

Czekaj-Zastawny 2008a

342. Łapczyca, site 37

1. Bochnia comm., Bochnia distr., Małopolskie voiv.
2. Raba river basin/upper Vistula river basin
3. 49°58'06.4"N, 20°22'22.2"E
4. Valley border

A –

B

1. Approx. 0.5 ha
2. LBK, Želiezovce phase

C

Czekaj-Zastawny 2008a

343. Ławy, site 2

1. Opatowiec comm., Kazimierza Wielka distr., Świętokrzyskie voiv.
2. Nidzica stream basin/upper Vistula river basin
3. 50°12'22"N, 20°39'28.1"E
4. Valley low terrace

A –

B

1. Approx. 100 m^2
2. LBK?

C

Czekaj-Zastawny 2008a; Machnik 1957

344. Łazany, site 12

1. Biskupice comm., Wieliczka distr., Małopolskie voiv.

2. Raba river basin/upper Vistula river basin
3. 49°56'28.2"N, 20°09'27.5"E
4. Valley border
A –
B
   1. Approx. 15 ha
   2. LBK
C
   Czekaj-Zastawny 2008a

345. Łazy, site 41
   1. Rzezawa comm., Bochnia distr., Małopolskie voiv.
   2. Upper Vistula river basin
   3. 49°58'17.7"N, 20°31'11.3"E
   4. Valley slope
A –
B
   1. Approx. 0.5 ha
   2. LBK
C
   Czekaj-Zastawny 2008a

346. Łazy, site 42
   1. Rzezawa comm., Bochnia distr., Małopolskie voiv.
   2. Upper Vistula river basin
   3. 49°58'08.4"N, 20°31'04.5"E
   4. Valley border
A –
B
   1. Approx. 1 ha
   2. LBK
C
   Czekaj-Zastawny 2008a

347. Łętkowice, site 2
   1. Radziemice comm., Proszowice distr., Małopolskie voiv.
   2. Szreniawa river basin/upper Vistula river basin
   3. 50°15'05.5"N, 20°10'07.5"E
   4. Outside valleys
A –
B
   1. Approx. 100 m²
   2. LBK?
C
   Czekaj-Zastawny 2008a

348. Łętkowice, site 22
   1. Radziemice comm., Proszowice distr., Małopolskie voiv.
   2. Szreniawa river basin/upper Vistula river basin
   3. 50°15'21.4"N, 20°11'09.4"E
   4. Outside valleys
A –
B
   1. Approx. 100 m²
   2. LBK?
C
   Czekaj-Zastawny 2008a

349. Łężkowice, site 1
   1. Kłaj comm., Wieliczka distr., Małopolskie voiv.
   2. Raba river basin/upper Vistula river basin
   3. 49°57'42.5"N, 20°17'32.8"E
   4. Valley slope/valley low terrace
A
   1. A Kulczycka-Leciejewiczowa, Z. Woźniak
   2. 1963-64

3. 200 m²
4. Settlement trace; no features, few pottery fragments
5. LBK, Music Note phase
B
   1. Approx. 100 m²
   2. LBK
C
   Czekaj-Zastawny 2008a; Woźniak 1966

350. Łężkowice, site 2
   1. Kłaj comm., Wieliczka distr., Małopolskie voiv.
   2. Raba river basin/upper Vistula river basin
   3. 49°58'04.6"N, 20°17'07.7"E
   4. Valley slope/valley low terrace
A
   1. A Kulczycka-Leciejewiczowa, Z. Woźniak
   2. 1966
   3. 350 m²
   4. Camp or settlement trace; no features, few pottery fragments
   5. LBK
B
   1. Approx. 100 m²
   2. LBK
C
   Czekaj-Zastawny 2008a; Rook & Woźniak 1968

351. Łoniowa, site 1
   1. Dębno comm., Brzesko distr., Małopolskie voiv.
   2. Dunajec river basin/upper Vistula river basin
   3. 49°55'06.5"N, 20°41'41.7"E
   4. Valley slope
A –
B
   1. Approx. 0.5 ha
   2. LBK
C
   Czekaj-Zastawny 2008a

352. Łoniowa, site 8
   1. Dębno comm., Brzesko distr., Małopolskie voiv.
   2. Dunajec river basin/upper Vistula river basin
   3. 49°55'13.5"N, 20°42'02"E
   4. Valley border
A –
B
   1. Approx. 0.5 ha
   2. LBK
C
   Czekaj-Zastawny 2008a

353. Łoniowa, site 18
   1. Dębno comm., Brzesko distr., Małopolskie voiv.
   2. Dunajec river basin/upper Vistula river basin
   3. 49°54'40"N, 20°39'57.9"E
   4. Valley border
A
   1. P. Valde-Nowak
   2. 1997, 2003, 2004
   3. 1100 m²
   4. Settlement; ca. 100 features (2-4 long houses in it and 1-2 human graves)
   5. LBK, Music Note phase, Želiezovce phase; imports of Bükk culture
   6230±40 BP, 6340±40 BP, 6220±40 BP

B

    1. Approx. 1 ha

    2. LBK

C

    Czekaj-Zastawny 2008a; Valde-Nowak 1997-1998; 2007;
    2008a; 2008b

354. Łoniowa, site 23

    1. Dębno comm., Brzesko distr., Małopolskie voiv.

    2. Dunajec river basin/upper Vistula river basin

    3. 49°54'09.7"N, 20°41'23.6"E

    4. Valley border

A –

B

    1. Approx. 0.5 ha

    2. LBK

C

    Czekaj-Zastawny 2008a

355. Łowce, site 13

    1. Chłopice comm., Jarosław distr., Podkarpackie voiv.

    2. San river basin/upper Vistula river basin

    3. 49°56'25.5"N, 22°42'38.1"E

    4. Valley slope

A –

B

    1. Approx. 100 m^2

    2. LBK?

C

    Czekaj-Zastawny 2008a

356. Łowczów, site 2

    1. Tuchów comm., Tarnów distr., Małopolskie voiv.

    2. Biała stream basin/Dunajec river basin/upper Vistula river
    basin

    3. 49°54'41.9"N, 20°58'32"E

    4. Valley border

A –

B

    1. Approx. 100 m^2

    2. LBK?

C

    Czekaj-Zastawny 2008a

357. Łuczyce, site 14

    1. Przemyśl comm., Przemyśl distr., Podkarpackie voiv.

    2. Wiar stream basin/San river basin/upper Vistula river basin

    3. 49°44'33.2"N, 22°50'13.9"E

    4. Valley slope

A –

B

    1. Approx. 100 m^2

    2. LBK

C

    Czekaj-Zastawny 2008a

358. Łysa Góra, site 38

    1. Dębno comm., Brzesko distr., Małopolskie voiv.

    2. Dunajec river basin/upper Vistula river basin

    3. 49°55'39.1"N, 20°44'23.1"E

    4. Valley border

A –

B

    1. Approx. 100 m^2

    2. LBK

C

    Czekaj-Zastawny 2008a

359. Łysa Góra, site 4

    1. Werbkowice comm., Hrubieszów distr., Lubelskie voiv.

    2. Huczwa stream basin/Bug river basin/upper Vistula river
    basin

    3. 50°43'58"N, 23°45'25.4"E

    4. Valley slope

A –

B

    1. Approx. 100 m^2

    2. LBK

C

    Czekaj-Zastawny 2008a

360. Mała Wieś, site 4

    1. Wieliczka comm., Wieliczka distr., Małopolskie voiv.

    2. Upper Vistula river basin

    3. 50°00'02.3"N, 20°05'50.4"E

    4. Valley slope

A –

B

    1. Approx. 100 m^2

    2. LBK

C

    Czekaj-Zastawny 2008a; Szybowicz 1980

361. Marcinkowice, site 8

    1. Charsznica comm., Miechów distr., Małopolskie voiv.

    2. Mierzawa stream basin/Nida river basin/upper Vistula river
    basin

    3. 50°26'33.4"N, 19°54'24.2"E

    4. Valley slope nad floor

A –

B

    1. Approx. 100 m^2

    2. LBK?

C

    Czekaj-Zastawny 2008a

362. Markowa, site 36

    1. Markowa comm., Łańcut distr., Podkarpackie voiv.

    2. Mleczka stream basin/Wisłok river basin/San river
    basin/upper Vistula river basin

    3. 50°00'55.3"N, 22°18'05.8"E

    4. Valley slope

A –

B

    1. Approx. 15 ha

    2. LBK

C

    Czekaj-Zastawny 2008a

363. Markowa, site 52

    1. Markowa comm., Łańcut distr., Podkarpackie voiv.

    2. Mleczka stream basin/Wisłok river basin/San river
    basin/upper Vistula river basin

    3. 50°00'54.7"N, 22°19'05.3"E

    4. Valley slope

A

    1. T. Seile, M. Posselt

    2. 2002

    3. 1 ha of geophisical prospecting

    4. Settlement; traces of several dozen features

    5. LBK

B

1. Approx. 5 ha
2. LBK

C

Czekaj-Zastawny 2008a; Saile *et al.* 2008

364. Markowa, site 55

1. Markowa comm., Łańcut distr., Podkarpackie voiv.
2. Mleczka stream basin/Wisłok river basin/San river basin/upper Vistula river basin
3. 50°00'52.7"N, 22°20'12.8"E
4. Valley slope

A –

B

1. Approx. 5 ha
2. LBK, Music Note phase

C

Czekaj-Zastawny 2008a

365. Markowa, site 62

1. Markowa comm., Łańcut distr., Podkarpackie voiv.
2. Mleczka stream basin/Wisłok river basin/San river basin/upper Vistula river basin
3. 50°00'50.3"N, 22°20'59.4"E
4. Valley slope

A

1. T. Seile, M. Posselt
2. 2002
3. 1 ha of geophisical prospecting
4. Settlement; traces of several dozen features (5 long houses in it)
5. LBK

B

1. Approx. 15 ha
2. LBK

C

Czekaj-Zastawny 2008a; Posselt & Seile 2003; Saile *et al.* 2008

366. Markowa, site 66

1. Markowa comm., Łańcut distr., Podkarpackie voiv.
2. Mleczka stream basin/Wisłok river basin/San river basin/upper Vistula river basin
3. 50°01'03.8"N, 22°21'37.4"E
4. Valley slope

A

1. T. Seile, M. Posselt
2. 2002
3. 1 ha of geophisical prospecting
4. Settlement; traces of several dozen features (1long house in it)
5. LBK

B

1. Approx. 1 ha
2. LBK, Music Note phase

C

Czekaj-Zastawny 2008a; Saile *et al.* 2008

367. Marszowice, site 1

1. Gdów comm., Wieliczka distr., Małopolskie voiv.
2. Raba river basin/upper Vistula river basin
3. 49°54'26"N, 20°14'44"E
4. Valley slope nad border

A –

B

1. Approx. 100 m^2

2. LBK

C

Czekaj-Zastawny 2008a; Szybowicz 1980

368. Marszowice, site 12

1. Gdów comm., Wieliczka distr., Małopolskie voiv.
2. Raba river basin/upper Vistula river basin
3. 49°54'34.3"N, 20°15'36.4"E
4. Valley low terrace

A –

B

1. Approx. 100 m^2
2. LBK

C

Czekaj-Zastawny 2008a

369. Masłomęcz, site 14

1. Hrubieszów comm., Hrubieszów distr., Lubelskie voiv.
2. Bug river basin/upper Vistula river basin
3. 50°43'44"N, 23°53'01.4"E
4. Valley slope

A –

B

1. Approx. 100 m^2
2. LBK

C

Czekaj-Zastawny 2008a

370. Maszyce, site 10

1. Skała comm., Kraków distr., Małopolskie voiv.
2. Prądnik river basin/upper Vistula river basin
3. 50°10'40.7"N, 19°50'49.7"E
4. "Maszycka" Cave

A

1. G. Ossowski; S. K. Kozłowski
2. 1883; 1962-66
3. Cave sediments completely explorated; cave entrance terrace
4. Cave camp
5. LBK, Ia (*Gniechowice*) phase

B

1. –
2. LBK

C

Czekaj-Zastawny 2008a; Rook 1980

371. Maszyce, site 12

1. Skała comm., Kraków distr., Małopolskie voiv.
2. Prądnik river basin/upper Vistula river basin
3. 50°10'43.5"N, 19°50'20.6"E
4. "Górna w Ogrojcu" Cave

A

1. S. Czarnowski
2. 1901
3. Part of cave entrance terrace and cave sediments
4. Cave camp
5. LBK

B

1. –
2. LBK

C

Czekaj-Zastawny 2008a; Rook 1980

372. Medyka, site 19

1. Medyka comm., Przemyśl distr., Podkarpackie voiv.
2. San river basin/upper Vistula river basin

3. 49°47'49.3"N, 22°55'42.2"E
4. Valley slope
A –
B

1. Approx. 100 m^2
2. LBK?
C

Czekaj-Zastawny 2008a

373. Michałowice, site 3
1. Michałowice comm., Kraków distr., Małopolskie voiv.
2. Dłubnia river basin/upper Vistula river basin
3. 50°08'53.8"N, 19°58'50.5"E
4. Valley low terrace
A –
B

1. Approx. 1 ha
2. LBK
C

Czekaj-Zastawny 2008a; Kruk 1969

374. Michałowice, site 4
1. Michałowice comm., Kraków distr., Małopolskie voiv.
2. Dłubnia river basin/upper Vistula river basin
3. 50°09'18.9"N, 19°59'32.2"E
4. Border zone of upland
A –
B

1. Approx. 5 ha
2. LBK
C

Czekaj-Zastawny 2008a; Kruk 1969

375. Michałowice, site 27
1. Michałowice comm., Kraków distr., Małopolskie voiv.
2. Dłubnia river basin/upper Vistula river basin
3. 50°09'51.7"N, 19°59'15.9"E
4. Valley upper terrace/valley slope
A

1. S. Milisauskas, J. Kruk, J. Machnik
2. 1967
3. 150 m^2
4. Settlement; 3 features
5. LBK, Music Note phase; imports of Bükk culture
B

1. Approx. 15 ha
2. LBK
C

Czekaj-Zastawny 2008a; Czekaj-Zastawny & Milisauskas 1997; 1998; Kruk 1969

376. Miechów, site 3
1. Miechów comm., Kraków distr., Małopolskie voiv.
2. Szreniawa river basin/upper Vistula river basin
3. 50°19'36.6"N, 20°05'13.6"E
4. Valley slope and border
A

1. S. J. Czarnowski
2. 1897-1905
3. ?
4. Settlement or camp; no features, ca. 50 pottery fragments
5. LBK
B

1. Approx. 15 ha
2. LBK

C

Czarnowski 1908; Czekaj-Zastawny 2008a

377. Miechów, site 8
1. Miechów comm., Kraków distr., Małopolskie voiv.
2. Szreniawa river basin/upper Vistula river basin
3. 50°23'20.5"N, 20°01'50.9"E
4. Valley border
A –
B

1. Approx. 100 m^2
2. LBK?
C

Czekaj-Zastawny 2008a

378. Miechów, site 8
1. Miechów comm., Kraków distr., Małopolskie voiv.
2. Szreniawa river basin/upper Vistula river basin
3. 50°22'15.4"N, 20°01'23.6"E
4. Valley slope
A –
B

1. Approx. 0.5 ha
2. LBK
C

Czekaj-Zastawny 2008a

379. Miechów, site 38
1. Miechów comm., Kraków distr., Małopolskie voiv.
2. Szreniawa river basin/upper Vistula river basin
3. 50°19'53"N, 20°07'28.5"E
4. Outside valleys
A –
B

1. Approx. 100 m^2
2. LBK
C

Czekaj-Zastawny 2008a

380. Miechów, site 39
1. Miechów comm., Kraków distr., Małopolskie voiv.
2. Szreniawa river basin/upper Vistula river basin
3. 50°21'16.6"N, 20°06'20.7"E
4. Outside valleys
A –
B

1. Approx. 100 m^2
2. LBK
C

Czekaj-Zastawny 2008a

381. Miechów, site 40
1. Miechów comm., Kraków distr., Małopolskie voiv.
2. Szreniawa river basin/upper Vistula river basin
3. 50°19'38.3"N, 20°02'15.3"E
4. Outside valleys
A –
B

1. Approx. 100 m^2
2. LBK?
C

Czekaj-Zastawny 2008a

382. Miechów, site 65
1. Miechów comm., Kraków distr., Małopolskie voiv.
2. Szreniawa river basin/upper Vistula river basin

3. 50°22'45.6"N, 20°03'08.1"E
4. Outside valleys

A

1. Accidental find
2. 2004
3. –
4. One complete vessel (amphora) – grave?
5. LBK; Ib (*Zofipole*) phase

B

1. ?
2. LBK; Ib (*Zofipole*) phase

C

Czekaj-Zastawny 2008a

383. Mieniany, site 7
1. Hrubieszów comm., Hrubieszów distr., Lubelskie voiv.
2. Bug river basin/upper Vistula river basin
3. 50°43'06.8"N, 23°57'28.9"E
4. Valley slope

A –

B

1. Approx. 0.5 ha
2. LBK

C

Czekaj-Zastawny 2008a

384. Mieniany, site 13
1. Hrubieszów comm., Hrubieszów distr., Lubelskie voiv.
2. Bug river basin/upper Vistula river basin
3. 50°44'52.2"N, 23°57'17.1"E
4. Valley slope

A –

B

1. Approx. 100 m²
2. LBK

C

Czekaj-Zastawny 2008a

385. Mietel, site 4
1. Stopnica comm., Busko Zdrój distr., Świętokrzyskie voiv.
2. Wschodnia stream basin/upper Vistula river basin
3. 50°25'35.2"N, 20°57'58.8"E
4. Valley slope

A –

B

1. Approx. 100 m²
2. LBK?

C

Czekaj-Zastawny 2008a

386. Miętkie Kolonia, site 17
1. Mircze comm., Hrubieszów distr., Lubelskie voiv.
2. Huczwa stream basin/Bug river basin/upper Vistula river basin
3. 50°39'15.6"N, 23°48'54.3"E
4. Valley slope

A –

B

1. Approx. 0.5 ha
2. LBK?

C

Czekaj-Zastawny 2008a

387. Milówka, site 12
1. Wojnicz comm., Tarnów distr., Małopolskie voiv.
2. Dunajec river basin/upper Vistula river basin

3. 49°55'12.5"N, 20°47'41.5"E
4. Valley border

A –

B

1. Approx. 100 m²
2. LBK

C

Czekaj-Zastawny 2008a

388. Miłocice, site 8
1. Słomniki comm., Kraków distr., Małopolskie voiv.
2. Szreniawa river basin/upper Vistula river basin
3. 50°14'00.4"N, 20°03'35.6"E
4. Valley upper terrace

A –

B

1. Approx. 100 m²
2. LBK

C

Czekaj-Zastawny 2008a

389. Minoga, site 5
1. Skała comm., Kraków distr., Małopolskie voiv.
2. Dłubnia river basin/upper Vistula river basin
3. 50°14'39.2"N, 19°53'18.5"E
4. Valley slope

A –

B

1. Approx. 0.5 ha
2. LBK?

C

Czekaj-Zastawny 2008a

390. Minoga, site 10
1. Skała comm., Kraków distr., Małopolskie voiv.
2. Dłubnia river basin/upper Vistula river basin
3. 50°15'25.5"N, 19°51'58.5"E
4. Outside valleys

A –

B

1. Approx. 100 m²
2. LBK?

C

Czekaj-Zastawny 2008a

391. Minoga, site 14
1. Skała comm., Kraków distr., Małopolskie voiv.
2. Dłubnia river basin/upper Vistula river basin
3. 50°14'44.8"N, 19°54'37.9"E
4. Valley border

A –

B

1. Approx. 0.5 ha
2. LBK?

C

Czekaj-Zastawny 2008a

392. Młodzawy Małe, site 1
1. Pińczów comm., Pińczów distr., Świętokrzyskie voiv.
2. Nida river basin/upper Vistula river basin
3. 50°27'36"N, 20°30'56.3"E
4. Valley slope

A –

B

1. Approx. 100 m²
2. LBK

C

Czekaj-Zastawny 2008a; Dąbrowska 1965a; 1965b

393. Młodziejowice, site 4
1. Michałowice comm., Kraków distr., Małopolskie voiv.
2. Dłubnia river basin/upper Vistula river basin
3. 50°08'39.9"N, 19°59'44.6"E
4. Valley low terrace

A –

B
1. Approx. 0.5 ha
2. LBK

C

Czekaj-Zastawny 2008a; Kruk 1969

394. Mników, site 2
1. Liszki comm., Kraków distr., Małopolskie voiv.
2. Sanka stream basin/upper Vistula river basin
3. 50°02'58"N, 19°43'06.1"E
4. Valley slope – "Na Gaiku I" rocky shelter

A
1. G. Ossowski
2. 1881
3. Cave sediments completely explorated
4. Cave camp
5. LBK

B
1. –
2. LBK

C

Czekaj-Zastawny 2008a; Rook 1980

395. Mników, site 7
1. Liszki comm., Kraków distr., Małopolskie voiv.
2. Sanka stream basin/upper Vistula river basin
3. 50°04'06.8"N, 19°42'18.7"E
4. Valley floor – "Na Łopiankach I" Cave

A
1. P. Umiński, J. Sadowski; G. Ossowski
2. 1876; 1880-81
3. Cave sediments completely explorated
4. Cave camp
5. LBK

B
1. –
2. LBK

C

Czekaj-Zastawny 2008a; Rook 1980

396. Mników, site 8
1. Liszki comm., Kraków distr., Małopolskie voiv.
2. Sanka stream basin/upper Vistula river basin
3. 50°03'57.3"N, 19°42'42.8"E
4. Valley floor – "Na Łopiankach II" Cave

A
1. G. Ossowski
2. 1881-82
3. Cave sediments completely explorated
4. Cave camp
5. LBK

B
1. –
2. LBK

C

Czekaj-Zastawny 2008a; Rook 1980

397. Mniszów Kolonia, site 4
1. Brzesko comm., Brzesko distr., Małopolskie voiv.
2. Szreniawa river basin/upper Vistula river basin
3. 50°10'30.4"N, 20°23'11.3"E
4. Valley low terrace

A –

B
1. Approx. 5 ha
2. LBK

C

Czekaj-Zastawny 2008a

398. Modlniczka, site 2
1. Wielka Wieś comm., Kraków distr., Małopolskie voiv.
2. Rudawa river basin/upper Vistula river basin
3. 50°07'06.1"N, 19°51'54.5"E
4. Valley slope and floor

A
1. M. Przybyła (The Cracow Team for Archaeological Supervision of Motorway Construction, Institute of Archaeology and Ethnology Polish Academy of Sciences, Museum of Archaeology Cracow, Jagiellonian University)
2. 2008
3. 39583 m^2
4. Cemetery; ca. 38 cremation graves; few features
5. LBK, Music Note phase?

B
1. Approx. 1 ha
2. LBK

C

Czekaj-Zastawny *et al.* in press

399. Modlnica, site 3
1. Wielka Wieś como., Kraków bistr., Małopolskie volv.
2. Rudawa river basin/upper Vistula river basin
3. 50°07'40"N, 19°51'52.8"E
4. Valley slope and border

A
1. R. Czerniak
2. 2008
3. 150 m^2
4. Settlement; a few hundred features (1 long houses in it)
5. LBK

B
1. Approx. 1 ha
2. LBK

C

Information from R. Czerniak

400. Modlnica, site 5
1. Wielka Wieś como., Kraków bistr., Małopolskie volv.
2. Rudawa river basin/upper Vistula river basin
3. 50°07'48.8"N, 19°52'05.4"E
4. Valley slope and border

A
1. B Konieczny (The Cracow Team for Archaeological Supervision of Motorway Construction, Institute of Archaeology and Ethnology Polish Academy of Sciences, Museum of Archaeology Cracow, Jagiellonian University)
2. 2008
3. 261314 m^2
4. Settlement; a few hundred features (ca. 7 long houses in it)
5. LBK, Ia (*Gniechowice*) phase, Ib (*Zofipole*) phase, Music Note phase

B
1. Approx. 5 ha

2. LBK

C

Konieczny 2008

401. Modryniec, site 2
1. Mircze comm., Hrubieszów distr., Lubelskie voiv.
2. Bug river basin/upper Vistula river basin
3. 50°41'12.2"N, 23°53'13.2"E
4. Valley slope

A –

B

1. Approx. 100 m²
2. LBK

C

Czekaj-Zastawny 2008a

402. Modryniec, site 5
1. Mircze comm., Hrubieszów distr., Lubelskie voiv.
2. Bug river basin/upper Vistula river basin
3. 50°41'26"N, 23°53'41.7"E
4. Valley floor

A –

B

1. Approx. 100 m²
2. LBK

C

Czekaj-Zastawny 2008a

403. Modrzany, site 1
1. Koszyce comm., Proszowice distr., Małopolskie voiv.
2. Szreniawa river basin/upper Vistula river basin
3. 50°10'01.5"N, 20°29'48.1"E
4. Border zone of upland

A –

B

1. Approx. 100 m²
2. LBK

C

Czekaj-Zastawny 2008a; Rydzewski 1972

404. Mogielnica, site 3
1. Boguchwała comm., Rzeszów distr., Podkarpackie voiv.
2. Wisłok river basin/San river basin/upper Vistula river basin
3. 49°58'32.1"N, 21°53'35.2"E
4. Valley border

A –

B

1. Approx. 1 ha
2. LBK?

C

Czekaj-Zastawny 2008a

405. Mogielnica, site 4
1. Boguchwała comm., Rzeszów distr., Podkarpackie voiv.
2. Wisłok river basin/San river basin/upper Vistula river basin
3. 49°58'37.6"N, 21°54'26.2"E
4. Valley border

A –

B

1. Approx. 100 m²
2. LBK?

C

Czekaj-Zastawny 2008a

406. Mokoszyn, site 1
1. Sandomierz comm., Sandomierz distr., Świętokrzyskie

voiv.
2. Upper Vistula river basin
3. 50°41'48.4"N, 21°46'25.3"E
4. Border zone of upland

A –

B

1. Approx. 0.5 ha
2. LBK?

C

Czekaj-Zastawny 2008a

407. Morawiany, site 2
1. Bejsce comm., Kazimierza Wielka distr., Świętokrzyskie voiv.
2. Nidzica river basin/upper Vistula river basin
3. 50°13'47.5"N, 20°37'39.7"E
4. Border zone of upland

A –

B

1. Approx. 100 m²
2. LBK?

C

Czekaj-Zastawny 2008a

408. Morawiany, site 6
1. Bejsce comm., Kazimierza Wielka distr., Świętokrzyskie voiv.
2. Nidzica river basin/upper Vistula river basin
3. 50°12'54.1"N, 20°40'39"E
4. Valley floor

A –

B

1. Approx. 5 ha
2. LBK

C

Czekaj-Zastawny 2008a

409. Morawiany, site 8
1. Bejsce comm., Kazimierza Wielka distr., Świętokrzyskie voiv.
2. Nidzica river basin/upper Vistula river basin
3. 50°13'26.8"N, 20°40'04.6"E
4. Valley upper terrace

A –

B

1. Approx. 100 m²
2. LBK

C

Czekaj-Zastawny 2008a

410. Morawiany, site 9
1. Bejsce comm., Kazimierza Wielka distr., Świętokrzyskie voiv.
2. Nidzica river basin/upper Vistula river basin
3. 50°13'15.7"N, 20°40'57.6"E
4. Valley low terrace

A –

B

1. Approx. 0.5 ha
2. LBK

C

Czekaj-Zastawny 2008a

411. Morawiany, site 11
1. Bejsce comm., Kazimierza Wielka distr., Świętokrzyskie voiv.

2. Nidzica river basin/upper Vistula river basin
3. 50°13'12.7"N, 20°41'55.7"E
4. Valley low terrace

A –
B

1. Approx. 15 ha
2. LBK?

C

Czekaj-Zastawny 2008a

412. Mostek, site 6
1. Gołcza comm., Miechów distr., Małopolskie voiv.
2. Szreniawa river basin/upper Vistula river basin
3. 50°20'44.7"N, 19°50'12.7"E
4. Outside valleys

A –
B

1. Approx. 100 m^2
2. LBK?

C

Czekaj-Zastawny 2008a

413. Mrowla, site 6
1. Świlcza comm., Rzeszów distr., Podkarpackie voiv.
2. Wisłok river basin/San river basin/upper Vistula river basin
3. 50°05'59"N, 21°54'50.5"E
4. Valley low terrace

A –
B

1. Approx. 100 m^2
2. LBK

C

Czekaj-Zastawny 2008a

414. Muniaczkowice, site 6
1. Koniusza comm., Proszowice distr., Małopolskie voiv.
2. Szreniawa river basin/upper Vistula river basin
3. 50°12'43.6"N, 20°12'10.8"E
4. Valley low terrace

A –
B

1. Approx. 0.5 ha
2. LBK

C

Czekaj-Zastawny 2008a

415. Myczkowce, site 16
1. Solina comm., Lesko distr., Podkarpackie voiv.
2. San river basin/upper Vistula river basin
3. 49°26'59.3"N, 22°24'38.9"E
4. Valley slope

A –
B

1. Approx. 100 m^2
2. LBK?

C

Czekaj-Zastawny 2008a

416. Mysławczyce, site 2
1. Proszowice comm., Proszowice distr., Małopolskie voiv.
2. Szreniawa river basin/upper Vistula river basin
3. 50°11'04.8"N, 20°24'48.2"E
4. Valley low terrace

A –
B

1. Approx. 100 m^2

2. LBK

C

Czekaj-Zastawny 2008a; Rydzewski 1972

417. Nehrybka, site 21
1. Przemyśl comm., Przemyśl distr., Podkarpackie voiv.
2. Wiar stream basin/San river basin/upper Vistula river basin
3. 49°45'00.5"N, 22°47'35.6"E
4. Valley slope

A –
B

1. Approx. 1 ha
2. LBK, Želiezovce phase

C

Czekaj-Zastawny 2008a

418. Niedzieliska, site 13
1. Szczebrzeszyn comm., Zamość distr., Lubelskie voiv.
2. Wieprz river basin/upper Vistula river basin
3. 50°42'42.4"N, 23°04'29.2"E
4. Valley slope

A –
B

1. Approx. 100 m^2
2. LBK

C

Czekaj-Zastawny 2008a

419. Niedźwice, site 9
1. Koprzywnica comm., Sandomierz distr., Świętokrzyskie voiv.
2. Koprzywianka stream basin/upper Vistula river basin
3. 50°36'42"N, 21°30'46.8"E
4. Valley border

A –
B

1. Approx. 100 m^2
2. LBK

C

Czekaj-Zastawny 2008a; Kowalewska-Marszałek 1992

420. Niedźwiedź, site 15
1. Słomniki comm., Kraków distr., Małopolskie voiv.
2. Szreniawa river basin/upper Vistula river basin
3. 50°13'35.8"N, 20°05'39.5"E
4. Valley upper terrace

A –
B

1. Approx. 5 ha
2. LBK

C

Czekaj-Zastawny 2008a; Kruk 1970

421. Niedźwiedź, site 16
1. Słomniki comm., Kraków distr., Małopolskie voiv.
2. Szreniawa river basin/upper Vistula river basin
3. 50°13'30.2"N, 20°06'23.8"E
4. Valley low terrace

A –
B

1. Approx. 0.5 ha
2. LBK

C

Czekaj-Zastawny 2008a

422. Niedźwiedź, site 17
1. Słomniki comm., Kraków distr., Małopolskie voiv.
2. Szreniawa river basin/upper Vistula river basin
3. 50°13'36.3"N, 20°05'50.8"E
4. Valley low terrace
A –
B
  1. Approx. 5 ha
  2. LBK
C
  Czekaj-Zastawny 2008a; Kruk 1970

423. Niegardów, site 1
1. Koniusza comm., Proszowice distr., Małopolskie voiv.
2. Szreniawa river basin/upper Vistula river basin
3. 50°12'50.5"N, 20°11'21.2"E
4. Valley upper terrace
A –
B
  1. Approx. 0.5 ha
  2. LBK
C
  Czekaj-Zastawny 2008a; Kruk 1970

424. Niegardów, site 2
1. Koniusza comm., Proszowice distr., Małopolskie voiv.
2. Szreniawa river basin/upper Vistula river basin
3. 50°12'27.8"N, 20°12'05.9"E
4. Valley upper terrace
A –
B
  1. Approx. 100 m^2
  2. LBK
C
  Czekaj-Zastawny 2008a; Kruk 1970

425. Niegardów, site 4
1. Koniusza comm., Proszowice distr., Małopolskie voiv.
2. Szreniawa river basin/upper Vistula river basin
3. 50°12'16.4"N, 20°12'04"E
4. Valley border
A –
B
  1. Approx. 100 m^2
  2. LBK
C
  Czekaj-Zastawny 2008a

426. Niegardów, site 6
1. Koniusza comm., Proszowice distr., Małopolskie voiv.
2. Szreniawa river basin/upper Vistula river basin
3. 50°12'56"N, 20°10'54.6"E
4. Valley border
A –
B
  1. Approx. 0.5 ha
  2. LBK
C
  Czekaj-Zastawny 2008a; Kruk 1970

427. Niegardów, site 8
1. Koniusza comm., Proszowice distr., Małopolskie voiv.
2. Szreniawa river basin/upper Vistula river basin
3. 50°12'15.8"N, 20°11'19.5"E
4. Valley border
A –

B
  1. Approx. 15 ha
  2. LBK
C
  Czekaj-Zastawny 2008a; Kruk 1970

428. Niegoszowice, site 1
1. Zabierzów comm., Kraków distr., Małopolskie voiv.
2. Rudawa stream basin/upper Vistula river basin
3. 50°07'08.3"N, 19°44'50"E
4. Valley slope
A –
B
  1. Approx. 1 ha
  2. LBK
C
  Czekaj-Zastawny 2008a

429. Niemienice, site IB
1. Sadowie comm., Opatów distr., Świętokrzyskie voiv.
2. Opatówka stream basin/upper Vistula river basin
3. 50°49'42.6"N, 21°19'44.4"E
4. Valley border
A –
B
  1. Approx. 200 m^2
  2. LBK
C
  Bąbel 1975; Czekaj-Zastawny 2008a; Kowalewska-Marszałek 1992

430. Nienadówka, site 1
1. Sokołów Małopolski comm., Rzeszów distr., Podkarpackie voiv.
2. San river basin/upper Vistula river basin
3. 50°11'57.5"N, 22°05'47.6"E
4. Valley slope
A –
B
  1. Approx. 100 m^2
  2. LBK?
C
  Czekaj-Zastawny 2008a

431. Nieprowice, site 2
1. Złota Pińczowska comm., Pińczów distr., Świętokrzyskie voiv.
2. Nida river basin/upper Vistula river basin
3. 50°24'25.9"N, 20°34'16.3"E
4. Outside valleys
A –
B
  1. Approx. 100 m^2
  2. LBK
C
  Czekaj-Zastawny 2008a; Dąbrowska 1965a

432. Nieprowice, site 16
1. Złota Pińczowska comm., Pińczów distr., Świętokrzyskie voiv.
2. Nida river basin/upper Vistula river basin
3. 50°23'50.4"N, 20°35'45.2"E
4. Outside valleys
A –
B
  1. Approx. 100 m^2

2. LBK

C

Czekaj-Zastawny 2008a

433. Nieszków, site 1
1. Słaboszów comm., Miechów distr., Małopolskie voiv.
2. Nidzica river basin/upper Vistula river basin
3. 50°22'55.1"N, 20°16'44.8"E
4. Valley low terrace

A –

B

1. Approx. 100 m²
2. LBK

C

Czekaj-Zastawny 2008a

434. Nieszków, site 4
1. Słaboszów comm., Miechów distr., Małopolskie voiv.
2. Nidzica river basin/upper Vistula river basin
3. 50°22'45.4"N, 20°17'19.5"E
4. Valley upper terrace

A –

B

1. Approx. 5 ha
2. LBK

C

Czekaj-Zastawny 2008a; Liguzińska-Kruk 1982

435. Nieznanowice, site 10
1. Gdów comm., Wieliczka distr., Małopolskie voiv.
2. Raba river basin/upper Vistula river basin
3. 49°54'58.3"N, 20°16'08.5"E
4. Valley low terrace

A –

B

1. Approx. 100 m²
2. LBK

C

Czekaj-Zastawny 2008a

436. Nowa Wieś, site 3
1. Skała comm., Kraków distr., Małopolskie voiv.
2. Dłubnia river basin/upper Vistula river basin
3. 50°14'15.8"N, 19°54'04.1"E
4. Valley slope

A –

B

1. Approx. 0.5 ha
2. LBK

C

Czekaj-Zastawny 2008a; Kruk 1969

437. Nowa Wieś, site 4
1. Skała comm., Kraków distr., Małopolskie voiv.
2. Dłubnia river basin/upper Vistula river basin
3. 50°13'42.9"N, 19°54'38.2"E
4. Valley slope

A –

B

1. Approx. 0.5 ha
2. LBK

C

Czekaj-Zastawny 2008a

438. Nowosielce, site 6
1. Przeworsk comm., Przeworsk distr., Podkarpackie voiv.

2. Wisłok river basin/San river basin/upper Vistula river basin
3. 50°05'02.9"N, 22°24'48.1"E
4. Valley border

A –

B

1. Approx. 100 m²
2. LBK

C

Czekaj-Zastawny 2008a

439. Nowosielce, site 8
1. Przeworsk comm., Przeworsk distr., Podkarpackie voiv.
2. Wisłok river basin/San river basin/upper Vistula river basin
3. 50°04'28.2"N, 22°24'26.3"E
4. Valley upper terrace

A –

B

1. Approx. 100 m²
2. LBK

C

Czekaj-Zastawny 2008a

440. Nowosielce, site 9
1. Przeworsk comm., Przeworsk distr., Podkarpackie voiv.
2. Wisłok river basin/San river basin/upper Vistula river basin
3. 50°02'55.1"N, 22°21'54.6"E
4. Outside valleys

A –

B

1. Approx. 100 m²
2. LBK?

C

Czekaj-Zastawny 2008a

441. Nowosielce, site 13
1. Przeworsk comm., Przeworsk distr., Podkarpackie voiv.
2. Wisłok river basin/San river basin/upper Vistula river basin
3. 50°02'33.5"N, 22°22'57.5"E
4. Valley low terrace

A –

B

1. Approx. 100 m²
2. LBK?

C

Czekaj-Zastawny 2008a

442. Obrażejowice, site 18
1. Radziemice comm., Proszowice distr., Małopolskie voiv.
2. Szreniawa river basin/upper Vistula river basin
3. 50°15'38.6"N, 20°09'30.9"E
4. Valley slope and border

A –

B

1. Approx. 100 m²
2. LBK

C

Czekaj-Zastawny 2008a

443. Oficjałów, site 6
1. Opatów comm., Opatów distr., Świętokrzyskie voiv.
2. Opatówka river basin/upper Vistula river basin
3. 50°47'12.4"N, 21°26'42.9"E
4. Valley slope

A –

B

1. Approx. 1 ha

2. LBK

C

Czekaj-Zastawny 2008a; Kowalewska-Marszałek 1992

444. Ojców, site 2
1. Skała comm., Kraków distr., Małopolskie voiv.
2. Prądnik river basin/upper Vistula river basin
3. 50°11'22.3"N, 19°50'13.9"E
4. Valley slope – "Główna w Okopach", Cave

A

1. S. Czarnowski
2. 1898
3. Cave entrance terrace
4. Cave camp; 3 pottery fragments
5. LBK

B

1. –
2. LBK

C

Czekaj-Zastawny 2008a; Rook 1980

445. Ojców, site 3
1. Skała comm., Kraków distr., Małopolskie voiv.
2. Prądnik river basin/upper Vistula river basin
3. 50°11'25.2"N, 19°50'10.7"E
4. Valley slope – "Okopy Wielka Dolna" Cave

A

1. J. Zawisza; S. Czarnowski
2. 1874; 1895, 1898
3. Upper layer of cave sediments completely explorated
4. Cave camp; 1 vessel and 15 pottery fragments
5. LBK, Ia (*Gniechowice*) phase, Music Note phase, Želiezovce phase

B

1. –
2. LBK

C

Czekaj-Zastawny 2008a; Rook 1980

446. Ojców, site 16
1. Skała comm., Kraków distr., Małopolskie voiv.
2. Prądnik river basin/upper Vistula river basin
3. 50°11'31.5"N, 19°50'06"E
4. Valley border – "W Krzyżowej Skale Większe" rocky shelter

A

1. S. Czarnowski
2. 1905
3. Rocky shelter sediments completely explorated
4. Cave camp; 3 pottery fragments
5. LBK

B

1. –
2. LBK

C

Czekaj-Zastawny 2008a; Rook 1980

447. Ojców, site 18
1. Skała comm., Kraków distr., Małopolskie voiv.
2. Prądnik river basin/upper Vistula river basin
3. 50°11'47.1"N, 19°49'57.8"E
4. Valley slope – "Ciemna-Oborzysko Wielkie" Cave

A

1. S. Czarnowski; S. Krukowski; S. Kowalski
2. 1901-1902; 1918-1919; 1963-1968
3. Cave entrance terrace, part of entrance, part of Northern

Tunnel and Ogrojec
4. Cave camp; 1 vessel and 159 pottery fragments
5. LBK, Music Note phase, Želiezovce phase; imports of Bükk culture

B

1. –
2. LBK

C

Czekaj-Zastawny 2008a; Rook 1980

448. Ojców, site 19
1. Skała comm., Kraków distr., Małopolskie voiv.
2. Prądnik river basin/upper Vistula river basin
3. 50°11'49.2"N, 19°49'52.9"E
4. Valley slope – "Oborzysko Małe" Cave

A

1. S. Czarnowski
2. 1901
3. Upper layer of cave sediments
4. Cave camp; 3 pottery fragments
5. LBK

B

1. –
2. LBK

C

Czekaj-Zastawny 2008a; Rook 1980

449. Okocim, site 7
1. Brzesko comm., Brzesko distr., Małopolskie voiv.
2. Uszwica river basin/upper Vistula river basin
3. 49°56'24.1"N, 20°36'27.2"E
4. Valley border

A –

B

1. Approx. 100 m^2
2. LBK

C

Czekaj-Zastawny 2008a

450. Olchowa, site 4
1. Iwierzyce comm., Ropczyce-Sędziszów distr., Podkarpackie voiv.
2. Bystrzyca stream basin/Wisłoka river basin/upper Vistula river basin
3. 50°03'49.3"N, 21°44'37.5"E
4. Valley border

A –

B

1. Approx. 0.5 ha
2. LBK

C

Czekaj-Zastawny 2008a

451. Olchowa, site 19
1. Iwierzyce comm., Ropczyce-Sędziszów distr., Podkarpackie voiv.
2. Bystrzyca stream basin/Wisłoka river basin/upper Vistula river basin
3. 50°03'00"N, 21°46'25.9"E
4. Valley border

A –

B

1. Approx. 0.5 ha
2. LBK

C

Czekaj-Zastawny 2008a

452. Olchowa, site 20
1. Iwierzyce comm., Ropczyce-Sędziszów distr.,
   Podkarpackie voiv.
2. Bystrzyca stream basin/Wisłoka river basin/upper Vistula
   river basin
3. 50°02'57.4"N, 21°45'18.1"E
4. Valley slope and border

A
1. P. Mitura, R. Zych
2. 1999-2000, 2002
3. 1275 m^2
4. Settlement; 87 features (ca. 3 long houses and 1 human
   grave in it)
5. LBK, Music Note phase, Želiezovce phase (through IIb?);
   imports of Bükk culture

B
1. Approx. 13 ha
2. LBK

C
Czekaj-Zastawny 2008a; Mitura & Zych 1999; Saile *et al.*
2008

453. Oleśnica, site 1
1. Oleśnica comm., Staszów distr., Świętokrzyskie voiv.
2. Wschodnia stream basin/upper Vistula river basin
3. 50°26'47"N, 21°03'46.8"E
4. Valley slope

A –
B
1. Approx. 100 m^2
2. LBK?

C
Czekaj-Zastawny 2008a

454. Olimpów, site 1
1. Iwierzyce comm., Ropczyce-Sędziszów distr.,
   Podkarpackie voiv.
2. Bystrzyca stream basin/Wisłoka river basin/upper Vistula
   river basin
3. 50°00'26.6"N, 21°45'55.4"EE
4. Valley border

A –
B
1. Approx. 100 m^2
2. LBK

C
Czekaj-Zastawny 2008a

455. Olimpów, site 2
1. Iwierzyce comm., Ropczyce-Sędziszów distr.,
   Podkarpackie voiv.
2. Bystrzyca stream basin/Wisłoka river basin/upper Vistula
   river basin
3. 50°00'08.3"N, 21°45'39.1"E
4. Valley slope and border

A –
B
1. Approx. 1 ha
2. LBK

C
Czekaj-Zastawny 2008a

456. Opatów, site 2
1. Opatów comm., Opatów distr., Świętokrzyskie voiv.
2. Opatówka stream basin/upper Vistula river basin
3. 50°47'42"N, 21°26'24.5"E

4. Valley slope and border
A –
B
1. Approx. 100 m^2
2. LBK

C
Czekaj-Zastawny 2008a; Kowalewska-Marszałek 1992

457. Opatów, site 2
1. Opatów comm., Opatów distr., Świętokrzyskie voiv.
2. Opatówka stream basin/upper Vistula river basin
3. 50°48'38.1"N, 21°24'41.8"E
4. Valley slope and border

A –
B
1. Approx. 1 ha
2. LBK

C
Czekaj-Zastawny 2008a; Kowalewska-Marszałek 1992

458. Orłów, site 2
1. Słomniki comm., Kraków distr., Małopolskie voiv.
2. Szreniawa river basin/upper Vistula river basin
3. 50°17'28.8"N, 20°02'08.8"E
4. Valley border

A –
B
1. Approx. 5 ha
2. LBK

C
Czekaj-Zastawny 2008a; Kruk 1970

459. Paczółtowice, site 2
1. Krzeszowice comm., Kraków distr., Małopolskie voiv.
2. Rudawa stream basin/upper Vistula river basin
3. 50°10'27.1"N, 19°39'20.3"E
4. Outside valleys

A –
B
1. Approx. 0.5 ha
2. LBK?

C
Czekaj-Zastawny 2008a

460. Pałecznica, site 18
1. Pałecznica comm., Proszowice distr., Małopolskie voiv.
2. Nidzica river basin/upper Vistula river basin
3. 50°17'31.1"N, 20°18'22.6"E
4. Valley border

A –
B
1. Approx. 100 m^2
2. LBK?

C
Czekaj-Zastawny 2008a

461. Pamięcice, site 7
1. Pałecznica comm., Proszowice distr., Małopolskie voiv.
2. Nidzica river basin/upper Vistula river basin
3. 50°18'35.5"N, 20°17'21.9"E
4. Outside valleys

A –
B
1. Approx. 100 m^2
2. LBK?

C

Czekaj-Zastawny 2008a

462. Pantalowice, site 37
 1. Kańczuga comm., Przeworsk distr., Podkarpackie voiv.
 2. Mleczka stream basin/Wisłok river basin/San river basin/Vistula river basin
 3. 49°56'57.8"N, 22°26'53.2"E
 4. Valley slope and border
A –
B
 1. Approx. 8-9 ha
 2. LBK
C

Saile *et al.* 2008

463. Pantalowice, site 39
 1. Kańczuga comm., Przeworsk distr., Podkarpackie voiv.
 2. Mleczka stream basin/Wisłok river basin/San river basin/Vistula river basin
 3. 49°56'59"N, 22°26'29.2"E
 4. Valley slope
A –
B
 1. Approx. 1 ha
 2. LBK
C

Saile *et al.* 2008

464. Parkoszowice, site 1
 1. Miechów comm., Miechów distr., Małopolskie voiv.
 2. Szreniawa river basin/upper Vistula river basin
 3. 50°19'10"N, 20°03'14.4"E
 4. Valley border
A –
B
 1. Approx. 1 ha
 2. LBK
C

Czekaj-Zastawny 2008a; Kruk 1970

465. Pełkinie, site 15
 1. Jarosław comm., Jarosław distr., Podkarpackie voiv.
 2. San river basin/Vistula river basin
 3. 50°04'23.4"N, 22°38'04.2"E
 4. Valley slope
A –
B
 1. Approx. 100 m^2
 2. LBK
C

Czekaj-Zastawny 2008a

466. Pielgrzymowice, site 2
 1. Michałowice comm., Kraków distr., Małopolskie voiv.
 2. Dłubnia river basin/upper Vistula river basin
 3. 50°09'00.3"N, 20°03'30.2"E
 4. Valley slope
A –
B
 1. Approx. 100 m^2
 2. LBK
C

Czekaj-Zastawny 2008a; Kruk 1969

467. Pierzchów, site 1
 1. Gdów comm., Wieliczka distr., Małopolskie voiv.
 2. Raba river basin/upper Vistula river basin
 3. 49°55'42.5"N, 20°16'55.5"E
 4. Valley low terrace
A –
B
 1. Approx. 15 ha
 2. LBK
C

Czekaj-Zastawny 2008a; Szybowicz 1980

468. Piestrzec, site 12
 1. Solec Zdrój comm., Busko-Zdrój distr., Świętokrzyskie voiv.
 2. Strumień stream basin/upper Vistula river basin
 3. 50°23'28.6"N, 20°56'32"E
 4. Outside valleys
A –
B
 1. Approx. 100 m^2
 2. LBK?
C

Czekaj-Zastawny 2008a

469. Piestrzec, site 27
 1. Solec Zdrój comm., Busko-Zdrój distr., Świętokrzyskie voiv.
 2. Strumień stream basin/upper Vistula river basin
 3. 50°22'40.4"N, 20°57'02.5"E
 4. Border zone of upland/valley border
A –
B
 1. Approx. 5 ha
 2. LBK
C

Czekaj-Zastawny 2008a

470. Piotrkowice Wielkie, site 1
 1. Koniusza comm., Proszowice distr., Małopolskie voiv.
 2. Szreniawa river basin/upper Vistula river basin
 3. 50°13'18.3"N, 20°11'15"E
 4. Valley low terrace
A –
B
 1. Approx. 100 m^2
 2. LBK
C

Czekaj-Zastawny 2008a; Kruk 1970

471. Piotrkowice Wielkie, site 2
 1. Koniusza comm., Proszowice distr., Małopolskie voiv.
 2. Szreniawa river basin/upper Vistula river basin
 3. 50°13'31.3"N, 20°11'12.9"E
 4. Valley upper terrace
A –
B
 1. Approx. 100 m^2
 2. LBK
C

Czekaj-Zastawny 2008a; Kruk 1970

472. Piotrkowice Wielkie, site 8
 1. Koniusza comm., Proszowice distr., Małopolskie voiv.
 2. Szreniawa river basin/upper Vistula river basin
 3. 50°13'46.6"N, 20°10'43.3"E

4. Valley low terrace

A –

B

1. Approx. 0.5 ha
2. LBK

C

Czekaj-Zastawny 2008a

473. Piotrkowice Małe, site 2

1. Koniusza comm., Proszowice distr., Małopolskie voiv.
2. Szreniawa river basin/upper Vistula river basin
3. 50°11'48.7"N, 20°14'21.9"E
4. Valley low terrace

A –

B

1. Approx. 5 ha
2. LBK

C

Czekaj-Zastawny 2008a; Kruk 1970

474. Pniówek, site 1

1. Zamość comm., Zamość distr., Lubelskie voiv.
2. Wieprz river basin/upper Vistula river basin
3. 50°40'56.3"N, 23°18'42"E
4. Valley slope

A –

B

1. Approx. 1 ha
2. LBK

C

Czekaj-Zastawny 2008a

475. Podgaje, site 1

1. Skalbimierz comm., Kazimierza Wielka distr., Świętokrzyskie voiv.
2. Nidzica river basin/upper Vistula river basin
3. 50°20'33.5"N, 20°21'49.4"E
4. Valley low terrace

A

1. J. Rydzewski
2. 1973
3. 100 m^2
4. Camp or settlement trace; no features, 4 pottery fragments
5. LBK

B

1. Approx. 0.5 ha
2. LBK

C

Czekaj-Zastawny 2008a

476. Podhorce, site 2

1. Werbkowice comm., Hrubieszów distr., Lubelskie voiv.
2. Huczwa stream basin/Bug river basin/upper Vistula river basin
3. 50°46'20.4"N, 23°46'38"E
4. Valley floor

A –

B

1. Approx. 5 ha
2. LBK

C

Czekaj-Zastawny 2008a

477. Podhorce, site 11

1. Werbkowice comm., Hrubieszów distr., Lubelskie voiv.
2. Huczwa stream basin/Bug river basin/upper Vistula river

basin
3. 50°47'16.3"N, 23°47'57.4"E
4. Valley floor

A –

B

1. Approx. 100 m^2
2. LBK

C

Czekaj-Zastawny 2008a

478. Podhorce, site 33

1. Werbkowice comm., Hrubieszów distr., Lubelskie voiv.
2. Huczwa stream basin/Bug river basin/upper Vistula river basin
3. 50°46'42.6"N, 23°47'44.1"E
4. Valley slope

A –

B

1. Approx. 100 m^2
2. LBK

C

Czekaj-Zastawny 2008a

479. Podhorce, site 37

1. Werbkowice comm., Hrubieszów distr., Lubelskie voiv.
2. Huczwa stream basin/Bug river basin/upper Vistula river basin
3. 50°46'25.2"N, 23°48'03.6"E
4. Valley floor

A –

B

1. Approx. 0.5 ha
2. LBK

C

Czekaj-Zastawny 2008a

480. Podhorce, site 38

1. Werbkowice comm., Hrubieszów distr., Lubelskie voiv.
2. Huczwa stream basin/Bug river basin/upper Vistula river basin
3. 50°46'12.9"N, 23°47'59.1"E
4. Valley floor

A –

B

1. Approx. 100 m^2
2. LBK

C

Czekaj-Zastawny 2008a

481. Podhorce, site 52

1. Werbkowice comm., Hrubieszów distr., Lubelskie voiv.
2. Huczwa stream basin/Bug river basin/upper Vistula river basin
3. 50°47'20"N, 23°48'33.8"E
4. Valley border

A –

B

1. Approx. 0.5 ha
2. LBK

C

Czekaj-Zastawny 2008a

482. Podhorce, site 53

1. Werbkowice comm., Hrubieszów distr., Lubelskie voiv.
2. Huczwa stream basin/Bug river basin/upper Vistula river basin

3. 50°47'01.5"N, 23°48'28.7"E
4. Valley border
A –
B
1. Approx. 0.5 ha
2. LBK
C
Czekaj-Zastawny 2008a

483. Podole, site 1
1. Opatów comm., Opatów distr., Świętokrzyskie voiv.
2. Kamienna stream basin/upper Vistula river basin
3. 50°50'21.3"N, 21°27'06.3"E
4. Valley border
A –
B
1. Approx. 2 ha
2. LBK
C
Czekaj-Zastawny 2008a; Kowalewska-Marszałek 1992;
   Kowalski 1975

484. Pogwizdów, site 3
1. Charsznica comm., Miechów distr., Małopolskie voiv.
2. Mierzawa stream basin/Nida river basin/upper Vistula river
   basin
3. 50°25'36.6"N, 19°56'08.7"E
4. Outside valleys
A –
B
1. Approx. 0.5 ha
2. LBK?
C
Czekaj-Zastawny 2008a

485. Pojałowice, site 6
1. Miechów comm., Miechów distr., Małopolskie voiv.
2. Szreniawa river basin/upper Vistula river basin
3. 50°19'05.7"N, 20°05'42.7"E
4. Valley slope
A –
B
1. Approx. 1 ha
2. LBK
C
Czekaj-Zastawny 2008a

486. Polanów, site 4
1. Koprzywianka comm., Sandomierz distr., Świętokrzyskie
   voiv.
2. Kamienna stream basin/upper Vistula river basin
3. 50°39'44.2"N, 21°38'32.6"E
4. Border zone of upland
A –
B
1. Approx. 100 m^2
2. LBK
C
Czekaj-Zastawny 2008a; Kowalewska-Marszałek 1992

487. Polanów, site 5
1. Samborzec comm., Sandomierz distr., Świętokrzyskie voiv.
2. Koprzywianka stream basin/upper Vistula river basin
3. 50°39'34.3"N, 21°40'05.1"E
4. Valley slope
A –

B
1. Approx. 100 m^2
2. LBK
C
Czekaj-Zastawny 2008a; Kowalewska-Marszałek 1992

488. Polanów, site 11
1. Samborzec comm., Sandomierz distr., Świętokrzyskie voiv.
2. Koprzywianka stream basin/upper Vistula river basin
3. 50°39'16.5"N, 21°39'05.4"E
4. Valley border
A –
B
1. Approx. 1 ha
2. LBK
C
Czekaj-Zastawny 2008a; Kowalewska-Marszałek 1992

489. Polanów, site 12
1. Samborzec comm., Sandomierz distr., Świętokrzyskie voiv.
2. Koprzywianka stream basin/upper Vistula river basin
3. 50°39'51.7"N, 21°39'54.7"E
4. Valley slope
A –
B
1. Approx. 1 ha
2. LBK
C
Czekaj-Zastawny 2008a; Kowalewska-Marszałek 1992

490. Polanów, site 14
1. Samborzec comm., Sandomierz distr., Świętokrzyskie voiv.
2. Koprzywianka stream basin/upper Vistula river basin
3. 50°40'01.4"N, 21°40'21.4"E
4. Valley border
A –
B
1. Approx. 100 m^2
2. LBK
C
Czekaj-Zastawny 2008a; Kowalewska-Marszałek 1992

491. Polesie, site 2
1. Tomaszów Lubelski comm., Tomaszów Lubelski distr.,
   Lubelskie voiv.
2. Sołoikija stream basin/Bug river basin/upper Vistula river
   basin
3. 50°26'26.9"N, 23°28'44.8"E
4. Valley slope
A –
B
1. Approx. 0.5 ha
2. LBK
C
Czekaj-Zastawny 2008a

492. Płaza, site 4
1. Chrzanów comm., Chrzanów distr., Małopolskie voiv.
2. Upper Vistula river basin
3. 50°05'15.2"N, 19°26'58"E
4. Valley slope
A –
B
1. Approx. 100 m^2
2. LBK?

C

Czekaj-Zastawny 2008a

493. Poręba Laskowska, site 1
1. Skała comm., Kraków distr., Małopolskie voiv.
2. Dłubnia river basin/upper Vistula river basin
3. 50°15'35.5"N, 19°55'07.9"E
4. Outside valleys

A –

B

1. Approx. 0.5 ha
2. LBK?

C

Czekaj-Zastawny 2008a

494. Poręba Spytkowska, site 25
1. Brzesko comm., Brzesko distr., Małopolskie voiv.
2. Uszwica stream basin/upper Vistula river basin
3. 49°56'27.7"N, 20°34'21.1"E
4. Valley slope

A –

B

1. Approx. 0.5 ha
2. LBK

C

Czekaj-Zastawny 2008a

495. Poręba Spytkowska, site 27
1. Brzesko comm., Brzesko distr., Małopolskie voiv.
2. Uszwica stream basin/upper Vistula river basin
3. 49°56'09"N, 20°33'03.3"E
4. Valley border

A –

B

1. Approx. 100 m²
2. LBK?

C

Czekaj-Zastawny 2008a

496. Prandocin, site 1
1. Słomniki comm., Kraków distr., Małopolskie voiv.
2. Szreniawa river basin/upper Vistula river basin
3. 50°15'39.8"N, 20°05'55.3"E
4. Valley slope and border

A –

B

1. Approx. 2 ha
2. LBK

C

Czekaj-Zastawny 2008a; Kruk 1970

497. Przebieczany, site 2
1. Biskupice comm., Wieliczka distr., Małopolskie voiv.
2. Upper Vistula river basin
3. 49°58'49.1"N, 20°07'08.4"E
4. Valley slope

A –

B

1. Approx. 100 m²
2. LBK

C

Czekaj-Zastawny 2008a; Szybowicz 1980

498. Przeginia, site 7
1. Jerzmanowice-Przeginia comm., Kraków distr., Małopolskie voiv.

2. Prądnik river basin/upper Vistula river basin
3. 50°14'36.2"N, 19°41'48.8"E
4. Outside valleys

A –

B

1. Approx. 100 m²
2. LBK?

C

Czekaj-Zastawny 2008a

499. Przemęczany, site 12
1. Radziemice comm., Proszowice distr., Małopolskie voiv.
2. Szreniawa river basin/upper Vistula river basin
3. 50°16'18.2"N, 20°13'47.7"E
4. Valley border

A –

B

1. Approx. 1 ha
2. LBK

C

Czekaj-Zastawny 2008a

500. Przemyków, site 7
1. Koszyce comm., Proszowice distr., Małopolskie voiv.
2. Upper Vistula river basin
3. 50°11'25.5"N, 20°39'05.7"E
4. Valley low terrace

A –

B

1. Approx. 100 m²
2. LBK

C

Czekaj-Zastawny 2008a

501. Przemyśl, site 77
1. Przemyśl comm., Przemyśl distr., Podkarpackie voiv.
2. San river basin/Vistula river basin
3. 49°46'57.1"N, 22°46'26.1"E
4. Valley slope

A

1. A Koperski
2. 1970, 1989
3. ?
4. Settlement; 10 features
5. LBK

B

1. Approx. 1 ha
2. LBK

C

Czekaj-Zastawny 2008a; Koperski 2001

502. Przemyśl, site 285
1. Przemyśl comm., Przemyśl distr., Podkarpackie voiv.
2. San river basin/Vistula river basin
3. 49°47'21.8"N, 22°47'52.2"E
4. Valley slope

A –

B

1. Approx. 0.5 ha
2. LBK

C

Czekaj-Zastawny 2008a; Koperski 2001

503. Przeorsk, site 9
1. Tomaszów Lubelski comm., Tomaszów Lubelski distr., Lubelskie voiv.

2. Sołoikija stream basin/Bug river basin/upper Vistula river
basin
3. 50°25'02.1"N, 23°29'56.4"E
4. Valley low terrace

A –
B
1. Approx. 0.5 ha
2. LBK?
C
Czekaj-Zastawny 2008a

504. Przesławice, site 2
1. Miechów comm., Miechów distr., Małopolskie voiv.
2. Szreniawa river basin/upper Vistula river basin
3. 50°19'07.4"N, 20°00'29.1"E
4. Valley slope and border

A –
B
1. Approx. 0.5 ha
2. LBK
C
Czekaj-Zastawny 2008a; Kruk 1970

505. Przesławice, site 1
1. Koniusza comm., Proszowice distr., Małopolskie voiv.
2. Szreniawa river basin/upper Vistula river basin
3. 50°11'56.5"N, 20°13'02.1"E
4. Valley low terrace

A –
B
1. Approx. 5 ha
2. LBK
C
Czekaj-Zastawny 2008a; Kruk 1970

506. Przesławice, site 2
1. Koniusza comm., Proszowice distr., Małopolskie voiv.
2. Szreniawa river basin/upper Vistula river basin
3. 50°11'47.4"N, 20°12'40.9"E
4. Border zone of upland

A –
B
1. Approx. 1 ha
2. LBK
C
Czekaj-Zastawny 2008a; Kruk 1970

507. Przesławice, site 7
1. Koniusza comm., Proszowice distr., Małopolskie voiv.
2. Szreniawa river basin/upper Vistula river basin
3. 50°12'05.1"N, 20°12'30.8"E
4. Valley slope

A –
B
1. Approx. 100 m^2
2. LBK
C
Czekaj-Zastawny 2008a; Kruk 1973

508. Przesławice, site 8
1. Koniusza comm., Proszowice distr., Małopolskie voiv.
2. Szreniawa river basin/upper Vistula river basin
3. 50°12'20.2"N, 20°12'29.6"E
4. Valley low terrace

A –

B
1. Approx. 0.5 ha
2. LBK, Żeliezovce phase
C
Czekaj-Zastawny 2008a

509. Przybysławice, site 3
1. Skała comm., Kraków distr., Małopolskie voiv.
2. Dłubnia river basin/upper Vistula river basin
3. 50°13'51.4"N, 19°55'08"E
4. Border zone of upland/valley border

A –
B
1. Approx. 5 ha
2. LBK
C
Czekaj-Zastawny 2008a

510. Przybysławice, site 6
1. Skała comm., Kraków distr., Małopolskie voiv.
2. Dłubnia river basin/upper Vistula river basin
3. 50°13'25.2"N, 19°54'33.5"E
4. Valley slope

A –
B
1. Approx. 100 m^2
2. LBK?
C
Czekaj-Zastawny 2008a; Kruk 1969

511. Przybyszówka, site 11
1. Świlcza comm., Rzeszów distr., Podkarpackie voiv.
2. Wisłok river basin/San river basin/Vistula river basin
3. 50°02'22.3"N, 21°55'15.3"E
4. Valley slope

A –
B
1. Approx. 1 ha
2. LBK
C
Czekaj-Zastawny 2008a

512. Pstroszyce, site 5
1. Miechów comm., Miechów distr., Małopolskie voiv.
2. Szreniawa river basin/upper Vistula river basin
3. 50°24'00.4"N, 20°01'07"E
4. Valley slope and border

A –
B
1. Approx. 5 ha
2. LBK
C
Data from AZP card

513. Pstroszyce, site 10
1. Miechów comm., Miechów distr., Małopolskie voiv.
2. Szreniawa river basin/upper Vistula river basin
3. 50°23'07.7"N, 20°00'43.1"E
4. Outside valleys

A –
B
1. Approx. 100 m^2
2. LBK

C

Data from AZP card

514. Pstroszyce, site 16
1. Miechów comm., Miechów distr., Małopolskie voiv.
2. Szreniawa river basin/upper Vistula river basin
3. 50°23'42.4"N, 20°00'45.5"E
4. Valley slope and floor

A –

B

1. Approx. 0.5 ha
2. LBK

C

Data from AZP card

515. Pstroszyce, site ?
1. Miechów comm., Miechów distr., Małopolskie voiv.
2. Szreniawa stream basin/upper Vistula river basin
3. 50°24'00.2"N, 20°00'31.3"E
4. Valley border

A –

B

1. Approx. ?
2. LBK, Ib (*Zofipole*) phase

C

Czekaj-Zastawny 2008a; Kulczycka-Leciejewiczowa 2000

516. Racławówka, site 12
1. Boguchwała comm., Rzeszów distr., Podkarpackie voiv.
2. Wisłok river basin/San river basin/upper Vistula river basin
3. 50°00'02.1"N, 21°55'44.7"E
4. Valley slope

A –

B

1. Approx. 0.5 ha
2. LBK?

C

Czekaj-Zastawny 2008a

517. Radwanowice, site 5
1. Zabierzów comm., Kraków distr., Małopolskie voiv.
2. Rudawa stream basin/upper Vistula river basin
3. 50°09'06.6"N, 19°43'44.9"E
4. Outside valleys

A –

B

1. Approx. 0.5 ha
2. LBK?

C

Czekaj-Zastawny 2008a

518. Radziemice, site 13
1. Radziemice comm., Proszowice distr., Małopolskie voiv.
2. Szreniawa river basin/upper Vistula river basin
3. 50°15'18.1"N, 20°13'57.7"E
4. Valley border

A –

B

1. Approx. 100 m²
2. LBK

C

Czekaj-Zastawny 2008a

519. Radziemice, site 16
1. Radziemice comm., Proszowice distr., Małopolskie voiv.
2. Szreniawa river basin/upper Vistula river basin

3. 50°15'23.1"N, 20°14'17.3"E
4. Valley slope

A –

B

1. Approx. 100 m²
2. LBK?

C

Czekaj-Zastawny 2008a

520. Radziszów, site 45
1. Skawina comm., Kraków distr., Małopolskie voiv.
2. Skawa stream basin/upper Vistula river basin
3. 49°56'14.4"N, 19°49'17.6"E
4. Outside valleys

A –

B

1. Approx. 5 ha
2. LBK

C

Czekaj-Zastawny 2008a

521. Radziszów, site 48
1. Skawina comm., Kraków distr., Małopolskie voiv.
2. Skawa stream basin/upper Vistula river basin
3. 49°56'40.3"N, 19°49'28.4"E
4. Outside valleys

A –

B

1. Approx. 100 m²
2. LBK?

C

Czekaj-Zastawny 2008a

522. Ratajów, site 5
1. Słomniki comm., Kraków distr., Małopolskie voiv.
2. Szreniawa river basin/upper Vistula river basin
3. 50°13'44.3"N, 20°04'49.3"E
4. Valley upper terrace

A –

B

1. Approx. 100 m²
2. LBK

C

Czekaj-Zastawny 2008a

523. Rogów, site 3
1. Opatowiec comm., Kazimierza Wielka distr., Świętokrzyskie voiv.
2. Upper Vistula river basin
3. 50°13'49.6"N, 20°42'24.6"E
4. Valley slope

A –

B

1. Approx. 0.5 ha
2. LBK?

C

Czekaj-Zastawny 2008a

524. Rogóźno, site 1
1. Tomaszów Lubelski comm., Tomaszów Lubelski distr., Lubelskie voiv.
2. Sołoikija stream basin/Bug river basin/upper Vistula river basin
3. 50°27'59"N, 23°23'58.7"E
4. Valley slope

A –

B

1. Approx. 100 m²
2. LBK?

C

Czekaj-Zastawny 2008a

525. Rosiejów, site 10
1. Skalbimierz comm., Kazimierza Wielka distr.,
   Świętokrzyskie voiv.
2. Nidzica river basin/upper Vistula river basin
3. 50°19'18.6"N, 20°19'30.7"E
4. Valley border

A –

B

1. Approx. 100 m²
2. LBK

C

Czekaj-Zastawny 2008a

526. Rozbórz, site 29
1. Przeworsk comm., Przeworsk distr., Podkarpackie voiv.
2. Mleczka stream basin/Wisłok river basin/San river
   basin/upper Vistula river basin
3. 50°03'37.2"N, 22°32'53.6"E
4. Valley slope

A –

B

1. Approx. 100 m²
2. LBK, Želiezovce phase

C

Czekaj-Zastawny 2008a

527. Rożubowice, site 12
1. Przemyśl comm., Przemyśl distr., Podkarpackie voiv.
2. Wiar stream basin/San river basin/upper Vistula river basin
3. 49°44'02.8"N, 22°50'52.4"E
4. Valley slope

A –

B

1. Approx. 100 m²
2. LBK?

C

Czekaj-Zastawny 2008a

528. Rożubowice, site 15
1. Przemyśl comm., Przemyśl distr., Podkarpackie voiv.
2. Wiar stream basin/San river basin/upper Vistula river basin
3. 49°43'48.6"N, 22°51'14.5"E
4. Valley border

A –

B

1. Approx. 100 m²
2. LBK?

C

Czekaj-Zastawny 2008a

529. Ruszcza Płaszczyzna, site 23
1. Koprzywnica comm., Sandomierz distr., Świętokrzyskie
   voiv.
2. Koprzywianka stream basin/upper Vistula river basin
3. 50°34'31.5"N, 21°28'09.3"E
4. Valley slope

A –

B

1. Approx. 1 ha
2. LBK

C

Czekaj-Zastawny 2008a; Kowalewska-Marszałek 1992

530. Ruszków, site VI
1. Sadowie comm., Opatów distr., Świętokrzyskie voiv.
2. Opatówka stream basin/upper Vistula river basin
3. 50°51'25.6"N, 21°20'30.2"E
4. Valley slope

A –

B

1. Approx. 0.5 ha
2. LBK?

C

Bąbel 1975; Czekaj-Zastawny 2008a; Kowalewska-Marszałek
1992

531. Rzeplin, site IV
1. Pruchnik comm., Jarosław distr., Podkarpackie voiv.
2. Mleczka stream basin/Wisłok river basin/San river
   basin/upper Vistula river basin
3. 49°55'54.6"N, 22°27'58.7"E
4. Valley slope and border

A –

B

1. Approx. 5 ha
2. LBK

C

Czekaj-Zastawny 2008a

532. Rzeplin, site VII
1. Pruchnik comm., Jarosław distr., Podkarpackie voiv.
2. Mleczka stream basin/Wisłok river basin/San river
   basin/upper Vistula river basin
3. 49°55'39.4"N, 22°28'21.7"E
4. Valley slope and border

A –

B

1. Approx. 0.5 ha
2. LBK

C

Czekaj-Zastawny 2008a

533. Rzeplin, site 1
1. Skała comm., Kraków distr., Małopolskie voiv.
2. Dłubnia river basin/upper Vistula river basin
3. 50°13'05.5"N, 19°53'57.7"E
4. Valley border

A –

B

1. Approx. 0.5 ha
2. LBK?

C

Czekaj-Zastawny 2008a

534. Rzeplin, site 9
1. Skała comm., Kraków distr., Małopolskie voiv.
2. Dłubnia river basin/upper Vistula river basin
3. 50°13'10.8"N, 19°54'59.2"E
4. Valley border

A –

B

1. Approx. 0.5 ha
2. LBK?

C

Czekaj-Zastawny 2008a

535. Rzeplin, site 10
1. Skała comm., Kraków distr., Małopolskie voiv.
2. Dłubnia river basin/upper Vistula river basin
3. 50°13'02.6"N, 19°54'41.3"E
4. Valley border

A –
B
1. Approx. 15 ha
2. LBK

C
Czekaj-Zastawny 2008a; Lech *et al.* 1984

536. Rzeszów, site 3
1. Rzeszów comm., Rzeszów distr., Podkarpackie voiv.
2. Wisłok river basin/San river basin/upper Vistula river basin
3. 50°02'41.4"N, 22°00'24.2"E
4. Valley upper terrace

A
1. T. Aksamit, A. Gruszczyńska, A. Talar
2. 1965-69
3. 1 ha
4. Settlement; 33 features (elongated pits belongs to long houses in it)
5. LBK, Ib (*Zofipole*) phase, Music Note phase, Želiezovce phase (through ŽIIb); imports of Tisadob-Kapušany group and Bükk culture

B
1. Approx. 10 ha
2. LBK

C
Czekaj-Zastawny 2008a; Czopek 1999; Kadrow 1997; Saile *et al.* 2008

537. Rzeszów, site 4
1. Rzeszów comm., Rzeszów distr., Podkarpackie voiv.
2. Wisłok river basin/San river basin/upper Vistula river basin
3. 50°02'44.2"N, 22°01'15.9"E
4. Valley slope

A –
B
1. Approx. 1 ha
2. LBK

C
Barłowski 1968; Czekaj-Zastawny 2008a

538. Rzeszów, site 8
1. Rzeszów comm., Rzeszów distr., Podkarpackie voiv.
2. Wisłok river basin/San river basin/upper Vistula river basin
3. 50°03'51.9"N, 22°01'44.3"E
4. Valley upper terrace

A –
B
1. Approx. 100 m^2
2. LBK

C
Barłowski 1968; Czekaj-Zastawny 2008a; Moskwa 1974

539. Rzeszów, site 9
1. Rzeszów comm., Rzeszów distr., Podkarpackie voiv.
2. Wisłok river basin/San river basin/upper Vistula river basin
3. 50°01'51.7"N, 22°00'59.7"E
4. Valley slope

A –
B
1. Approx. 100 m^2
2. LBK?

C
Czekaj-Zastawny 2008a; Moskwa 1964

540. Rzeszów, site 16
1. Rzeszów comm., Rzeszów distr., Podkarpackie voiv.
2. Wisłok river basin/San river basin/upper Vistula river basin
3. 50°01'43.3"N, 21°59'40.2"E
4. Valley upper terrace

A
1. T. Aksamit
2. 1960-65
3. ?
4. Settlement; 85 features (ca. 17-19 household in it)
5. LBK, Ia (*Gniechowice*) phase, Ib (*Zofipole*) phase, Music Note phase, Želiezovce phase; imports of Alföld Linear Pottery culture (AVK), Tisadob-Kapušany group and Bükk culture

B
1. Approx. 6 ha
2. LBK

C
Czopek 1999; Czekaj-Zastawny 2008a; Kadrow 1990a; Moskwa 1974; Saile *et al.* 2008

541. Rzeszów, site 23
1. Rzeszów comm., Rzeszów distr., Podkarpackie voiv.
2. Wisłok river basin/San river basin/upper Vistula river basin
3. 50°00'36.6"N, 21°59'11.9"E
4. Valley upper terrace

A
1. T. Aksamit
2. 1963
3. 10 m^2
4. Settlement trace; no features, 1 pottery fragment
5. LBK

B
1. Approx. 100 m^2
2. LBK

C
Aksamit 1964b; Czekaj-Zastawny 2008a

542. Rzeszów, site 24
1. Rzeszów comm., Rzeszów distr., Podkarpackie voiv.
2. Wisłok river basin/San river basin/upper Vistula river basin
3. 50°00'23.7"N, 21°58'50.2"E
4. Valley upper terrace

A
1. T. Aksamit
2. 1963
3. 150 m^2
4. Camp or settlement trace; no features, few pottery fragments
5. LBK

B
1. Approx. 100 m^2
2. LBK

C
Aksamit 1964b; Czekaj-Zastawny 2008a; Czopek 1999

543. Rzeszów, site 34
1. Rzeszów comm., Rzeszów distr., Podkarpackie voiv.
2. Wisłok river basin/San river basin/upper Vistula river basin
3. 50°03'11.3"N, 22°01'11.2"E
4. Valley upper terrace

A
1. A Talar

2. 1970
3. 225 m^2
4. Settlement; 56 features (2-3 long houses in it)
5. LBK, Music Note phase; imports of Tisadob-Kapušany group

B

1. Approx. 1 ha
2. LBK

C

Czekaj-Zastawny 2008a; informations from S. Kadrow

544. Rzeszów, site 42
1. Rzeszów comm., Rzeszów distr., Podkarpackie voiv.
2. Wisłok river basin/San river basin/upper Vistula river basin
3. 50°02'58.9"N, 22°01'29.7"E
4. Outside valleys

A –

B

1. Approx. 0.5 ha
2. LBK

C

Czekaj-Zastawny 2008a

545. Rzeszów, site 50
1. Rzeszów comm., Rzeszów distr., Podkarpackie voiv.
2. Wisłok river basin/San river basin/upper Vistula river basin
3. 50°02'47.5"N, 22°01'47.5"E
4. Valley border

A –

B

1. Approx. 100 m^2
2. LBK

C

Czekaj-Zastawny 2008a

546. Rzeszów, site 55
1. Rzeszów comm., Rzeszów distr., Podkarpackie voiv.
2. Wisłok river basin/San river basin/upper Vistula river basin
3. 50°02'05.5"N, 22°01'44.9"E
4. Valley slope

A

1. P. Mitura
2. 1997-98
3. 900 m^2
4. Settlement; 6 features (probably fragm. of 1 long house in it)
5. LBK

B

1. Approx. 1 ha
2. LBK

C

Czekaj-Zastawny 2008a; Czopek 1999; Saile *et al.* 2008

547. Rzeszów, site 65
1. Rzeszów comm., Rzeszów distr., Podkarpackie voiv.
2. Wisłok river basin/San river basin/upper Vistula river basin
3. 50°01'49.3"N, 22°01'51.9"E
4. Valley slope

A –

B

1. Approx. 0.5 ha
2. LBK

C

Czekaj-Zastawny 2008a

548. Rzeszów, site 96
1. Rzeszów comm., Rzeszów distr., Podkarpackie voiv.
2. Wisłok river basin/San river basin/upper Vistula river basin
3. 50°02'59.6"N, 22°02'40.7"E
4. Valley slope

A –

B

1. Approx. 5 ha
2. LBK

C

Barłowski 1971; Czekaj-Zastawny 2008a

549. Rzeszów, site 97
1. Rzeszów comm., Rzeszów distr., Podkarpackie voiv.
2. Wisłok river basin/San river basin/upper Vistula river basin
3. 50°02'58"N, 22°02'21.3"E
4. Valley slope

A –

B

1. Approx. 1 ha
2. LBK

C

Czekaj-Zastawny 2008a

550. Rzeszów, site 114
1. Rzeszów comm., Rzeszów distr., Podkarpackie voiv.
2. Wisłok river basin/San river basin/upper Vistula river basin
3. 50°02'32.2"N, 21°57'57.7"E
4. Valley slope

A –

B

1. Approx. 100 m^2
2. LBK?

C

Czekaj-Zastawny 2008a

551. Rzędowice, site 10
1. Książ Wielki comm., Miechów distr., Małopolskie voiv.
2. Nidzica river basin/upper Vistula river basin
3. 50°26'29"N, 20°05'20.4"E
4. Valley slope

A –

B

1. Approx. 0.5 ha
2. LBK

C

Czekaj-Zastawny 2008a

552. Samborzec, site 1
1. Samborzec comm., Sandomierz distr., Świętokrzyskie voiv.
2. Koprzywianka stream basin/upper Vistula river basin
3. 50°38'14.2"N, 21°38'50.8"E
4. Valley upper terrace

A

1. K. Salewicz; B. Burchard , J. Kamieńska, A. Kulczycka-Leciejewiczowa
2. 1930; 1960-66
3. 5000 m^2
4. Settlement; ca. 60 features (probably few long houses in it; 5 human graves)
5. LBK, Ia (*Gniechowice*) phase, Ib (*Zofipole*) phase, Music Note phase, Želiezovce phase; imports of Bükk culture

B

1. Approx. 11 ha
2. LBK

C

Czekaj-Zastawny 2008a; Kamieńska 1964a; 1964b; 1965;
1966; 1968; Kamieńska & Kulczycka-Leciejewiczowa 1970;
Kulczycka-Leciejewiczowa 2008; Podkowińska 1960

553. Samborzec, site II
1. Samborzec comm., Sandomierz distr., Świętokrzyskie voiv.
2. Koprzywianka stream basin/upper Vistula river basin
3. 50°38'38.7"N, 21°39'10.2"E
4. Valley border

A –

B

1. Approx. 0.5 ha
2. LBK

C

Czekaj-Zastawny 2008a; Kowalewska-Marszałek 1992;
   Podkowińska 1960

554. Samborzec, site III
1. Samborzec comm., Sandomierz distr., Świętokrzyskie voiv.
2. Koprzywianka stream basin/upper Vistula river basin
3. 50°39'13"N, 21°39'26.8"E
4. Valley border

A –

B

1. Approx. 0.5 ha
2. LBK

C

Czekaj-Zastawny 2008a; Kowalewska-Marszałek 1992;
   Podkowińska 1960

555. Sandomierz, site 3
1. Sandomierz comm., Sandomierz distr., Świętokrzyskie
   voiv.
2. Upper Vistula river basin
3. 50°41'20.4"N, 21°46'37.6"E
4. Border zone of upland

A

1. IAE PAN (Institute of Archaeology and Ethnology Polish
   Academy of Sciences)
2. 1969
3. ?
4. Settlement or camp; no features, ca. 100 pottery fragments
5. LBK

B

1. Approx. 1 ha
2. LBK

C

Czekaj-Zastawny 2008a; Kowalewska-Marszałek 1992

556. Sandomierz, site 5
1. Sandomierz comm., Sandomierz distr., Świętokrzyskie
   voiv.
2. Upper Vistula river basin
3. 50°40'39.5"N, 21°45'29.8"E
4. Valley low terrace

A

1. E. Tabaczyńska, S. Tabaczyński;
   H. Kowalewska-Marszałek
2. 1971; 1980
3. 250 m^2
4. Settlement?; no features, 103 pottery fragments
5. LBK, Music Note phase, Żeliezovce phase (through ŽIIb);
   imports of Eastern Linear Pottery culture and Bükk culture

B

1. Approx. 0.5 ha

2. LBK

C

Czekaj-Zastawny 2008a; Kowalewska-Marszałek 1981; 1992;
   1996; Tabaczyńska 1972

557. Sandomierz, site 7
1. Sandomierz comm., Sandomierz distr., Świętokrzyskie
   voiv.
2. Upper Vistula river basin
3. 50°41'56.6"N, 21°45'16.4"E
4. Border zone of upland and valley border

A

1. H. Wróbel
2. 1981-82
3. 170 m^2
4. Settlement or camp; 1 feature
5. LBK, Żeliezovce phase

B

1. Approx. 100 m^2
2. LBK

C

Czekaj-Zastawny 2008a; Kowalewska-Marszałek 1992;
   Kulczycka-Leciejewiczowa 1968; Wróbel 1982; 1983

558. Sandomierz, site 11
1. Sandomierz comm., Sandomierz distr., Świętokrzyskie
   voiv.
2. Upper Vistula river basin
3. 50°41'55"N, 21°43'26.8"E
4. Border zone of upland and valley border

A

1. J. Żurowski
2. 1929
3. ?
4. Settlement; 3 features
5. LBK, Music Note phase

B

1. Approx. 1 ha
2. LBK

C

Burchard 1960; Czekaj-Zastawny 2008a;
   Kowalewska-Marszałek 1992

559. Sandomierz, site 12
1. Sandomierz comm., Sandomierz distr., Świętokrzyskie
   voiv.
2. Upper Vistula river basin
3. 50°40'59"N, 21°46'23.2"E
4. Valley border

A –

B

1. Approx. 100 m^2
2. LBK

C

Czekaj-Zastawny 2008a; Kowalewska-Marszałek 1992

560. Sandomierz, site 20
1. Sandomierz comm., Sandomierz distr., Świętokrzyskie
   voiv.
2. Upper Vistula river basin
3. 50°41'49"N, 21°45'32.3"E
4. Border zone of upland

A

1. G. Miliszkiewicz; H. Taras; J., J. Ścibior
2. 1979; 1980-82; 1983-85
3. 440 m^2

4. Settlement; 5 features (probably 1 long house in it)
5. LBK, Ib (*Zofipole*) phase, Music Note phase, Żeliezovce
   phase (through ŻIIb); imports of Bükk culture

B

1. Approx. 1 ha
2. LBK

C

Czekaj-Zastawny 2008a; Kowalewska-Marszałek 1992;
Michalak-Ścibior & Taras 1995

561. Sandomierz, site 29
1. Sandomierz comm., Sandomierz distr., Świętokrzyskie
   voiv.
2. Upper Vistula river basin
3. 50°41'16.5"N, 21°45'00.1"E
4. Border zone of upland/valley border

A

1. J. Żurowski
2. 1928
3. ?
4. Camp or settlement trace; no features, few pottery
   fragments
5. LBK

B

1. Approx. 0.5 ha
2. LBK

C

Czekaj-Zastawny 2008a; Jakimowicz 1935;
Kowalewska-Marszałek 1992

562. Sandomierz, site 30
1. Sandomierz comm., Sandomierz distr., Świętokrzyskie
   voiv.
2. Upper Vistula river basin
3. 50°41'02.6"N, 21°44'31.6"E
4. Border zone of upland/valley border

A –

B

1. Approx. 100 m²
2. LBK?

C

Czekaj-Zastawny 2008a; Kowalewska-Marszałek 1992

563. Sandomierz, site 32
1. Sandomierz comm., Sandomierz distr., Świętokrzyskie
   voiv.
2. Upper Vistula river basin
3. 50°40'41.5"N, 21°43'43"E
4. Border zone of upland/valley border

A –

B

1. Approx. 100 m²
2. LBK

C

Czekaj-Zastawny 2008a; Kowalewska-Marszałek 1992

564. Sąspów, site 34
1. Jerzmanowice-Przeginia comm., Kraków distr.,
   Małopolskie voiv.
2. Prądnik river basin/upper Vistula river basin
3. 50°13'50"N, 19°45'57.1"E
4. Outside valleys

A –

B

1. Approx. 100 m²
2. LBK?

C

Czekaj-Zastawny 2008a

565. Sąspów, site 80
1. Jerzmanowice-Przeginia comm., Kraków distr.,
   Małopolskie voiv.
2. Prądnik river basin/upper Vistula river basin
3. 50°13'33.2"N, 19°47'37.1"E
4. Outside valleys

A –

B

1. Approx. 100 m²
2. LBK?

C

Czekaj-Zastawny 2008a

566. Sieciechowice, site 1
1. Iwanowice comm., Kraków distr., Małopolskie voiv.
2. Dłubnia river basin/upper Vistula river basin
3. 50°14'45.7"N, 19°58'12.9"E
4. Valley low terrace/valley slope

A –

B

1. Approx. 0.5 ha
2. LBK

C

Czekaj-Zastawny 2008a; Kruk 1969

567. Sieciechowice, site 28
1. Iwanowice comm., Kraków distr., Małopolskie voiv.
2. Dłubnia river basin/upper Vistula river basin
3. 50°15'27.7"N, 19°59'10.4"E
4. Outside valleys

A –

B

1. Approx. 100 m²
2. LBK

C

Czekaj-Zastawny 2008a

568. Sieciechowice, site 30
1. Iwanowice comm., Kraków distr., Małopolskie voiv.
2. Dłubnia river basin/upper Vistula river basin
3. 50°14'38.6"N, 19°59'46.6"E
4. Outside valleys

A –

B

1. Approx. 100 m²
2. LBK

C

Czekaj-Zastawny 2008a

569. Sieciechowice, site 45
1. Iwanowice comm., Kraków distr., Małopolskie voiv.
2. Dłubnia river basin/upper Vistula river basin
3. 50°14'48.6"N, 20°00'33.8"E
4. Outside valleys

A –

B

1. Approx. 100 m²
2. LBK

C

Czekaj-Zastawny 2008a

570. Sieciechowice, site 48
1. Iwanowice comm., Kraków distr., Małopolskie voiv.
2. Dłubnia river basin/upper Vistula river basin
3. 50°15'05.4"N, 20°00'09.9"E
4. Outside valleys

A –
B
  1. Approx. 100 m^2
  2. LBK
C
  Czekaj-Zastawny 2008a

571. Siedleczka, site 5
1. Kańczuga comm., Przeworsk distr., Podkarpackie voiv.
2. Mleczka stream basin/Wisłok river basin/San river basin/upper Vistula river basin
3. 49°57'39"N, 22°23'04.7"E
4. Valley slope

A –
B
  1. Approx. 5 ha
  2. LBK
C
  Czekaj-Zastawny 2008a

572. Siedliska, site 3
1. Miechów comm., Miechów distr., Małopolskie voiv.
2. Szreniawa river basin/upper Vistula river basin
3. 50°22'22"N, 20°01'20.8"E
4. Valley border

A –
B
  1. Approx. 100 m^2
  2. LBK
C
  Data from AZP card

573. Siedliska, site 13
1. Miechów comm., Miechów distr., Małopolskie voiv.
2. Szreniawa river basin/upper Vistula river basin
3. 50°22'45.1"N, 20°01'41.6"E
4. Valley slope and floor

A –
B
  1. Approx. 1 ha
  2. LBK
C
  Data from AZP card

574. Siedliska, site 16
1. Miechów comm., Miechów distr., Małopolskie voiv.
2. Szreniawa river basin/upper Vistula river basin
3. 50°22'55.4"N, 20°02'00.5"E
4. Valley border/outside valleys

A –
B
  1. Approx. 0.5 ha
  2. LBK
C
  Data from AZP card

575. Siedliska, site 20
1. Miechów comm., Miechów distr., Małopolskie voiv.
2. Szreniawa river basin/upper Vistula river basin
3. 50°22'29.1"N, 20°01'42.9"E
4. Outside valleys

A –
B
  1. Approx. 0.5 ha
  2. LBK
C
  Data from AZP card

576. Siedliska, site 3
1. Medyka comm., Przemyśl distr., Podkarpackie voiv.
2. San river basin/upper Vistula river basin
3. 49°45'46.4"N, 22°52'24.5"E
4. Valley upper terrace

A –
B
  1. Approx. 0.5 ha
  2. LBK
C
  Czekaj-Zastawny 2008a

577. Sielec, site 5
1. Iwierzyce comm., Ropczyce-Sędziszów distr., Podkarpackie voiv.
2. Wielopolka stream basin/Wisłoka river basin/upper Vistula river basin
3. 50°02'55.6"N, 21°44'52.5"E
4. Valley slope

A –
B
  1. Approx. 100 m^2
  2. LBK
C
  Czekaj-Zastawny 2008a

578. Sierakośce, site 125
1. Fredropol comm., Przemyśl distr., Podkarpackie voiv.
2. Wiar stream basin/San river basin/upper Vistula river basin
3. 49°39'05.8"N, 22°45'40.6"E
4. Valley slope

A –
B
  1. Approx. 100 m^2
  2. LBK?
C
  Czekaj-Zastawny 2008a

579. Siercza, site 15
1. Wieliczka comm., Wieliczka distr., Małopolskie voiv.
2. Raba river basin/upper Vistula river basin
3. 49°58'20.6"N, 20°02'07.3"E
4. Outside valleys

A –
B
  1. Approx. 0.5 ha
  2. LBK?
C
  Czekaj-Zastawny 2008a; Szybowicz 1980

580. Siesławice, site 3
1. Busko-Zdrój comm., Busko Zdrój distr., Świętokrzyskie voiv.
2. Nida river basin/upper Vistula river basin
3. 50°27'29.8"N, 20°41'18.4"E
4. Outside valleys

A –
B
  1. Approx. 100 m^2

2. LBK

C

Czekaj-Zastawny 2008a

581. Sietesz, site 50
1. Kańczuga comm., Przeworsk distr., Podkarpackie voiv.
2. Mleczka stream basin/Wisłok river basin/San river basin/upper Vistula river basin
3. 49°59'20.8"N, 22°20'28.9"E
4. Valley slope

A –

B

1. Approx. 0.5 ha
2. LBK

C

Czekaj-Zastawny 2008a

582. Sietesz, site 52
1. Kańczuga comm., Przeworsk distr., Podkarpackie voiv.
2. Mleczka stream basin/Wisłok river basin/San river basin/upper Vistula river basin
3. 50°00'08.1"N, 22°20'44.2"E
4. Valley slope

A –

B

1. Approx. 0.5 ha
2. LBK

C

Czekaj-Zastawny 2008a

583. Sietesz, site 58
1. Kańczuga comm., Przeworsk distr., Podkarpackie voiv.
2. Mleczka stream basin/Wisłok river basin/San river basin/upper Vistula river basin
3. 49°59'27.7"N, 22°21'15.2"E
4. Outside valleys

A –

B

1. Approx. 0.5 ha
2. LBK

C

Czekaj-Zastawny 2008a

584. Skała, site 3
1. Skała comm., Kraków distr., Małopolskie voiv.
2. Prądnik river basin/upper Vistula river basin
3. 50°13'08.7"N, 19°51'07.4"E
4. Outside valleys

A –

B

1. Approx. 0.5 ha
2. LBK?

C

Czekaj-Zastawny 2008a

585. Skrobaczów, site 9
1. Stopnica comm., Busko Zdrój distr., Świętokrzyskie voiv.
2. Wschodnia stream basin/upper Vistula river basin
3. 50°27'51.9"N, 20°54'46.7"E
4. Valley slope

A –

B

1. Approx. 100 m^2
2. LBK

C

Czekaj-Zastawny 2008a

586. Skrobaczów, site 11
1. Stopnica comm., Busko Zdrój distr., Świętokrzyskie voiv.
2. Wschodnia stream basin/upper Vistula river basin
3. 50°27'25.6"N, 20°54'06.6"E
4. Valley slope

A –

B

1. Approx. 100 m^2
2. LBK

C

Czekaj-Zastawny 2008a

587. Skorczów, site 4
1. Kazimierza Wielka comm., Kazimierza Wielka distr., Świętokrzyskie voiv.
2. Nidzica river basin/upper Vistula river basin
3. 50°15'13.7"N, 20°26'08.9"E
4. Valley slope

A –

B

1. Approx. 0.5 ha
2. LBK

C

Czekaj-Zastawny 2008a; Rydzewski 1973

588. Słabuszewice, site 39
1. Lipnik comm., Opatów distr., Świętokrzyskie voiv.
2. Nidzica river basin/upper Vistula river basin
3. 50°45'03.4"N, 21°32'38.1"E
4. Valley border

A –

B

1. Approx. 100 m^2
2. LBK?

C

Czekaj-Zastawny 2008a; Kowalewska-Marszałek 1992

589. Sławice Szlacheckie, site 1
1. Miechów comm., Miechów distr., Małopolskie voiv.
2. Szreniawa river basin/upper Vistula river basin
3. 50°19'09.1"N, 20°04'21.4"E
4. Valley slope and border

A –

B

1. Approx. 15 ha
2. LBK

C

Czekaj-Zastawny 2008a; Kruk 1970

590. Sławice Szlacheckie, site 2
1. Miechów comm., Miechów distr., Małopolskie voiv.
2. Szreniawa river basin/upper Vistula river basin
3. 50°18'55.4"N, 20°04'42.2"E
4. Valley slope

A –

B

1. Approx. 0.5 ha
2. LBK

C

Czekaj-Zastawny 2008a; Kruk 1970

591. Sławice Szlacheckie, site 3
1. Miechów comm., Miechów distr., Małopolskie voiv.
2. Szreniawa river basin/upper Vistula river basin
3. 50°19'03.2"N, 20°04'15.6"E
4. Valley slope

A –
B
    1. Approx. 100 m²
    2. LBK
C
    Czekaj-Zastawny 2008a; Kruk 1970

592. Sławice Szlacheckie, site ?
    1. Miechów comm., Miechów distr., Małopolskie voiv.
    2. Szreniawa river basin/upper Vistula river basin
    3. 50°19'08.9"N, 20°04'42.1"E
    4. Valley slope
A –
B
    1. Approx. 100 m²
    2. LBK?
C
    Czekaj-Zastawny 2008a

593. Sławkowice, site 5
    1. Biskupice comm., Wieliczka distr., Małopolskie voiv.
    2. Raba river basin/upper Vistula river basin
    3. 49°55'54.1"N, 20°08'48.7"E
    4. Outside valleys
A –
B
    1. Approx. 0.5 ha
    2. LBK
C
    Czekaj-Zastawny 2008a

594. Sławkowice, site 6
    1. Biskupice comm., Wieliczka distr., Małopolskie voiv.
    2. Raba river basin/upper Vistula river basin
    3. 49°55'48.1"N, 20°08'26"E
    4. Outside valleys
A –
B
    1. Approx. 100 m²
    2. LBK
C
    Czekaj-Zastawny 2008a

595. Sławkowice, site 14
    1. Biskupice comm., Wieliczka distr., Małopolskie voiv.
    2. Raba river basin/upper Vistula river basin
    3. 49°55'55.6"N, 20°08'05.3"E
    4. Outside valleys
A –
B
    1. Approx. 100 m²
    2. LBK
C
    Czekaj-Zastawny 2008a

596. Sławkowice, site 19
    1. Biskupice comm., Wieliczka distr., Małopolskie voiv.
    2. Raba river basin/upper Vistula river basin
    3. 49°56'27.3"N, 20°08'54.3"E
    4. Valley border
A –
B
    1. Approx. 0.5 ha
    2. LBK
C
    Czekaj-Zastawny 2008a

597. Słomniki, site 4
    1. Słomniki comm., Kraków distr., Małopolskie voiv.
    2. Szreniawa river basin/upper Vistula river basin
    3. 50°14'12.5"N, 20°07'30.2"E
    4. Border zone of upland
A –
B
    1. Approx. 0.5 ha
    2. LBK?
C
    Czekaj-Zastawny 2008a

598. Słomniki, site 6
    1. Słomniki comm., Kraków distr., Małopolskie voiv.
    2. Szreniawa river basin/upper Vistula river basin
    3. 50°13'38.8"N, 20°06'29.6"E
    4. Valley low terrace
A –
B
    1. Approx. 100 m²
    2. LBK
C
    Czekaj-Zastawny 2008a

599. Słupów, site 15
    1. Słaboszów comm., Miechów distr., Małopolskie voiv.
    2. Nidzica river basin/upper Vistula river basin
    3. 50°21'22.7"N, 20°19'54.8"E
    4. Valley low terrace
A –
B
    1. Approx. 1 ha
    2. LBK
C
    Czekaj-Zastawny 2008a; Liguzińska-Kruk 1982

600. Smardzowice, site 8
    1. Skała comm., Kraków distr., Małopolskie voiv.
    2. Prądnik river basin/upper Vistula river basin
    3. 50°11'26.5"N, 19°50'41.9"E
    4. Outside valleys
A –
B
    1. Approx. 0.5 ha
    2. LBK?
C
    Czekaj-Zastawny 2008a

601. Smroków, site 15
    1. Słomniki comm., Kraków distr., Małopolskie voiv.
    2. Szreniawa river basin/upper Vistula river basin
    3. 50°16'50.2"N, 20°01'59.4"E
    4. Valley low terrace
A –
B
    1. Approx. 100 m²
    2. LBK
C
    Czekaj-Zastawny 2008a; Kruk 1970

602. Sośniczany, site 10
    1. Koprzywnica comm., Sandomierz distr., Świętokrzyskie voiv.
    2. Koprzywianka stream basin/upper Vistula river basin
    3. 50°37'11.4"N, 21°36'31.2"E
    4. Border zone of upland

A –

B

1. Approx. 1 ha
2. LBK

C

Czekaj-Zastawny 2008a; Kowalewska-Marszałek 1992

603. Sośniczany, site 20

1. Koprzywnica comm., Sandomierz distr., Świętokrzyskie voiv.
2. Koprzywianka stream basin/upper Vistula river basin
3. 50°36'53.2"N, 21°36'58.7"E
4. Valley low terrace

A –

B

1. Approx. 1 ha
2. LBK

C

Czekaj-Zastawny 2008a; Kowalewska-Marszałek 1992

604. Sośniczany, site 31

1. Koprzywnica comm., Sandomierz distr., Świętokrzyskie voiv.
2. Koprzywianka stream basin/upper Vistula river basin
3. 50°36'48.7"N, 21°36'26.7"E
4. Border zone of upland

A –

B

1. Approx. 1 ha
2. LBK, Ia (*Gniechowice*) phase

C

Czekaj-Zastawny 2008a; Kowalewska-Marszałek 1992

605. Sośniczany, site 40

1. Koprzywnica comm., Sandomierz distr., Świętokrzyskie voiv.
2. Koprzywianka stream basin/upper Vistula river basin
3. 50°36'32.5"N, 21°35'45.8"E
4. Border zone of upland

A –

B

1. Approx. 1 ha
2. LBK

C

Czekaj-Zastawny 2008a; Kowalewska-Marszałek 1992

606. Sośniczany, site 53

1. Koprzywnica comm., Sandomierz distr., Świętokrzyskie voiv.
2. Koprzywianka stream basin/upper Vistula river basin
3. 50°36'26.1"N, 21°36'16.4"E
4. Valley upper terrace

A –

B

1. Approx. 1 ha
2. LBK

C

Czekaj-Zastawny 2008a; Kowalewska-Marszałek 1992

607. Spytkowice, site 26

1. Spytkowice comm., Wadowice distr., Małopolskie voiv.
2. Skawa stream basin/upper Vistula river basin
3. 50°00'20.9"N, 19°31'01.9"E
4. Valley border

A

1. S. Dryja

2. 1992-1996
3. 504 m^2
4. Settlement; ca. 20 features (probably fragm. of 1 long house in it)
5. LBK, Ib (*Zofipole*) phase, Music Note phase; imports of Eastern Linear Pottery culture and Alföld Linear Pottery culture (AVK)

B

1. Approx. 2-3 ha
2. LBK

C

Czekaj-Zastawny 2008a; Dryja 1997; 1998a; 1998b; 1998c; Stryjowska 2007

608. Sroczków, site 2

1. Pacanów comm., Busko Zdrój distr., Świętokrzyskie voiv.
2. Wschodnia stream basin/upper Vistula river basin
3. 50°25'43.5"N, 21°02'38.2"E
4. Valley slope

A –

B

1. Approx. 100 m^2
2. LBK?

C

Czekaj-Zastawny 2008a

609. Sroczków, site 8

1. Pacanów comm., Busko Zdrój distr., Świętokrzyskie voiv.
2. Upper Vistula river basin
3. 50°25'16.8"N, 21°03'58.9"E
4. Valley slope

A –

B

1. Approx. 100 m^2
2. LBK, Music Note phase

C

Czekaj-Zastawny 2008a

610. Stary Korczyn, site 16

1. Nowy Korczyn comm., Busko Zdrój distr., Świętokrzyskie voiv.
2. Nida river basin/upper Vistula river basin
3. 50°17'26.7"N, 20°44'20"E
4. Valley low terrace

A –

B

1. Approx. 100 m^2
2. LBK

C

Czekaj-Zastawny 2008a

611. Sternalice, site 7

1. Lipnik comm., Opatów distr., Świętokrzyskie voiv.
2. Koprzywianka stream basin/upper Vistula river basin
3. 50°41'45.6"N, 21°30'16.6"E
4. Valley slope

A –

B

1. Approx. 5 ha
2. LBK

C

Czekaj-Zastawny 2008a; Kowalewska-Marszałek 1992

612. Sternalice, site 22

1. Lipnik comm., Opatów distr., Świętokrzyskie voiv.
2. Koprzywianka stream basin/upper Vistula river basin

3. 50°41'43.9"N, 21°29'57"E
4. Valley slope

A –

B

1. Approx. 100 m²
2. LBK

C

Czekaj-Zastawny 2008a; Kowalewska-Marszałek 1992

613. Stoki, site 1
1. Skała comm., Kraków distr., Małopolskie voiv.
2. Dłubnia river basin/upper Vistula river basin
3. 50°13'14.4"N, 19°53'30.1"E
4. Valley border

A –

B

1. Approx. 0.5 ha
2. LBK?

C

Czekaj-Zastawny 2008a

614. Stręgoborzyce, site 4
1. Igołomia-Wawrzeńczyce comm., Kraków distr., Małopolskie voiv.
2. Upper Vistula river basin
3. 50°07'36.9"N, 20°17'37.1"E
4. Valley slope

A –

B

1. Approx. 1 ha
2. LBK

C

Czekaj-Zastawny 2008a

615. Strumiany, site 5
1. Wieliczka comm., Wieliczka distr., Małopolskie voiv.
2. Upper Vistula river basin
3. 50°00'46.3"N, 20°06'17.9"E
4. Valley border

A

1. R. Czerniak
2. 2006
3. ca. 100 m²
4. Settlement; 4 features
5. LBK

B

1. Approx. 1 ha
2. LBK

C

Czerniak 2006

616. Strzeżów, site 22
1. Miechów comm., Miechów distr., Małopolskie voiv.
2. Szreniawa river basin/upper Vistula river basin
3. 50°22'39.4"N, 20°03'17.9"E
4. Outside valleys

A –

B

1. Approx. 5 ha
2. LBK

C

Data from AZP card

617. Sufczyce-Budy, site 1
1. Oleśnica comm., Staszów distr., Świętokrzyskie voiv.
2. Wschodnia stream basin/upper Vistula river basin

3. 50°28'19.7"N, 21°04'11.8"E
4. Valley low terrace

A –

B

1. Approx. 0.5 ha
2. LBK

C

Czekaj-Zastawny 2008a

618. Sufczyn, site 25
1. Dębno comm., Brzesko distr., Małopolskie voiv.
2. Kisielina stream basin/upper Vistula river basin
3. 49°56'53.3"N, 20°45'08.5"E
4. Valley slope

A –

B

1. Approx. 0.5 ha
2. LBK

C

Czekaj-Zastawny 2008a

619. Sufczyn, site 32
1. Dębno comm., Brzesko distr., Małopolskie voiv.
2. Kisielina stream basin/upper Vistula river basin
3. 49°57'25.5"N, 20°46'17.2"E
4. Valley slope

A –

B

1. Approx. 1 ha
2. LBK

C

Czekaj-Zastawny 2008a

620. Suliszów, site 5
1. Łoniów comm., Sandomierz distr., Świętokrzyskie voiv.
2. Koprzywianka stream basin/upper Vistula river basin
3. 50°34'52.7"N, 21°29'57.1"E
4. Valley slope

A –

B

1. Approx. 1 ha
2. LBK

C

Czekaj-Zastawny 2008a; Kowalewska-Marszałek 1992

621. Suliszów, site 6
1. Łoniów comm., Sandomierz distr., Świętokrzyskie voiv.
2. Koprzywianka stream basin/upper Vistula river basin
3. 50°34'47.2"N, 21°29'25.9"E
4. Valley slope

A –

B

1. Approx. 100 m²
2. LBK

C

Czekaj-Zastawny 2008a; Kowalewska-Marszałek 1992

622. Suliszów, site 7
1. Łoniów comm., Sandomierz distr., Świętokrzyskie voiv.
2. Koprzywianka stream basin/upper Vistula river basin
3. 50°34'38.6"N, 21°29'11.6"E
4. Valley slope

A –

B

1. Approx. 100 m²
2. LBK

C

Czekaj-Zastawny 2008a; Kowalewska-Marszałek 1992

623. Suliszów, site 9
1. Łoniów comm., Sandomierz distr., Świętokrzyskie voiv.
2. Koprzywianka stream basin/upper Vistula river basin
3. 50°34'42.6"N, 21°30'09.6"E
4. Valley slope

A –
B

1. Approx. 100 m^2
2. LBK

C

Czekaj-Zastawny 2008a; Kowalewska-Marszałek 1992

624. Sułkowice, site 5
1. Iwanowice comm., Kraków distr., Małopolskie voiv.
2. Dłubnia river basin/upper Vistula river basin
3. 50°13'17.8"N, 19°56'09"E
4. Border zone of upland

A –
B

1. Approx. 0.5 ha
2. LBK?

C

Czekaj-Zastawny 2008a; Kruk 1969

625. Sułkowice, site 6
1. Iwanowice comm., Kraków distr., Małopolskie voiv.
2. Dłubnia river basin/upper Vistula river basin
3. 50°13'46.7"N, 19°56'32.2"E
4. Valley low terrace

A –
B

1. Approx. 100 m^2
2. LBK?

C

Czekaj-Zastawny 2008a

626. Sułkowice, site 7
1. Iwanowice comm., Kraków distr., Małopolskie voiv.
2. Dłubnia river basin/upper Vistula river basin
3. 50°13'40.7"N, 19°56'01.4"E
4. Border zone of upland and valley slope

A –
B

1. Approx. 100 m^2
2. LBK?

C

Czekaj-Zastawny 2008a

627. Sułkowice, site 13
1. Iwanowice comm., Kraków distr., Małopolskie voiv.
2. Dłubnia river basin/upper Vistula river basin
3. 50°13'12.1"N, 19°55'05"E
4. Valley border/outside valleys

A –
B

1. Approx. 0.5 ha
2. LBK?

C

Czekaj-Zastawny 2008a

628. Sułkowice, site 14
1. Iwanowice comm., Kraków distr., Małopolskie voiv.
2. Dłubnia river basin/upper Vistula river basin

3. 50°12'49.3"N, 19°56'06.9"E
4. Outside valleys

A –
B

1. Approx. 0.5 ha
2. LBK?

C

Czekaj-Zastawny 2008a

629. Sułoszowa, site 12
1. Sułoszowa comm., Kraków distr., Małopolskie voiv.
2. Prądnik river basin/upper Vistula river basin
3. 50°16'11"N, 19°44'37.7"E
4. Outside valleys

A –
B

1. Approx. 0.5 ha
2. LBK?

C

Czekaj-Zastawny 2008a; Lech *et al.* 1984

630. Sułoszowa, site 39
1. Sułoszowa comm., Kraków distr., Małopolskie voiv.
2. Prądnik river basin/upper Vistula river basin
3. 50°15'21.7"N, 19°46'01.1"E
4. Outside valleys

A –
B

1. Approx. 100 m^2
2. LBK?

C

Czekaj-Zastawny 2008a

631. Sułoszowa, site 41
1. Sułoszowa comm., Kraków distr., Małopolskie voiv.
2. Prądnik river basin/upper Vistula river basin
3. 50°15'50.6"N, 19°46'25.9"E
4. Outside valleys

A –
B

1. Approx. 0.5 ha
2. LBK?

C

Czekaj-Zastawny 2008a

632. Sułoszowa, site 115
1. Sułoszowa comm., Kraków distr., Małopolskie voiv.
2. Prądnik river basin/upper Vistula river basin
3. 50°15'21.4"N, 19°44'09.4"E
4. Outside valleys

A –
B

1. Approx. 100 m^2
2. LBK?

C

Czekaj-Zastawny 2008a

633. Sumin, site 1(?)
1. Tarnawatka comm., Tomaszów Lubelski distr., Lubelskie voiv.
2. Wieprz river basin/upper Vistula river basin
3. 50°32'43.7"N, 23°24'12"E
4. Valley slope

A –
B

1. ?

2. LBK, Ib (*Zofipole*) phase

C

Kulczycka-Leciejewiczowa 2000

634. Suskrajowice, site 5
1. Chmielnik comm., Kielce distr., Świętokrzyskie voiv.
2. Wschodnia stream basin/upper Vistula river basin
3. 50°33'44.3"N, 20°47'15.4"E
4. Valley slope

A –

B

1. Approx. 100 m^2
2. LBK

C

Czekaj-Zastawny 2008a

635. Szarbia Zwierzyniecka, site 5
1. Skalbimierz comm., Kazimierza Wielka distr.,
Świętokrzyskie voiv.
2. Nidzica river basin/upper Vistula river basin
3. 50°19'41.6"N, 20°22'22.4"E
4. Valley border

A –

B

1. Approx. 100 m^2
2. LBK

C

Czekaj-Zastawny 2008a

636. Szarów, site 9
1. Kłaj comm., Wieliczka distr., Małopolskie voiv.
2. Tusznica stream basin/Raba river basin/upper Vistula river
basin
3. 49°59'49.9"N, 20°15'51.1"E
4. Valley slope and border

A

1. The Cracow Team for Archaeological Supervision of
Motorway Construction, Institute of Archaeology and
Ethnology Polish Academy of Sciences, Museum of
Archaeology Cracow, Jagiellonian University –
E. Schellner, M. Anioła
2. 2004-2005
3. 15000 m^2
4. Settlement; 81 features (2 long houses in it)
5. LBK, Želiezovce phase

B

1. Approx. 1.5 ha
2. LBK

C

Czekaj-Zastawny 2008a; Czerniak *et al.* 2006

637. Szczepanowice, site 1
1. Miechów comm., Miechów distr., Małopolskie voiv.
2. Szreniawa river basin/upper Vistula river basin
3. 50°17'58.5"N, 20°01'34.7"E
4. Valley border

A –

B

1. Approx. 0.5 ha
2. LBK?

C

Czekaj-Zastawny 2008a; Kruk 1970

638. Szczepanowice, site 3
1. Miechów comm., Miechów distr., Małopolskie voiv.
2. Szreniawa river basin/upper Vistula river basin

3. 50°17'45.3"N, 20°01'59.5"E
4. Valley slope and border

A –

B

1. Approx. 5 ha
2. LBK

C

Czekaj-Zastawny 2008a; Kruk 1970; 1973

639. Szczepanowice, site 5
1. Miechów comm., Miechów distr., Małopolskie voiv.
2. Szreniawa river basin/upper Vistula river basin
3. 50°18'53.9"N, 20°02'52"E
4. Outside valleys

A –

B

1. Approx. 5 ha
2. LBK

C

Czekaj-Zastawny 2008a; Kruk 1970; 1973

640. Szczepanowice, site 6
1. Miechów comm., Miechów distr., Małopolskie voiv.
2. Szreniawa river basin/upper Vistula river basin
3. 50°18'51.4"N, 20°03'39"E
4. Valley border

A –

B

1. Approx. 5 ha
2. LBK

C

Czekaj-Zastawny 2008a; Kruk 1970

641. Szczepanowice, site 7
1. Miechów comm., Miechów distr., Małopolskie voiv.
2. Szreniawa river basin/upper Vistula river basin
3. 50°18'37.5"N, 20°03'20"E
4. Valley border

A –

B

1. Approx. 5 ha
2. LBK

C

Czekaj-Zastawny 2008a; Kruk 1970

642. Szczepanowice, site 9
1. Miechów comm., Miechów distr., Małopolskie voiv.
2. Szreniawa river basin/upper Vistula river basin
3. 50°18'21.7"N, 20°02'52.1"E
4. Valley slope and border

A –

B

1. Approx. 0.5 ha
2. LBK

C

Czekaj-Zastawny 2008a; Kruk 1970; 1973

643. Szczepanowice, site 11
1. Miechów comm., Miechów distr., Małopolskie voiv.
2. Szreniawa river basin/upper Vistula river basin
3. 50°18'53.2"N, 20°03'09.9"E
4. Valley slope and border

A –

B

1. Approx. 0.5 ha
2. LBK

C

Czekaj-Zastawny 2008a; Kruk 1970

644. Szczepanowice, site 23
1. Miechów comm., Miechów distr., Małopolskie voiv.
2. Szreniawa river basin/upper Vistula river basin
3. 50°18'41.1"N, 20°04'21.7"E
4. Valley border

A –

B

1. Approx. 0.5 ha
2. LBK

C

Czekaj-Zastawny 2008a

645. Szczepiatyn, site 27
1. Ulhówek comm., Tomaszów Lubelski distr., Lubelskie voiv.
2. Sołokija stream basin/Bug river basin/upper Vistula river basin
3. 50°25'22.5"N, 23°49'45.5"E
4. Valley slope

A –

B

1. Approx. 0.5 ha
2. LBK

C

Czekaj-Zastawny 2008a

646. Szczotkowice, site 1
1. Działoszyce comm., Pińczów distr., Świętokrzyskie voiv.
2. Nidzica river basin/upper Vistula river basin
3. 50°21'16"N, 20°20'26.9"E
4. Valley low terrace

A

1. A Krauss
2. 1961
3. Accidental find
4. ?; 1 human grave
5. LBK, Music Note phase

B

1. ?
2. LBK

C

Czekaj-Zastawny 2008a; Krauss 1964

647. Szczytniki, site 7
1. Gdów comm., Wieliczka distr., Małopolskie voiv.
2. Raba river basin/upper Vistula river basin
3. 49°58'00.8"N, 20°14'18.3"E
4. Valley slope

A –

B

1. Approx. 100 m^2
2. LBK

C

Czekaj-Zastawny 2008a

648. Szewna, site I
1. Bodzechów comm., Ostrowiec Świętokrzyski distr., Świętokrzyskie voiv.
2. Kamienna stream basin/upper Vistula river basin
3. 50°54'23.1"N, 21°22'13.5"E
4. Valley border

A –

B

1. Approx. 100 m^2
2. LBK

C

Bąbel 1975; Czekaj-Zastawny 2008a; Kowalewska-Marszałek 1992

649. Szewna, site V
1. Bodzechów comm., Ostrowiec Świętokrzyski distr., Świętokrzyskie voiv.
2. Kamienna stream basin/upper Vistula river basin
3. 50°54'12.2"N, 21°22'01.4"E
4. Valley slope

A –

B

1. Approx. 100 m^2
2. LBK

C

Bąbel 1975; Czekaj-Zastawny 2008a; Kowalewska-Marszałek 1992

650. Szlatyn, site 10
1. Jarczów comm., Tomaszów Lubelski distr., Lubelskie voiv.
2. Sołokija stream basin/Bug river basin/upper Vistula river basin
3. 50°26'31.4"N, 23°40'31.6"E
4. Valley slope

A –

B

1. Approx. 100 m^2
2. LBK

C

Czekaj-Zastawny 2008a

651. Szyce, site 1
1. Wielka Wieś comm., Kraków distr., Małopolskie voiv.
2. Prądnik river basin/upper Vistula river basin
3. 50°09'20.2"N, 19°51'44.7"E
4. Outside valleys

A

1. J. Żurowski
2. 1926
3. ?
4. Settlement or camp; any informations about features
5. LBK

B

1. Approx. 1 ha
2. LBK

C

Czekaj-Zastawny 2008a; Żurowski 1926

652. Szyce, site 6
1. Wielka Wieś comm., Kraków distr., Małopolskie voiv.
2. Prądnik river basin/upper Vistula river basin
3. 50°09'04.8"N, 19°51'23.4"E
4. Outside valleys

A –

B

1. Approx. 1 ha
2. LBK

C

Czekaj-Zastawny 2008a

653. Szyce, site 8
1. Wielka Wieś comm., Kraków distr., Małopolskie voiv.
2. Prądnik river basin/upper Vistula river basin

3. 50°09'23.5"N, 19°51'23.8"E
4. Outside valleys

A

1. E. Rook
2. 1980
3. 120 m^2
4. Settlement or camp; no features, ca. 40 pottery fragments
5. LBK

B

1. Approx. 0.5 ha
2. LBK

C

Czekaj-Zastawny 2008a; Lech *et al.* 1984; Rook 1981

654. Szyce, site 9

1. Wielka Wieś comm., Kraków distr., Małopolskie voiv.
2. Prądnik river basin/upper Vistula river basin
3. 50°08'39.2"N, 19°51'53.7"E
4. Outside valleys

A –

B

1. Approx. 100 m^2
2. LBK?

C

Czekaj-Zastawny 2008a; Lech *et al.* 1984

655. Śmiłowice, site 6

1. Nowe Brzesko comm., Proszowice distr., Małopolskie voiv.
2. Upper Vistula river basin
3. 50°08'52.9"N, 20°27'00.9"E
4. Border zone of upland

A –

B

1. Approx. 100 m^2
2. LBK

C

Czekaj-Zastawny 2008a; Rydzewski 1972

656. Świlcza, site 22

1. Świlcza comm., Rzeszów distr., Podkarpackie voiv.
2. Wisłok river basin/San river basin/upper Vistula river basin
3. 50°03'50.1"N, 21°54'00.1"E
4. Valley slope

A –

B

1. Approx. 1 ha
2. LBK, Želiezovce phase

C

Czekaj-Zastawny 2008a

657. Świniary, site 1

1. Solec Zdrój comm., Busko Zdrój distr., Świętokrzyskie voiv.
2. Strumień stream basin/upper Vistula river basin
3. 50°21'12.4"N, 20°56'14"E
4. Valley upper terrace

A –

B

1. Approx. 100 m^2
2. LBK

C

Czekaj-Zastawny 2008a

658. Świniary, site 2

1. Solec Zdrój comm., Busko Zdrój distr., Świętokrzyskie voiv.

2. Strumień stream basin/upper Vistula river basin
3. 50°21'17.6"N, 20°57'14.2"E
4. Valley upper terrace

A –

B

1. Approx. 100 m^2
2. LBK?

C

Czekaj-Zastawny 2008a

659. Targowisko, site 1

1. Kłaj comm., Wieliczka distr., Małopolskie voiv.
2. Tusznica stream basin/Raba river basin/upper Vistula river basin
3. 49°58'48.6"N, 20°19'29.1"E
4. Valley slope/valley low terrace

A

1. S. Nosek; A Kulczycka-Leciejewiczowa, Z. Woźniak
2. 1949; 1963-65
3. 952 m^2
4. Settlement; 7 features
5. LBK, Music Note phase, Želiezovce phase; imports of Bükk culture

B

1. Approx. 10 ha
2. LBK

C

Czekaj-Zastawny 2008a; Kulczycka-Leciejewiczowa 1973b; Rook 1968; Woźniak 1966

660. Targowisko, site 2

1. Kłaj comm., Wieliczka distr., Małopolskie voiv.
2. Tusznica stream basin/Raba river basin/upper Vistula river basin
3. 49°59'03.6"N, 20°19'13.4"E
4. Valley slope/valley low terrace

A

1. S. Nosek; K. Bielenin, A. Krauss; A. Kulczycka-Leciejewiczowa, Z. Woźniak
2. 1948-49; 1950; 1963-65
3. 1800 m^2
4. Settlement; 24 features (probably fragm. of long house in it)
5. LBK, Music Note phase, Želiezovce phase; imports of Bükk culture

B

1. Approx. 5 ha
2. LBK

C

Czekaj-Zastawny 2008a; Kulczycka-Leciejewiczowa 1964; 1965; 1973a;1973b; Rook 1968

661. Targowisko, site 11

1. Kłaj comm., Wieliczka distr., Małopolskie voiv.
2. Tusznica stream basin/Raba river basin/upper Vistula river basin
3. 49°59'15.9"N, 20°17'55.7"E
4. Valley slope/valley low terrace

A

1. The Cracow Team for Archaeological Supervision of Motorway Construction, Institute of Archaeology and Ethnology Polish Academy of Sciences, Museum of Archaeology Cracow, Jagiellonian University – B Konieczny, B Grabowska
2. 1996, 2000-2005
3. 6 ha
4. Settlement; 206 features (3 long houses in it)

5. LBK, Ib (*Zofipole*) phase, Music Note phase, Želiezovce phase; imports of Bükk culture

B

1. Approx. 5 ha
2. LBK

C

Czekaj-Zastawny *et al.* 2002; Czekaj-Zastawny *et al.* 2003; Czekaj-Zastawny 2008a

662. Targowisko, site 12, 13
1. Kłaj comm., Wieliczka distr., Małopolskie voiv.
2. Tusznica stream basin/Raba river basin/upper Vistula river basin
3. 49°59'27"N, 20°17'29.5"E
4. Valley low terrace

A

1. The Cracow Team for Archaeological Supervision of Motorway Construction, Institute of Archaeology and Ethnology Polish Academy of Sciences, Museum of Archaeology Cracow, Jagiellonian University – A. Golański, J. Nowacka
2. 2003-2005
3. 3.5 ha
4. Settlement; 1002 features (20 long houses in it)
5. LBK, Želiezovce phase; imports of Bükk culture

B

1. Approx. 5 ha
2. LBK

C

Czekaj-Zastawny 2008a; Czerniak *et al.* 2006

663. Targowisko, site 14
1. Kłaj comm., Wieliczka distr., Małopolskie voiv.
2. Tusznica stream basin/Raba river basin/upper Vistula river basin
3. 49°59'36.7"N, 20°16'57.5"E
4. Valley low terrace

A

1. The Cracow Team for Archaeological Supervision of Motorway Construction, Institute of Archaeology and Ethnology Polish Academy of Sciences, Museum of Archaeology Cracow, Jagiellonian University – J. Rozen, J. Kokolus
2. 1996, 2003-2005
3. 3.5 ha
4. Settlement; ca. 300 features (7 long houses in it)
5. LBK, Želiezovce phase; imports of Bükk culture

B

1. Approx. 5 ha
2. LBK

C

Czekaj-Zastawny *et al.* 2002; Czekaj- Zastawny *et al.* 2003; Czerniak *et al.* 2006; Czekaj-Zastawny 2008a

664. Targowisko, site 16
1. Kłaj comm., Wieliczka distr., Małopolskie voiv.
2. Tusznica stream basin/Raba river basin/upper Vistula river basin
3. 49°59'23.5"N, 20°16'37.9"E
4. Valley low terrace/border zone of upland

A

1. The Cracow Team for Archaeological Supervision of Motorway Construction, Institute of Archaeology and Ethnology Polish Academy of Sciences, Museum of Archaeology Cracow, Jagiellonian University – P. Włodarczak, P. Olejarczyk, W. Gliński, B Chmielewski, R.

Czerniak, K. Łach
2. 1996, 2000-2005
3. 15 ha
4. Settlement; few thousand features (20 long houses in it)
5. LBK, Želiezovce phase (through ŽIIb); imports of Bükk culture

B

1. Approx. 15 ha
2. LBK

C

Czekaj-Zastawny *et al.* 2002; Czekaj- Zastawny *et al.* 2003; Włodarczak 2006; Czekaj-Zastawny 2008a

665. Tarnawatka, site 6
1. Tarnawatka comm., Tomaszów Lubelski distr., Lubelskie voiv.
2. Wieprz river basin/upper Vistula river basin
3. 50°31'17.1"N, 23°23'16.6"E
4. Valley low terrace

A –

B

1. Approx. 0.5 ha
2. LBK

C

Czekaj-Zastawny 2008a

666. Tarnawatka, site 6
1. Tarnawatka comm., Tomaszów Lubelski distr., Lubelskie voiv.
2. Wieprz river basin/upper Vistula river basin
3. 50°32'42.2"N, 23°23'16.4"E
4. Valley floor, slope and border

A –

B

1. Approx. 0.5 ha
2. LBK

C

Czekaj-Zastawny 2008a

667. Tarnoszyn, site 1
1. Ulhówek comm., Tomaszów Lubelski distr., Lubelskie voiv.
2. Sołokija stream basin/Bug river basin/upper Vistula river basin
3. 50°25'16.8"N, 23°46'48.6"E
4. Valley slope

A

1. I. Chorostowska
2. ?
3. ?
4. ?; any information about features
5. LBK, Music Note phase

B

1. Approx. 1 ha
2. LBK

C

Czekaj-Zastawny 2008a; Gurba 1971

668. Tarnoszyn, site 33
1. Ulhówek comm., Tomaszów Lubelski distr., Lubelskie voiv.
2. Sołokija stream basin/Bug river basin/upper Vistula river basin
3. 50°25'40.7"N, 23°46'47.8"E
4. Valley slope

A –

B

1. Approx. 100 m²
2. LBK

C

Czekaj-Zastawny 2008a

669. Topola, site 4

1. Skalbimierz comm., Kazimierza Wielka distr.,
   Świętokrzyskie voiv.
2. Nidzica river basin/upper Vistula river basin
3. 50°18'38.5"N, 20°26'38.5"E
4. Border zone of upland

A –

B

1. Approx. 100 m²
2. LBK

C

Czekaj-Zastawny 2008a

670. Topola, site 7

1. Skalbimierz comm., Kazimierza Wielka distr.,
   Świętokrzyskie voiv.
2. Nidzica river basin/upper Vistula river basin
3. 50°18'41.2"N, 20°25'54"E
4. Border zone of upland

A –

B

1. Approx. 100 m²
2. LBK

C

Czekaj-Zastawny 2008a

671. Topola, site 10

1. Skalbimierz comm., Kazimierza Wielka distr.,
   Świętokrzyskie voiv.
2. Nidzica river basin/upper Vistula river basin
3. 50°18'52.1"N, 20°26'31.6"E
4. Valley low terrace

A –

B

1. Approx. 100 m²
2. LBK

C

Czekaj-Zastawny 2008a

672. Trąbki, site 4

1. Biskupice comm., Wieliczka distr., Małopolskie voiv.
2. Raba river basin/upper Vistula river basin
3. 49°57'37"N, 20°08'21.8"E
4. Valley slope

A –

B

1. Approx. 5 ha
2. LBK

C

Czekaj-Zastawny 2008a; Szybowicz 1980

673. Trąbki, site 8

1. Biskupice comm., Wieliczka distr., Małopolskie voiv.
2. Raba river basin/upper Vistula river basin
3. 49°57'54.7"N, 20°09'11.3"E
4. Valley slope

A –

B

1. Approx. 5 ha

2. LBK

C

Czekaj-Zastawny 2008a; Szybowicz 1980

674. Tropiszów, site 1

1. Igołomia-Wawrzeńczyce comm., Kraków distr.,
   Małopolskie voiv.
2. Upper Vistula river basin
3. 50°06'04.2"N, 20°11'58"E
4. Valley slope

A

1. T. Reyman
2. 1924, 1930, 1934
3. ?
4. Settlement trace; no features, 2 pottery fragments
5. LBK

B

1. Approx. 5 ha
2. LBK

C

Czekaj-Zastawny 2008a; Reyman 1931

675. Trzciana, site 9

1. Świlcza comm., Rzeszów distr., Podkarpackie voiv.
2. Wisłok river basin/San river basin/upper Vistula river basin
3. 50°04'30.5"N, 21°49'31.4"E
4. Valley low terrace

A –

B

1. Approx. 0.5 ha
2. LBK

C

Czekaj-Zastawny 2008a

676. Trzciana, site 20

1. Świlcza comm., Rzeszów distr., Podkarpackie voiv.
2. Wisłok river basin/San river basin/upper Vistula river basin
3. 50°03'02.9"N, 21°48'23.4"E
4. Valley slope and border

A –

B

1. Approx. 100 m²
2. LBK

C

Czekaj-Zastawny 2008a

677. Trzebiesławice, site 1

1. Łoniów comm., Sandomierz distr., Świętokrzyskie voiv.
2. Koprzywianka stream basin/upper Vistula river basin
3. 50°34'39.9"N, 21°31'14.8"E
4. Valley slope

A

1. J. Żurowski
2. 1929
3. ?
4. Settlement; any information about features; ca. 400 pottery
   fragments
5. LBK, Music Note phase

B

1. Approx. 1 ha
2. LBK

C

Burchard 1959; Czekaj-Zastawny 2008a; Kamieńska 1963;
   Kowalewska-Marszałek 1992

678. Trzebiesławice, site 5
1. Łoniów comm., Sandomierz distr., Świętokrzyskie voiv.
2. Koprzywianka stream basin/upper Vistula river basin
3. 50°34'17.5"N, 21°31'43.7"E
4. Valley border
A –
B
  1. Approx. 1 ha
  2. LBK
C
  Czekaj-Zastawny 2008a; Kowalewska-Marszałek 1992

679. Turkowice Kolonia, site 7
1. Werbkowice comm., Hrubieszów distr., Lubelskie voiv.
2. Huczwa stream basin/Bug river basin/upper Vistula river basin
3. 50°39'49.3"N, 23°43'39.6"E
4. Valley border
A –
B
  1. Approx. 100 m^2
  2. LBK
C
  Czekaj-Zastawny 2008a

680. Tworkowa, site 4
1. Czchów comm., Brzesko distr., Małopolskie voiv.
2. Dunajec river basin/upper Vistula river basin
3. 49°51'34.8"N, 20°39'10.9"E
4. Outside valleys
A –
B
  1. Approx. 0.5 ha
  2. LBK
C
  Czekaj-Zastawny 2008a

681. Tworkowa, site 16
1. Czchów comm., Brzesko distr., Małopolskie voiv.
2. Dunajec river basin/upper Vistula river basin
3. 49°51'16"N, 20°39'17.5"E
4. Valley border
A –
B
  1. Approx. 1 ha
  2. LBK
C
  Czekaj-Zastawny 2008a

682. Tworkowa, site 19
1. Czchów comm., Brzesko distr., Małopolskie voiv.
2. Dunajec river basin/upper Vistula river basin
3. 49°50'56.9"N, 20°39'41.7"E
4. Valley slope
A –
B
  1. Approx. 1 ha
  2. LBK
C
  Czekaj-Zastawny 2008a

683. Tworkowa, site 39
1. Czchów comm., Brzesko distr., Małopolskie voiv.
2. Dunajec river basin/upper Vistula river basin
3. 49°51'06.9"N, 20°40'47"E
4. Valley upper terrace

A –
B
  1. Approx. 0.5 ha
  2. LBK
C
  Czekaj-Zastawny 2008a

684. Tyrawa Solna, site 12
1. Sanok comm., Sanok distr., Podkarpackie voiv.
2. San river basin/upper Vistula river basin
3. 49°36'22.9"N, 22°17'32.6"E
4. Valley low terrace
A –
B
  1. Approx. 100 m^2
  2. LBK?
C
  Czekaj-Zastawny 2008a

685. Tyszowce, site 4
1. Tyszowce comm., Tomaszów Lubelski distr., Lubelskie voiv.
2. Huczwa stream basin/Bug river basin/upper Vistula river basin
3. 50°37'04.8"N, 23°45'20.8"E
4. Valley low terrace
A –
B
  1. Approx. 100 m^2
  2. LBK?
C
  Czekaj-Zastawny 2008a

686. Tyszowce, site 6
1. Tyszowce comm., Tomaszów Lubelski distr., Lubelskie voiv.
2. Huczwa stream basin/Bug river basin/upper Vistula river basin
3. 50°38'27.8"N, 23°42'24.7"E
4. Valley low terrace
A –
B
  1. Approx. 100 m^2
  2. LBK?
C
  Czekaj-Zastawny 2008a

687. Ublinek, site 24
1. Lipnik comm., Opatów distr., Świętokrzyskie voiv.
2. Koprzywianka stream basin/upper Vistula river basin
3. 50°44'31.6"N, 21°24'03.4"E
4. Valley slope
A –
B
  1. Approx. 100 m^2
  2. LBK
C
  Czekaj-Zastawny 2008a; Kowalewska-Marszałek 1992

688. Ucisków, site 6
1. Nowy Korczyn comm., Busko Zdrój distr., Świętokrzyskie voiv.
2. Nida river basin/upper Vistula river basin
3. 50°19'26.6"N, 20°47'46.8"E
4. Outside valleys
A –

B

1. Approx. 100 m^2
2. LBK

C

Czekaj-Zastawny 2008a

689. Uników, site 1

1. Pińczów comm., Pińczów distr., Świętokrzyskie voiv.
2. Nida river basin/upper Vistula river basin
3. 50°32'26.8"N, 20°37'44.6"E
4. Valley border

A –
B

1. Approx. 0.5 ha
2. LBK?

C

Czekaj-Zastawny 2008a; Kozłowski 1923

690. Usarzów, site 4

1. Lipnik comm., Opatów distr., Świętokrzyskie voiv.
2. Opatówka stream basin/upper Vistula river basin
3. 50°42'46.1"N, 21°30'28.9"E
4. Valley slope and border

A –
B

1. Approx. 100 m^2
2. LBK

C

Czekaj-Zastawny 2008a; Kowalewska-Marszałek 1992

691. Usarzów, site 28

1. Lipnik comm., Opatów distr., Świętokrzyskie voiv.
2. Opatówka stream basin/upper Vistula river basin
3. 50°42'30.8"N, 21°30'42.8"E
4. Valley border

A –
B

1. Approx. 0.5 ha
2. LBK?

C

Czekaj-Zastawny 2008a; Kowalewska-Marszałek 1992

692. Usarzów, site 64

1. Lipnik comm., Opatów distr., Świętokrzyskie voiv.
2. Opatówka stream basin/upper Vistula river basin
3. 50°42'16"N, 21°31'18"E
4. Valley slope

A –
B

1. Approx. 100 m^2
2. LBK

C

Czekaj-Zastawny 2008a; Kowalewska-Marszałek 1992

693. Uszew, site 19

1. Gnojnik comm., Brzesko distr., Małopolskie voiv.
2. Uszwica stream basin/upper Vistula river basin
3. 49°55'57.4"N, 20°36'34.3"E
4. Valley slope

A –
B

1. Approx. 1 ha
2. LBK

C

Czekaj-Zastawny 2008a

694. Wawrzeńczyce, site 2

1. Igołomia-Wawrzeńczyce comm., Kraków distr.,
   Małopolskie voiv.
2. Upper Vistula river basin
3. 50°06'14.5"N, 20°17'08.7"E
4. Valley low terrace

A –
B

1. Approx. 100 m^2
2. LBK

C

Czekaj-Zastawny 2008a

695. Wawrzeńczyce, site 3

1. Igołomia-Wawrzeńczyce comm., Kraków distr.,
   Małopolskie voiv.
2. Upper Vistula river basin
3. 50°06'16.2"N, 20°17'42.7"E
4. Valley low terrace

A –
B

1. Approx. 100 m^2
2. LBK

C

Czekaj-Zastawny 2008a; Machnik 1957

696. Wawrzeńczyce, site 10

1. Igołomia-Wawrzeńczyce comm., Kraków distr.,
   Małopolskie voiv.
2. Upper Vistula river basin
3. 50°06'11.6"N, 20°18'21.3"E
4. Valley low terrace

A

1. T. Rodak, A. Zastawny
2. 1999
3. 20 m^2
4. Settlement trace; no features, 3 pottery fragments
5. LBK

B

1. Approx. 100 m^2
2. LBK

C

Czekaj-Zastawny 2008a

697. Wawrzeńczyce, site 24

1. Igołomia-Wawrzeńczyce comm., Kraków distr.,
   Małopolskie voiv.
2. Upper Vistula river basin
3. 50°06'20.4"N, 20°19'11.5"E
4. Valley low terrace

A –
B

1. Approx. 100 m^2
2. LBK

C

Czekaj-Zastawny 2008a; Machnik 1957

698. Wawrzeńczyce, site 32

1. Igołomia-Wawrzeńczyce comm., Kraków distr.,
   Małopolskie voiv.
2. Upper Vistula river basin
3. 50°06'44.7"N, 20°20'02.2"E
4. Valley low terrace

A –
B

1. Approx. 1.5 ha

2. LBK, Music Note phase, Želiezovce phase

C

Czekaj-Zastawny 2008a

699. Wawrzeńczyce, site 35
1. Igołomia-Wawrzeńczyce comm., Kraków distr., Małopolskie voiv.
2. Upper Vistula river basin
3. 50°06'53.8"N, 20°20'18.6"E
4. Valley low terrace

A –

B

1. Approx. 100 m^2
2. LBK, Želiezovce phase

C

Czekaj-Zastawny 2008a

700. Wawrzeńczyce, site 37
1. Igołomia-Wawrzeńczyce comm., Kraków distr., Małopolskie voiv.
2. Upper Vistula river basin
3. 50°06'59.8"N, 20°20'44.6"E
4. Valley low terrace

A –

B

1. Approx. 100 m^2
2. LBK?

C

Czekaj-Zastawny 2008a

701. Wawrzeńczyce, site 41
1. Igołomia-Wawrzeńczyce comm., Kraków distr., Małopolskie voiv.
2. Upper Vistula river basin
3. 50°07'08.8"N, 20°21'12.3"E
4. Valley border

A

1. K. Tunia
2. 2007
3. 400 m^2
4. Settlement; 1 feature
5. LBK, Music Note phase

B

1. Approx. 1 ha
2. LBK

C

Information from K. Tunia; Gajewski 1963b

702. Wawrzeńczyce, site 63
1. Igołomia-Wawrzeńczyce comm., Kraków distr., Małopolskie voiv.
2. Upper Vistula river basin
3. 50°06'36.7"N, 20°18'01"E
4. Valley low terrace

A –

B

1. Approx. 1 ha
2. LBK

C

Czekaj-Zastawny 2008a; Gajewski 1963b

703. Wawrzeńczyce, site 65
1. Igołomia-Wawrzeńczyce comm., Kraków distr., Małopolskie voiv.
2. Upper Vistula river basin

3. 50°06'40.5"N, 20°18'33.3"E
4. Valley low terrace

A –

B

1. Approx. 100 m^2
2. LBK

C

Czekaj-Zastawny 2008a

704. Wawrzeńczyce, site 66
1. Igołomia-Wawrzeńczyce comm., Kraków distr., Małopolskie voiv.
2. Upper Vistula river basin
3. 50°07'00.1"N, 20°18'45.2"E
4. Valley low terrace

A –

B

1. Approx. 100 m^2
2. LBK

C

Czekaj-Zastawny 2008a

705. Wąworków, site 1
1. Opatów comm., Opatów distr., Świętokrzyskie voiv.
2. Opatówka stream basin/upper Vistula river basin
3. 50°47'42"N, 21°26'53.5"E
4. Valley border

A

1. Milicer; W. Antoniewicz
2. 1913; 1922
3. ?
4. ?; any information about features
5. LBK

B

1. Approx. 0.5 ha
2. LBK

C

Czekaj-Zastawny 2008a; Kowalewska-Marszałek 1992

706. Werbkowice, site 1
1. Werbkowice comm., Hrubieszów distr., Lubelskie voiv.
2. Huczwa stream basin/Bug river basin/upper Vistula river basin
3. 50°43'13.2"N, 23°44'20.1"E
4. Valley floor

A

1. J. Kowalczyk, T. Liana, T. Piętka-Dąbrowska
2. 1959-60
3. 2100 m^2
4. Settlement; 5 features
5. LBK, Music Note phase

B

1. Approx. 5 ha
2. LBK

C

Czekaj-Zastawny 2008a; Dąbrowska & Liana 1963; Liana & Piętka-Dąbrowska 1962

707. Werbkowice, site 4
1. Werbkowice comm., Hrubieszów distr., Lubelskie voiv.
2. Huczwa stream basin/Bug river basin/upper Vistula river basin
3. 50°45'17.3"N, 23°45'36.5"E
4. Valley slope

A –

B

1. Approx. 100 m^2
2. LBK

C

Czekaj-Zastawny 2008a

708. Wężerów, site 18

1. Słomniki comm., Kraków distr., Małopolskie voiv.
2. Szreniawa river basin/upper Vistula river basin
3. 50°16'53"N, 20°02'55.1"E
4. Valley low terrace

A –

B

1. Approx. 1 ha
2. LBK

C

Czekaj-Zastawny 2008a

709. Wiatowice, site 1

1. Gdów comm., Wieliczka distr., Małopolskie voiv.
2. Raba river basin/upper Vistula river basin
3. 49°56'35.6"N, 20°12'26"
4. Valley border

A –

B

1. Approx. 15 ha
2. LBK

C

Czekaj-Zastawny 2008a

710. Wiatowice, site 2

1. Gdów comm., Wieliczka distr., Małopolskie voiv.
2. Raba river basin/upper Vistula river basin
3. 49°56'36.8"N, 20°12'51.7"E
4. Valley border

A –

B

1. Approx. 100 m^2
2. LBK

C

Czekaj-Zastawny 2008a; Szybowicz 1980

711. Widnica, site 18

1. Miechów comm., Miechów distr., Małopolskie voiv.
2. Szreniawa river basin/upper Vistula river basin
3. 50°23'36.9"N, 20°01'21.2"E
4. Outside valleys

A –

B

1. Approx. 5 ha
2. LBK

C

Data from AZP card

712. Widnica, site 19

1. Miechów comm., Miechów distr., Małopolskie voiv.
2. Szreniawa river basin/upper Vistula river basin
3. 50°23'44"N, 20°01'41.7"E
4. Valley slope and border

A –

B

1. Approx. 0.5 ha
2. LBK

C

Data from AZP card

713. Widnica, site 20

1. Miechów comm., Miechów distr., Małopolskie voiv.
2. Szreniawa river basin/upper Vistula river basin
3. 50°23'47.5"N, 20°01'58"E
4. Valley slope and border

A –

B

1. Approx. 1 ha
2. LBK

C

Data from AZP card

714. Widnica, site 22

1. Miechów comm., Miechów distr., Małopolskie voiv.
2. Szreniawa river basin/upper Vistula river basin
3. 50°23'38.3"N, 20°02'34.3"E
4. Valley slope and border/outside valleys

A –

B

1. Approx. 0.5 ha
2. LBK

C

Data from AZP card

715. Widuchowa, site 3

1. Busko Zdrój comm., Busko Zdrój distr., Świętokrzyskie voiv.
2. Wschodnia stream basin/upper Vistula river basin
3. 50°29'32.8"N, 20°47'49.5"E
4. Valley slope

A –

B

1. Approx. 100 m^2
2. LBK

C

Czekaj-Zastawny 2008a

716. Wielka Wieś, site 8

1. Wielka Wieś comm., Kraków distr., Małopolskie voiv.
2. Prądnik river basin/upper Vistula river basin
3. 50°09'46.9"N, 19°51'30.5"E
4. Valley floor and slope

A –

B

1. Approx. 0.5 ha
2. LBK?

C

Czekaj-Zastawny 2008a; Lech *et al.* 1984

717. Wielka Wieś, site 9

1. Wielka Wieś comm., Kraków distr., Małopolskie voiv.
2. Prądnik river basin/upper Vistula river basin
3. 50°09'26.3"N, 19°51'07.5"E
4. Outside valleys

A –

B

1. Approx. 0.5 ha
2. LBK?

C

Czekaj-Zastawny 2008a; Lech *et al.* 1984

718. Wielka Wieś, site 49

1. Wielka Wieś comm., Kraków distr., Małopolskie voiv.
2. Prądnik river basin/upper Vistula river basin
3. 50°08'59.3"N, 19°50'04.8"
4. Outside valleys

A –
B
1. Approx. 0.5 ha
2. LBK?
C
Czekaj-Zastawny 2008a

719. Wieliczka, site 27
1. Wieliczka comm., Wieliczka distr., Małopolskie voiv.
2. Upper Vistula river basin
3. 49°59'41.5"N, 20°05'03.8"E
4. Valley slope
A –
B
1. Approx. 100 m²
2. LBK
C
Czekaj-Zastawny 2008a; Szybowicz 1980

720. Wiercany, site 7
1. Iwierzyce comm., Ropczyce-Sędziszów distr., Podkarpackie voiv.
2. Wielopolka strem basin/Wisłoka river basin/upper Vistula river basin
3. 50°00'53.7"N, 21°45'30.4"E
4. Valley slope
A –
B
1. Approx. 100 m²
2. LBK
C
Czekaj-Zastawny 2008a

721. Wiercany, site 8
1. Iwierzyce comm., Ropczyce-Sędziszów distr., Podkarpackie voiv.
2. Wielopolka strem basin/Wisłoka river basin/upper Vistula river basin
3. 50°01'13"N, 21°45'45.2"E
4. Valley slope and border
A –
B
1. Approx. 100 m²
2. LBK
C
Czekaj-Zastawny 2008a

722. Wierzbica, site 7
1. Lubycza Królewska comm., Tomaszów Lubelski distr., Lubelskie voiv.
2. Sołokija stream basin/Bug river basin/upper Vistula river basin
3. 50°20'26.1"N, 23°40'10.1"E
4. Valley slope
A –
B
1. Approx. 100 m²
2. LBK
C
Czekaj-Zastawny 2008a

723. Wierzbica, site 9
1. Lubycza Królewska comm., Tomaszów Lubelski distr., Lubelskie voiv.
2. Sołokija stream basin/Bug river basin/upper Vistula river basin
3. 50°20'12.8"N, 23°39'26.6"E
4. Valley slope
A –
B
1. Approx. 0.5 ha
2. LBK
C
Czekaj-Zastawny 2008a

724. Wierzbica, site 1
1. Radziemice comm., Proszowice distr., Małopolskie voiv.
2. Szreniawa river basin/upper Vistula river basin
3. 50°14'18.5"N, 20°08'56.9"E
4. Valley low terrace
A –
B
1. Approx. 0.5 ha
2. LBK
C
Czekaj-Zastawny 2008a; Kruk 1970

725. Wierzchowie, site 1
1. Wielka Wieś comm., Kraków distr., Małopolskie voiv.
2. Kluczwoda stream basin/Rudawa stream basin/upper Vistula river basin
3. 50°10'14"N, 19°48'19.1"E
4. "Mamutowa (Wierzchowiska Dolna)" Cave
A
1. J. Zawisza; L. Kozłowski; B. Ginter, S. Kowalski, J. K. Kozłowski; S. Kowalski
2. 1874-82; 1913; 1957, 1960, 1962; 1963
3. Part of cave sediments of main chamber; part of cave entrance terrace and front chamber; front chamber, main chamber, side niche, NE corridor; front chamber, main chamber, side niche, NE corridor
4. Cave camp; 1 pottery fragment
5. LBK, Želiezovce phase
B
1. –
2. LBK
C
Czekaj-Zastawny 2008a; Rook 1980

726. Wierzchowie, site 2
1. Wielka Wieś comm., Kraków distr., Małopolskie voiv.
2. Kluczwoda stream basin/Rudawa stream basin/upper Vistula river basin
3. 50°10'32.9"N, 19°48'24.3"E
4. "Wierzchowiska Górna" Cave
A
1. J. Zawisza; G. Ossowski; M. Mączyńska, E. Rook
2. 1871-1873; 1884-1886; 1970, 1974
3. Part of sediments of entrance I; front chamber, part of chambers Hala Wielka Dolna and Mała Dolna; part on the front of entrance II, cave entrance terrace
4. Cave camp; 22 pottery fragments
5. LBK, Želiezovce phase
B
1. –
2. LBK
C
Czekaj-Zastawny 2008a; Rook 1980

727. Więckowice, site 4
1. Zabierzów comm., Kraków distr., Małopolskie voiv.
2. Rudawa stream basin/upper Vistula river basin

3. 50°08'04.2"N, 19°45'32.5"E
4. Valley low terrace

A

1. A. Zastawny
2. 2006, 2007
3. ca. 700 m²
4. Settlement; 3 features
5. LBK, Music Note phase

B

1. Approx. 15 ha
2. LBK

C

Zastawny 2006

728. Wilczkowice, site 6
1. Michałowice comm., Kraków distr., Małopolskie voiv.
2. Dłubnia river basin/upper Vistula river basin
3. 50°11'20.8"N, 19°58'27.6"E
4. Valley low terrace

A –
B

1. Approx. 100 m²
2. LBK?

C

Czekaj-Zastawny 2008a; Kruk 1969

729. Wilków, site 13
1. Werbkowice comm., Hrubieszów distr., Lubelskie voiv.
2. Huczwa stream basin/Bug river basin/upper Vistula river basin
3. 50°47'02.7"N, 23°45'08.9"E
4. Valley floor

A –
B

1. Approx. 100 m²
2. LBK

C

Czekaj-Zastawny 2008a

730. Wilków, site 22
1. Werbkowice comm., Hrubieszów distr., Lubelskie voiv.
2. Huczwa stream basin/Bug river basin/upper Vistula river basin
3. 50°46'33.5"N, 23°45'37.9"E
4. Valley border

A –
B

1. Approx. 100 m²
2. LBK

C

Czekaj-Zastawny 2008a

731. Winiary, site 4
1. Nowy Korczyn comm., Busko Zdrój distr., Świętokrzyskie voiv.
2. Upper Vistula river basin
3. 50°17'14.7"N, 20°46'05.2"E
4. Valley upper terrace

A –
B

1. Approx. 0.5 ha
2. LBK

C

Czekaj-Zastawny 2008a

732. Winiary, site 15
1. Pałecznica comm., Proszowice distr., Małopolskie voiv.
2. Nidzica river basin/upper Vistula river basin
3. 50°17'21.3"N, 20°20'02.3"E
4. Valley slope

A –
B

1. Approx. 100 m²
2. LBK?

C

Czekaj-Zastawny 2008a

733. Winiary, site 18
1. Pałecznica comm., Proszowice distr., Małopolskie voiv.
2. Nidzica river basin/upper Vistula river basin
3. 50°17'55"N, 20°20'42.9"E
4. Valley slope

A –
B

1. Approx. 100 m²
2. LBK

C

Czekaj-Zastawny 2008a

734. Witoszyńce, site 8
1. Fredropol comm., Przemyśl distr., Podkarpackie voiv.
2. San river basin/upper Vistula river basin
3. 49°43'46.6"N, 22°44'01.1"E
4. Valley slope and border

A –
B

1. Approx. 0.5 ha
2. LBK

C

Czekaj-Zastawny 2008a

735. Włosnowice, site 7
1. Solec Zdrój comm., Busko Zdrój distr., Świętokrzyskie voiv.
2. Strumień stream basin/upper Vistula river basin
3. 50°22'45.7"N, 20°55'44.5"E
4. Valley slope

A –
B

1. Approx. 0.5 ha
2. LBK

C

Czekaj-Zastawny 2008a

736. Włostowice, site 5
1. Koszyce comm., Proszowice distr., Małopolskie voiv.
2. Szreniawa river basin/upper Vistula river basin
3. 50°09'58.3"N, 20°33'05.6"E
4. Valley upper terrace

A –
B

1. Approx. 0.5 ha
2. LBK

C

Czekaj-Zastawny 2008a; Rydzewski 1972

737. Wnorów, site 17
1. Łoniów comm., Sandomierz distr., Świętokrzyskie voiv.
2. Upper Vistula river basin
3. 50°33'39.5"N, 21°28'21.3"E
4. Valley border

117

A –
B
1. Approx. 1 ha
2. LBK
C

Czekaj-Zastawny 2008a; Kowalewska-Marszałek 1992

738. Wojnicz, site 34
1. Wojnicz comm., Tarnów distr., Małopolskie voiv.
2. Dunajec river basin/upper Vistula river basin
3. 49°57'31.7"N, 20°49'20.1"E
4. Valley border
A
1. The Cracow Team for Archaeological Supervision of
   Motorway Construction, Institute of Archaeology and
   Ethnology Polish Academy of Sciences, Museum of
   Archaeology Cracow, Jagiellonian University –
   M. Nowakowska, A. Jaremek
2. 2005
3. 34200 m^2
4. Camp; 1 feature
5. LBK
B
1. Approx. 4 ha
2. LBK
C

Nowakowska & Jaremek 2006

739. Wojnów, site 8
1. Oleśnica comm., Staszów distr., Świętokrzyskie voiv.
2. Wschodnia strem basin/upper Vistula river basin
3. 50°27'35.2"N, 21°05'31.1"E
4. Valley slope
A –
B
1. Approx. 0.5 ha
2. LBK
C

Czekaj-Zastawny 2008a

740. Wola Biechowska, site 3
1. Pacanów comm., Busko Zdrój distr., Świętokrzyskie voiv.
2. Strumień strem basin/upper Vistula river basin
3. 50°22'46.2"N, 21°01'11.5"E
4. Valley slope
A –
B
1. Approx. 0.5 ha
2. LBK
C

Czekaj-Zastawny 2008a

741. Wola Zgłobieńska, site 2
1. Boguchwała comm., Rzeszówl distr., Podkarpackie voiv.
2. Wisłok river/San river basin/upper Vistula river basin
3. 49°59'54.9"N, 21°48'07.1"E
4. Valley slope and border
A –
B
1. Approx. 0.5 ha
2. LBK
C

Czekaj-Zastawny 2008a

742. Wola Zgłobieńska, site 24
1. Boguchwała comm., Rzeszówl distr., Podkarpackie voiv.

2. Wisłok river/San river basin/upper Vistula river basin
3. 50°00'16.5"N, 21°49'39.4"E
4. Valley slope
A –
B
1. Approx. 0.5 ha
2. LBK
C

Czekaj-Zastawny 2008a

743. Wolwanowice, site 3
1. Proszowice comm., Proszowice distr., Małopolskie voiv.
2. Szreniawa river basin/upper Vistula river basin
3. 50°10'52.3"N, 20°25'22.6"E
4. Valley low terrace
A –
B
1. Approx. 100 m^2
2. LBK
C

Czekaj-Zastawny 2008a; Rydzewski 1972

744. Wójeczka, site 4
1. Pacanów comm., Busko Zdrój distr., Świętokrzyskie voiv.
2. Strumień strem basin/upper Vistula river basin
3. 50°24'14.7"N, 20°58'13.1"E
4. Outside valleys
A –
B
1. Approx. 100 m^2
2. LBK
C

Czekaj-Zastawny 2008a

745. Wójeczka, site 8
1. Pacanów comm., Busko Zdrój distr., Świętokrzyskie voiv.
2. Strumień strem basin/upper Vistula river basin
3. 50°23'53.5"N, 20°57'10.6"E
4. Outside valleys
A –
B
1. Approx. 0.5 ha
2. LBK
C

Czekaj-Zastawny 2008a

746. Wólka Gieraszowska, site 4
1. Łoniów comm., Sandomierz distr., Świętokrzyskie voiv.
2. Koprzywianka strem basin/upper Vistula river basin
3. 50°36'21.5"N, 21°28'35.7"E
4. Border zone of upland/valley slope and border
A –
B
1. Approx. 100 m^2
2. LBK
C

Czekaj-Zastawny 2008a; Kowalewska-Marszałek 1992

747. Wólka Gieraszowska, site 17
1. Łoniów comm., Sandomierz distr., Świętokrzyskie voiv.
2. Koprzywianka strem basin/upper Vistula river basin
3. 50°36'18.4"N, 21°27'44.2"E
4. Border zone of upland/valley slope and border
A –
B
1. Approx. 100 m^2

2. LBK

C

Czekaj-Zastawny 2008a; Kowalewska-Marszałek 1992

748. Wólka Pukarzowska, site 1
1. Łaszczów comm., Tomaszów Lubelski distr., Lubelskie voiv.
2. Huczwa stream basin/Bug river basin/upper Vistula river basin
3. 50°32'03.4"N, 23°39'53.7"E
4. Valley slope and border

A –

B
1. Approx. 100 m²
2. LBK?

C

Czekaj-Zastawny 2008a

749. Wychody, site 5
1. Zamość comm., Zamość distr., Lubelskie voiv.
2. Wieprz river basin/upper Vistula river basin
3. 50°40'13.1"N, 23°09'34.9"E
4. Valley slope

A –

B
1. Approx. 100 m²
2. LBK

C

Czekaj-Zastawny 2008a

750. Wysocice, site 8
1. Gołcza comm., Miechów distr., Małopolskie voiv.
2. Dłubnia river basin/upper Vistula river basin
3. 50°17'05.3"N, 19°55'02.6"E
4. Valley upper terrace

A –

B
1. Approx. 0.5 ha
2. LBK?

C

Czekaj-Zastawny 2008a

751. Zabłocie, site 5
1. Biskupice comm., Wieliczka distr., Małopolskie voiv.
2. Raba river basin/upper Vistula river basin
3. 49°58'29.8"N, 20°11'01.3"E
4. Outside valleys

A –

B
1. Approx. 100 m²
2. LBK

C

Czekaj-Zastawny 2008a

752. Zagaje Smrokowskie, site 2
1. Słomniki comm., Kraków distr., Małopolskie voiv.
2. Szreniawa river basin/upper Vistula river basin
3. 50°16'45.1"N, 20°00'35.3"E
4. Outside valleys

A –

B
1. Approx. 100 m²
2. LBK

C

Czekaj-Zastawny 2008a

753. Zagaje Smrokowskie, site 16
1. Słomniki comm., Kraków distr., Małopolskie voiv.
2. Szreniawa river basin/upper Vistula river basin
3. 50°16'23"N, 20°02'07.9"E
4. Valley low terrace

A –

B
1. Approx. 100 m²
2. LBK

C

Czekaj-Zastawny 2008a; Kruk 1970

754. Zagajów, site 1
1. Michałów comm., Pińczów distr., Świętokrzyskie voiv.
2. Mierzawa stream basin/Nida river basin/upper Vistula river basin
3. 50°29'32.7"N, 20°25'03.6"E
4. Valley upper terrace

A –

B
1. Approx. 100 m²
2. LBK

C

Czekaj-Zastawny 2008a; Dębowski 1972

755. Zagość, site 7
1. Pińczów comm., Pińczów distr., Świętokrzyskie voiv.
2. Nida river basin/upper Vistula river basin
3. 50°24'50.9"N, 20°35'31.4"E
4. Valley low terrace

A
1. J. Gromnicki
2. 1962-63
3. 650 m²
4. Settlement or camp; 2 features
5. LBK

B
1. Approx. 1 ha
2. LBK

C

Czekaj-Zastawny 2008a; Gromnicki 1965

756. Zagórzyce, site 1
1. Kazimierza Wielka comm., Kazimierza Wielka distr., Świętokrzyskie voiv.
2. Nidzica river basin/upper Vistula river basin
3. 50°16'29.9"N, 20°32'56.6"E
4. Valley low terrace

A
1. M. Grygiel, J. Pikulski
2. 2001-07
3. 3000 m²
4. Settlement or camp; 5 features
5. LBK, Ib (*Zofipole*) phase

B
1. Approx. 3.5 ha
2. LBK

C

Czekaj-Zastawny 2008a; Rygiel & Pikulski 2006; Grygiel *et al.* 2008

757. Zagórze, site 6
1. Babice comm., Chrzanów distr., Małopolskie voiv.
2. Upper Vistula river basin
3. 50°05'46.9"N, 19°24'05.9"E
4. Outside valleys

A –

B

1. Approx. 100 m^2
2. LBK?

C

Czekaj-Zastawny 2008a

758. Zagórze, site 2

1. Niepołomice comm., Wieliczka distr., Małopolskie voiv.
2. Drawinka stream basin/Raba river basin/upper Vistula river basin
3. 49°59'55.4"N, 20°11'44"E
4. Valley low terrace

A

1. The Cracow Team for Archaeological Supervision of Motorway Construction, Institute of Archaeology and Ethnology Polish Academy of Sciences, Museum of Archaeology Cracow, Jagiellonian University – M. Suchorska-Rola, J. Okoński
2. 1996, 2000-2005
3. 8 ha
4. Settlement; few hundred features (10 long houses in it)
5. LBK, Ib (*Zofipole*) phase, Music Note phase, Želiezovce phase (through ŽIIb)

B

1. Approx. 8 ha
2. LBK

C

Czekaj-Zastawny *et al.* 2002; Czekaj-Zastawny *et al.* 2003; Czekaj-Zastawny 2008a; Kadrow & Okoński 2008

759. Zagorzyce, site 4

1. Miechów comm., Miechów distr., Małopolskie voiv.
2. Szreniawa river basin/upper Vistula river basin
3. 50°22'56.3"N, 20°01'21.5"E
4. Valley slope

A –

B

1. Approx. 100 m^2
2. LBK?

C

Czekaj-Zastawny 2008a

760. Zakłodzie, site 4

1. Radecznica comm., Zamość distr., Lubelskie voiv.
2. Wieprz river basin/upper Vistula river basin
3. 50°45'23.7"N, 22°51'00"E
4. Valley floor

A –

B

1. Approx. 100 m^2
2. LBK?

C

Czekaj-Zastawny 2008a

761. Zakrzów, site 14

1. Niepołomice comm., Wieliczka distr., Małopolskie voiv.
2. Upper Vistula river basin
3. 50°00'15.1"N, 20°09'04.2"E
4. Outside valleys

A –

B

1. Approx. 0.5 ha
2. LBK?

C

Czekaj-Zastawny 2008a

762. Załęże, site 5

1. Krasne comm., Rzeszów distr., Podkarpackie voiv.
2. Wisłok river basin/San river basin/upper Vistula river basin
3. 50°03'08.3"N, 22°02'47.5"E
4. Valley floor

A –

B

1. Approx. 0.5 ha
2. LBK

C

Czekaj-Zastawny 2008a

763. Zamłynie, site 3

1. Tyszowce comm., Tomaszów Lubelski distr., Lubelskie voiv.
2. Huczwa stream basin/Bug river basin/upper Vistula river basin
3. 50°37'26.8"N, 23°41'47.3"E
4. Valley low terrace

A –

B

1. Approx. 0.5 ha
2. LBK

C

Czekaj-Zastawny 2008a

764. Zbigniewice, site 13

1. Koprzywnica comm., Sandomierz distr., Świętokrzyskie voiv.
2. Koprzywianka stream basin/upper Vistula river basin
3. 50°37'00.5"N, 21°30'16.3"E
4. Border zone of upland/valley border

A –

B

1. Approx. 100 m^2
2. LBK

C

Czekaj-Zastawny 2008a; Kowalewska-Marszałek 1992

765. Zelczyna, site 5

1. Skawina comm., Kraków distr., Małopolskie voiv.
2. Skawa stream basin/upper Vistula river basin
3. 49°57'07.8"N, 19°45'05.2"E
4. Border zone of upland

A –

B

1. Approx. 0.5 ha
2. LBK?

C

Czekaj-Zastawny 2008a

766. Zelczyna, site 8

1. Skawina comm., Kraków distr., Małopolskie voiv.
2. Skawa stream basin/upper Vistula river basin
3. 49°57'23.8"N, 19°45'15.9"E
4. Border zone of upland

A –

B

1. Approx. 0.5 ha
2. LBK?

C

Czekaj-Zastawny 2008a

767. Zelków, site 1

1. Zabierzów comm., Kraków distr., Małopolskie voiv.
2. Rudawa stream basin/upper Vistula river basin

3. 50°09'50.3"N, 19°47'31"E
4. Outside valleys

A –

B

1. Approx. 15 ha
2. LBK

C

Czekaj-Zastawny 2008a; Lech *et al.* 1984

768. Zelków, site 22
1. Zabierzów comm., Kraków distr., Małopolskie voiv.
2. Rudawa stream basin/upper Vistula river basin
3. 50°09'20.5"N, 19°48'06"E
4. Outside valleys

A –

B

1. Approx. 100 m²
2. LBK

C

Czekaj-Zastawny 2008a; Lech *et al.* 1984

769. Zgłobień, site 19
1. Boguchwała comm., Rzeszów distr., Podkarpackie voiv.
2. Wisłok river basin/San river basin/upper Vistula river basin
3. 50°00'42.3"N, 21°50'11.3"E
4. Valley slope

A –

B

1. Approx. 100 m²
2. LBK

C

Czekaj-Zastawny 2008a

770. Zielonki, site 11
1. Zielonki comm., Kraków distr., Małopolskie voiv.
2. Prądnik river basin/upper Vistula river basin
3. 50°07'13.7"N, 19°55'05.2"E
4. Valley floor

A –

B

1. Approx. 0.5 ha
2. LBK?

C

Czekaj-Zastawny 2008a; Lech *et al.* 1984

771. Złota, site 7
1. Czchów comm., Brzesko distr., Małopolskie voiv.
2. Dunajec river basin/upper Vistula river basin
3. 49°52'14.6"N, 20°41'04.3"E
4. Valley slope

A –

B

1. Approx. 0.5 ha
2. LBK

C

Czekaj-Zastawny 2008a

772. Złota (Grodzisko I), site 1
1. Samborzec comm., Sandomierz distr., Świętokrzyskie voiv.
2. Upper Vistula river basin
3. 50°39'00.9"N, 21°41'27.3"E
4. Border zone of upland

A

1. J. Żurowski
2. 1928
3. ?

4. Camp or settlement trace; no features, few pottery fragments
5. LBK

B

1. Approx. 100 m²
2. LBK

C

Czekaj-Zastawny 2008a; Kowalewska-Marszałek 1992; Rauhut 1970; Żurowski 1929c, 1934

773. Złota, site 22
1. Samborzec comm., Sandomierz distr., Świętokrzyskie voiv.
2. Koprzywianka stream basin/upper Vistula river basin
3. 50°39'26.1"N, 21°41'58.9"E
4. Border zone of upland/valley border

A –

B

1. Approx. 100 m²
2. LBK

C

Czekaj-Zastawny 2008a; Kowalewska-Marszałek 1992

774. Złota, site 22
1. Samborzec comm., Sandomierz distr., Świętokrzyskie voiv.
2. Upper Vistula river basin
3. 50°38'38.6"N, 21°40'41.1"E
4. Border zone of upland

A –

B

1. Approx. 1 ha
2. LBK

C

Czekaj-Zastawny 2008a; Kowalewska-Marszałek 1992

775. Złotniki, site 1
1. Igołomia-Wawrzeńczyce comm., Kraków distr., Małopolskie voiv.
2. Upper Vistula river basin
3. 50°05'51.8"N, 20°16'17.8"E
4. Valley low terrace

A

1. A. Dzieduszycka-Machnikowa
2. 1962-63
3. 440 m²
4. Settlement; 13 features (probably 3 human graves in it)
5. LBK, Music Note phase, Želiezovce phase; imports of Bükk culture

B

1. Approx. 1 ha
2. LBK

C

Czekaj-Zastawny 2008a; Dzieduszycka-Machnikowa 1964; Dzieduszycka-Machnikowa & Eker 1965

776. Zochcinek, site 13
1. Opatów comm., Opatów distr., Świętokrzyskie voiv.
2. Opatówka stream basin/upper Vistula river basin
3. 50°49'00.9"N, 21°23'42.1"E
4. Valley slope and border

A –

B

1. Approx. 100 m²
2. LBK

C

Czekaj-Zastawny 2008a; Kowalewska-Marszałek 1992

777. Zofipole, site 1
1. Igołomia-Wawrzeńczyce comm., Kraków distr.,
   Małopolskie voiv.
2. Upper Vistula river basin
3. 50°05'02.4"N, 20°13'56.9"E
4. Valley low terrace

A
1. T. Reyman, A. Żaki, S. Buratyński
2. 1946-49
3. 2950 m^2
4. Settlement; 15 features (probably 3 human graves in it)
5. LBK, Ia (*Gniechowice*) phase, Ib (*Zofipole*) phase, Music
   Note phase; imports of Tisadob-Kapušany group

B
1. Approx. 1.5 ha
2. LBK

C
Czekaj-Zastawny 2008a; Buratyński 1948; Kulczycka 1961;
Kulczycka-Leciejewiczowa 1983; Reyman 1947

778. Zofipole, site 2
1. Igołomia-Wawrzeńczyce comm., Kraków distr.,
   Małopolskie voiv.
2. Upper Vistula river basin
3. 50°05'12.5"N, 20°14'25.3"E
4. Valley low terrace

A –
B
1. Approx. 100 m^2
2. LBK

C
Czekaj-Zastawny 2008a

779. Zofipole, site 12
1. Igołomia-Wawrzeńczyce comm., Kraków distr.,
   Małopolskie voiv.
2. Upper Vistula river basin
3. 50°05'16.8"N, 20°14'04.5"E
4. Valley low terrace

A –
B
1. Approx. 100 m^2
2. LBK

C
Czekaj-Zastawny 2008a

780. Zofipole, site 14
1. Igołomia-Wawrzeńczyce comm., Kraków distr.,
   Małopolskie voiv.
2. Upper Vistula river basin
3. 50°05'19.4"N, 20°13'21"E
4. Valley slope

A –
B
1. Approx. 100 m^2
2. LBK

C
Czekaj-Zastawny 2008a

781. Zofipole, site 15
1. Igołomia-Wawrzeńczyce comm., Kraków distr.,
   Małopolskie voiv.
2. Upper Vistula river basin
3. 50°05'17.3"N, 20°14'06.9"E
4. Valley low terrace

A –
B
1. Approx. 100 m^2
2. LBK

C
Czekaj-Zastawny 2008a

782. Zwięczyca, site 2
1. Boguchwała comm., Rzeszów distr., Podkarpackie voiv.
2. Wisłok river basin/San river basin/upper Vistula river basin
3. 50°00'10.4"N, 21°57'47.6"E
4. Valley floor/border of a river

A –
B
1. Approx. 100 m^2
2. LBK

C
Czekaj-Zastawny 2008a

783. Zwięczyca, site 3
1. Boguchwała comm., Rzeszów distr., Podkarpackie voiv.
2. Wisłok river basin/San river basin/upper Vistula river basin
3. 49°59'56.3"N, 21°58'11.7"E
4. Valley low terrace

A
1. S. Czopek, K. Trybała; M. Dębiec, A. Dzbyński
2. 2003; 2005-2006
3. 740 m^2
4. Settlement; 158 features (2 long houses in it)
5. LBK, Music Note phase; imports of Tisadob-Kapušany
   group
6240±40 BP, 6170±40 BP, 6960± 60 BP, 6070± 40 BP

B
1. Approx. 11 ha
2. LBK

C
Dębiec & Dzbyński 2006; 2007; Saile *et al.* 2008

784. Zwięczyca, site 4
1. Boguchwała comm., Rzeszów distr., Podkarpackie voiv.
2. Wisłok river basin/San river basin/upper Vistula river basin
3. 49°59'34.9"N, 21°57'35"
4. Valley border

A
1. T. Dębowski
2. 1966
3. 1000 m^2
4. Settlement; 8 features
5. LBK, Music Note phase, Želiezovce phase; imports of
   Bükk culture

B
1. Approx. 1 ha
2. LBK

C
Czekaj-Zastawny 2008a; Czopek 1999; Dębowski 1968; Saile
et al. 2008

785. Żerków, site 1
1. Gnojnik comm., Brzesko distr., Małopolskie voiv.
2. Uszwica stream basin/Dunajec river basin/upper Vistula
   river basin
3. 49°54'19.4"N, 20°39'47.5"E
4. Valley border

A
1. P. Valde-Nowak
2. 2006-07

3. 340 m^2
4. Settlement; few features (a part of 1 long house in it)
5. LBK, Želiezovce phase
6210 ± 40 BP
B
1. Approx. 1 ha
2. LBK

C

Czekaj-Zastawny 2008a; Valde-Nowak 2007; 2008a

786. Żerniki Dolne, site 1
1. Stopnica comm., Busko Zdrój distr., Świętokrzyskie voiv.
2. Wschodnia stream basin/upper Vistula river basin
3. 50°29'54.7"N, 20°57'39.1"E
4. Valley low terrace/valley slope
A –
B
1. Approx. 100 m^2
2. LBK?
C

Czekaj-Zastawny 2008a

787. Zębocin, site 2
1. Proszowice comm., Proszowice distr., Małopolskie voiv.
2. Szreniawa river basin/upper Vistula river basin
3. 50°10'15.5"N, 20°19'32.8"E
4. Valley slope and floor
A –
B
1. Approx. 0.5 ha
2. LBK
C

Czekaj-Zastawny 2008a

788. Żurawica, site 30
1. Żurawica comm., Przemyśl distr., Podkarpackie voiv.
2. San river basin/upper Vistula river basin
3. 49°49'21"N, 22°46'44.2"E
4. Valley slope
A –
B
1. Approx. 0.5 ha
2. LBK
C

Czekaj-Zastawny 2008a

789. Żurawica, site 31
1. Żurawica comm., Przemyśl distr., Podkarpackie voiv.
2. San river basin/upper Vistula river basin
3. 49°49'29"N, 22°46'37.2"E
4. Valley floor
A –
B
1. Approx. 100 m^2
2. LBK
C

Czekaj-Zastawny 2008a

790. Żurawniki, site 2
1. Złota comm., Pińczów distr., Świętokrzyskie voiv.
2. Nida river basin/upper Vistula river basin
3. 50°22'36.9"N, 20°38'44.2"E
4. Valley low terrace
A –

B
1. Approx. 100 m^2
2. LBK
C

Czekaj-Zastawny 2008a; Dąbrowska 1965

791. Żurawniki, site 5
1. Złota comm., Pińczów distr., Świętokrzyskie voiv.
2. Nida river basin/upper Vistula river basin
3. 50°23'01.9"N, 20°38'02.9"E
4. Valley upper terrace
A –
B
1. Approx. 5 ha
2. LBK
C

Czekaj-Zastawny 2008a

792. Żydów, site 1
1. Igołomia-Wawrzeńczyce comm., Kraków distr., Małopolskie voiv.
2. Upper Vistula river basin
3. 50°07'46"N, 20°16'28.8"E
4. Valley slope
A –
B
1. Approx. 100 m^2
2. LBK
C

Czekaj-Zastawny 2008a

793. Żyłka, site 1
1. Jarczów comm., Tomaszów Lubelski distr., Lubelskie voiv.
2. Sołoikija stream basin/Bug river basin/upper Vistula river basin
3. 50°23'19.4"N, 23°29'35.9"E
4. Valley border
A –
B
1. Approx. 100 m^2
2. LBK?
C

Czekaj-Zastawny 2008a

REFERENCES

Aksamit T. 1964a. Badania archeologiczne na osadzie neolitycznej w Kraczkowej (stanowisko nr 1), pow. Łańcut w r. 1964. *Materiały i Sprawozdania Rzeszowskiego Ośrodka Archeologicznego* za rok 1964, 15–19.

Aksamit T. 1964b. Badania archeologiczne przeprowadzone w rejonie rzeszowskim w roku 1964. *Sprawozdania Rzeszowskiego Ośrodka Archeologicznego* za rok 1964, 12.

Aksamit T. 1966. Badania archeologiczne osady neolitycznej w Kormanicach, pow. Przemyśl. *Sprawozdania Rzeszowskiego Ośrodka Archeologicznego* za rok 1965, 23–27.

Aksamit T. 1968. Prace wykopaliskowe na osadzie neolitycznej we Fredropolu, pow. Przemyśl. *Sprawozdania Rzeszowskiego Ośrodka Archeologicznego* za rok 1968, 116–123.

Aksamit T. 1971. Z badań osady neolitycznej w Kormanicach pow. Przemyśl. *Materiały i Sprawozdania Rzeszowskiego Ośrodka Archeologicznego* za rok 1967, 107–113.

Bakels C. 1978. Four Linearbandkeramik settlements and their environment: a paleoecological study of Sittard, Stein, Elsloo and Hienheim. *Analecta Praehistorica Leidensia* 11, 1–244.

Balcer B. 1975. *Krzemień świeciechowski w kulturze pucharów lejkowatych. Eksploatacja, obróbka i rozprzestrzenienie.* Wrocław-Warszawa-Kraków.

Barłowski J. 1968. Wyniki badań przeprowadzonych na terenie Rzeszowa-Pobitno. *Materiały i Sprawozdania Rzeszowskiego Ośrodka Archeologicznego* za rok 1966, 265.

Barłowski J. 1971. Badania powierzchniowe na terenie Rzeszowa-Pobitno oraz wsi Wilkowyja i Krasne, Wólka w powiecie rzeszowskim. *Materiały i Sprawozdania Rzeszowskiego Ośrodka Archeologicznego* za rok 1967, 194.

Bąbel J. T. 1975. Badania powierzchniowe dorzecza rzeki Kamionki w pow. opatowskim. *Wiadomości Archeologiczne* 40, 531–581.

Behrends H. 1973. *Die Jungsteinzeit im Mittelelbe-Saale-Gebiet* (= Veröffentlichungen des Landesmuseums für Vorgeschichte in Halle 27). Halle.

Boiron L. 2006. Reflections on the functions of pits and the spatial distribution of finds in the early Neolithic of northern France and Belgium. Paper on *European Association of Archaeologists, 12th Annual Meeting, Cracow, Poland, 19-24 September 2006.*

Breitenfellner A. & Rook E. 1991. Sprawozdania z badań osady kultury ceramiki wstęgowej rytej w Bolechowicach-Zielonej, gm. Zabierzów, woj. Kraków, stanowisko 9. *Sprawozdania Archeologiczne* 43, 9–20.

Bukowski K. 2003. Określenie warunków geologicznych ze szczególnym uwzględnieniem możliwości występowania słonych źródeł dla rejonu stanowiska nr 27 Kraków-Bieżanów. In Kadrow S. (ed.), *Kraków-Bieżanów, stanowisko 27 i Kraków-Rżąka, stanowisko 1, osada kultury łużyckiej.* Kraków, 273–284.

Buratyński S. 1948. Wyniki prac wykopaliskowych w 1947 r. na terenie gminy Igołomia w pow. Miechów. *Sprawozdania z Czynności i Posiedzeń Polskiej Akademii Umiejętności* 49/3, 174–176.

Buratyński S. 1968. Wyniki ratowniczych badań archeologicznych na terenie osiedla Krzesławice w Nowej Hucie na stanowisku III. *Materiały Archeologiczne Nowej Huty* 1, 173–180.

Burchard B. 1959. Stanowisko kultury ceramiki wstęgowej rytej w Trzebiesławicach, pow. Sandomierz. *Materiały Archeologiczne* 1, 13–22.

Burchard B. 1960. Ziemianki kultury ceramiki wstęgowej rytej z Sandomierza-Krakówki. *Materiały Archeologiczne* 2, 5–9.

Cabalska M. 1960. Neolityczne narzędzia kamienne. *Zeszyty UJ* 28 (= Prace Archeologiczne 1), 175–178.

Cabalska M. 1969. Badania archeoligiczne w Chełmie, pow. Bochnia. *Sprawozdania Archeologiczne* 21, 47–55.

Cabalska M. 1975. Osadnictwo neolityczne na stanowisku w Chełmie, pow. Bochnia. *Materiały Starożytne i Wczesnośredniowieczne* 3, 7–40.

Childe G.V. 1929. *The Danube in prehistory.* Oxford.

Chmielewski W. & Madeyska T. 1976. Badania stanowiska archeologicznego Kraków-Zwierzyniec I w latach 1972-74. *Sprawozdania Archeologiczne* 28, 19–26.

Coudart A. 1998. *Architecture et société néolithique* (= Documents D'Archéologie Française 67). Paris.

Czarnowski S. 1908. Wykopaliska miechowskie. *Materiały Antropologiczno-Archeologiczne i Etnograficzne* 10, 3–24.

Czekaj-Zastawny A. 2000a. Groby kultury ceramiki wstęgowej rytej z Aleksandrowic, stan. 2, gm. Zabierzów, woj. małopolskie. *Sprawozdania Archeologiczne* 52, 97–112.

Czekaj-Zastawny A. 2000b. Kultura ceramiki wstęgowej rytej w zachodniej części Małopolski – materiały do badań nad geografią osadnictwa. *Sprawozdania Archeologiczne* 52, 49–95.

Czekaj-Zastawny A. 2001. Kultura ceramiki wstęgowej rytej na prawobrzeżu górnej Wisły – materiały do badań nad geografią osadnictwa. *Sprawozdania Archeologiczne* 53, 9–34.

Czekaj-Zastawny A. 2003. Znaczenie płci w obrządku pogrzebowym kultury ceramiki wstęgowej rytej. In W. Dzieduszycki & J. Wrzesiński (eds.), *Kobieta-Śmierć-Mężczyzna* (= Funeralia Lednickie 5). Poznań, 241–247.

Czekaj-Zastawny A. 2008a. *Osadnictwo społeczności kultury ceramiki wstęgowej rytej w dorzeczu górnej Wisły* [*Settlement of Linear Portery Communities in the upper Vistula river basin*]. Kraków.

Czekaj-Zastawny A. 2008b. Nowe źródła w badaniach nad zabudową osad wczesnoneolitycznych w Małopolsce. In J. Chochorowski (ed.), *Młodsza epoka kamienia – wybrane znaleziska* (= Via Archaeologica. Źródła z badań wykopaliskowych na trasie autostrady A4 w Małopolsce). Kraków, 23–42.

Czekaj-Zastawny A. 2008c. Pochówki kultury ceramiki wstęgowej rytej ze stanowiska 2 w Aleksandrowicach, pow. krakowski. In J. Chochorowski (ed.), *Młodsza epoka kamienia – wybrane znaleziska* (= Via Archaeologica. Źródła z badań wykopaliskowych na trasie autostrady A4 w Małopolsce). Kraków, 43–56.

Czekaj-Zastawny A. (ed.). in press. *Obrządek pogrzebowy kultur po- chodzenia naddunajskiego w neolicie Polski południowo-wschodniej.* [*Funerary site of the Danubian cultures in the Neolithic of Southeastern Poland*]. Kraków.

Czekaj-Zastawny A. & Milisauskas S. 1997. Neolityczne materiały z wielokulturowego stanowiska 27 (I) w Michałowicach, woj. krakowskie. *Sprawozdania Archeologiczne* 49, 39–94.

Czekaj-Zastawny A. & Milisauskas S. 1998. Osadnictwo z epoki brązu na wielokulturowym stanowisku 27 w Michałowicach, woj. krakowskie. *Sprawozdania Archeologiczne* 50, 169–204.

Czekaj-Zastawny A., Drobniewicz B., Jarosz P., Kadrow S., Kozłowski J.K., Machowski W., Mianowska I., Naglik R. & Rodak J. 2003. Sprawozdanie z badań ratowniczych przeprowadzonych w 2000 roku na stanowiskach na trasie projektowanej autostrady A4 w woj. małopolskim. In Bukowski Z. (ed.), *Ogólnopolski program ochrony archeologicznych dóbr kultury zagrożonych planowaną budową autostrad. Raport 2000.* Warszawa, 282–308.

Czekaj-Zastawny A., Jarosz P. & Kadrow S. 2002. Badania ratownicze na trasie projektowanej autostrady A4 w woj. małopolskim (sezon 2000–2001 – neolit i wczesna epoka brązu). *Acta Archaeologica Carpathica* 37, 19–44.

Czekaj-Zastawny A. & Zastawny A. 2006. Badania ratownicze w Brzeziu, gm. Kłaj, na stan. 17, woj. małopolskie, w latach 2003–2004. In Bukowski Z. & Gierlach M. (eds.), *Raport 2003–2004. Wstępne wyniki konserwatorskich badań archeologicznych w strefie budowy autostrad w Polsce za lata 2003–2004*. Warszawa, 509–522.

Czekaj-Zastawny A., Grabowska B., Rauba-Bukowska A. & Zastawny A. 2007. Results of mineralogical and petrographic Research on vessels of Linear Band Pottery Culture and Malice Culture from sites Brzezie 17 and Targowisko 11, Kłaj Commune, Małopolska Province [Technologia ceramiki KCWR i KML ze stanowisk 17 w Brzeziu i 11 w Targowisku, gm. Kłaj]. *Sprawozdania Archeologiczne* 59, 63–113.

Czekaj-Zastawny A., Przybyła M. & Trela-Kieferling E. *in press*. Cmentarzysko ciałopalne kultury ceramiki wstęgowej rytej ze stanowiska 2 w Modlniczce, pow. krakowski [Linear Band Pottery Cultures cremation cementary at site 2 in Modlniczka, Kraków District]. In conference materials "Otazky neolitu a eneolitu nasich zemi – Melnik 2009.

Czerniak L. 1994. *Wczesny i środkowy okres neolitu na Kujawach. 5400–3650 p.n.e.* Poznań.

Czerniak L., Golański A., Józwiak B., Kadrow S., Rozen J. & Rzepecki S. 2006. Sprawozdanie z archeologicznych badań wykopaliskowych przeprowadzonych w latach 2003–2004 na stanowiskach 3, 12–15 i 34 w Targowisku, gm. Kłaj, woj. małopolskie. In Bukowski Z. & Gierlach M. (eds.), *Raport 2003–2004. Wstępne wyniki konserwatorskich badań archeologicznych w strefie budowy autostrad w Polsce za lata 2003–2004*. Warszawa, 541–554.

Czerniak L., Golański A., Kadrow S. & Schellner E. 2006. Sprawozdanie z ratowniczych badań wykopaliskowych w zespole stanowisk nr 2, 9, 12, 13, 20 i 21 w Szarowie, gm. Kłaj, woj. małopolskie. In Bukowski Z. & Gierlach M. (eds.), *Raport 2003–2004. Wstępne wyniki konserwatorskich badań archeologicznych w strefie budowy autostrad w Polsce za lata 2003–2004*. Warszawa, 593–596.

Czerniak R. 2006. *Sprawozdanie z nadzoru archeologicznego i badań ratowniczych, związanego z budową domu w Stumianach, stan. 5, gmina Wieliczka, województwo małopolskie.* The typescript of report in Archaeological Museum in Kraków.

Czopek S. 1999. *Pradzieje Polski południowo-wschodniej*. Rzeszów.

Dąbrowska E. 1965a. *Studia nad osadnictwem wczesnośredniowiecznym Ziemi Wiślickiej*. Wrocław.

Dąbrowska E. 1965b. Sprawozdanie z badań powierzchniowych prowadzonych w dolinie dolnej Nidy 1961 roku. *Sprawozdania Archeologiczne* 17, 322.

Dębiec M. & Dzbyński A. 2006. Neue Funde der doppelschneidigen Geräte aus der Linearbandkeramischen Siedlung in Zwięczyca, Gemeinde Boguchwała, Wojewodeschaft Podkarpackie [Nowe znaleziska czekanów kamiennych z osady kultury ceramiki wstęgowej rytej w Zwięczycy, gm. Boguchwała, woj. Podkarpackie]. *Sprawozdania Archeologiczne* 58, 223–245.

Dębiec M. & Dzbyński A. 2007. Die ersten Radiokarbondatirungen aus der Siedlung der Linienbandkeramischen Kultur in Zwięczyca, gm. Boguchwała [Pierwsze daty ^{14}C z osady kultury ceramiki wstęgowej rytej w Zwięczycy, gm. Boguchwała]. *Sprawozdania Archeologiczne* 59, 53–62.

Dębowski T. 1968. Badania ratownicze na osadzie w Zwięczycy, pow. Rzeszów. *Materiały i Sprawozdania Rzeszowskiego Ośrodka Archeologicznego* za rok 1967, 107–110.

Dębowski T. 1972. *Sprawozdanie z badań powierzchniowych przeprowadzonych w 1972 roku na terenie pow. Pińczów*. PPPKZ Oddział w Krakowie Pracownia Archeologiczno-Konserwatorska. Kraków, 65–66.

Dryja S. 1997. Spytkowice, st. 26, gm. loco, woj. bielskie, AZP 103-52/26. *Informator Archeologiczny, Badania 1992*. Warszawa, 18.

Dryja S. 1998a. Spytkowice, st. 26, gm. loco, woj. bielskie, AZP 103-52/26. *Informator Archeologiczny, Badania 1993*. Warszawa, 21.

Dryja S. 1998b. Spytkowice, st. 26, gm. loco, woj. bielskie, AZP 103-52/26. *Informator Archeologiczny, Badania 1994*. Warszawa, 23.

Dryja S. 1998c. Spytkowice, st. 26, gm. loco, woj. bielskie, AZP 103-52/26. *Informator Archeologiczny, Badania 1995*. Warszawa, 23.

Dynowska I. 1991. Obieg wody. In Starkel L. (ed.), *Geografia Polski. Środowisko przyrodnicze*. Warszawa, 355–387.

Dzieduszycka A. 1959. Cmentarzysko i osada kultury starszej ceramiki wstęgowej w Giebułtowie, pow. Kraków. *Materiały Archeologiczne* 1, 23–44.

Dzieduszycka A. 1960. Stanowisko kultury ceramiki wstęgowej rytej w Boguchwale, pow. Rzeszów. *Materiały Archeologiczne* 2, 11–21.

Dzieduszycka A. 1964. Sprawozdanie z badań osady kultury ceramiki wstęgowej rytej i osady eneolitycznej w Złotnikach, pow. Proszowice, w 1962 roku. *Sprawozdania Archeologiczne* 16, 26–29.

Dzieduszycka-Machnikowa A. & Eker A. 1965. Sprawozdania z badań neolitycznej osady wielokulturowej w Złotnikach, pow. Proszowice w 1963 r. *Sprawozdania Archeologiczne* 17, 61–66.

Gajewski L. 1957. Sprawozdanie z badań terenowych w rejonie Igołomia-Wschód w 1955 r. *Sprawozdania Archeologiczne* 3, 57–74.

Gajewski L. 1959. Sprawozdanie z badań terenowych w Igołomi za rok 1956. *Sprawozdania Archeologiczne* 5, 41–48.

Gajewski L. 1963a. Wykopaliska w Igołomi, pow. Proszowice w 1961 roku. *Sprawozdania Archeologiczne* 15, 155–175.

Gajewski L. 1963b. Nowe znaleziska zabytków archeologicznych z miejscowości Wawrzeńczyce-Kolonia, pow. Proszowice. *Wiadomości Archeologiczne* 24/4, 362–363.

Gleń-Haduch E. 1989. Analiza antropologiczna szkieletów z okresu kultury ceramiki wstęgowej rytej z Samborca (woj. tarnobrzeskie) na tle wczesnoneolitycznych populacji europejskich. *Materiały i Prace Antropologiczne* 110, 43–59.

Gleń-Haduch E. 1995. Ocena stanu biologicznego populacji neolitycznych i wczesnobrązowych z Wyżyny Małopolskiej. In J. Schmager (ed.), *Prace Zakładu Antropologii Uniwersytetu Jagiellońskiego* (= Zeszyty Naukowe UJ, Prace Zoologiczne 41), 115–139.

Godłowska M. 1966. Materiały z osady neolitycznej w Nowej Hucie-Mogile w pow. krakowskim. *Przegląd Archeologiczny* 17, 45–59.

Godłowska M. 1976. Próba rekonstrukcji rozwoju osadnictwa neolitycznego w rejonie Nowej Huty. *Materiały Archeologiczne Nowej Huty* 5, 7–180.

Godłowska M. 1986. Neolityczne osadnictwo na stan. 76 w Krakowie-Nowej Hucie-Branicach. *Materiały Archeologiczne Nowej Huty* 10, 7–42.

Godłowska M. 1991. Osada kultury ceramiki wstęgowej rytej w Krakowie – Nowej Hucie na stan. 62 (Mogiła). Część I – materiały. *Materiały Archeologiczne Nowej Huty* 14, 7–68.

Godłowska M. 1992. Osada kultury ceramiki wstęgowej rytej w Krakowie – Nowej Hucie na stan. 62 (Mogiła). Część II – Analiza materiałów. *Materiały Archeologiczne Nowej Huty* 15, 7–52.

Godłowska M., Kozłowski J. K., Starkel L. & Wasylikowa K.

References

1987. Neolithic settlement at Pleszów and changes in the natural environment in the Vistula valley. *Przegląd Archeologiczny* 34, 133–159.

Godłowska M., Rook E. & Drobniewicz B. 1985. A settlement of the linear pottery culture at Pleszów. *Przegląd Archeologiczny* 33, 57–103.

Graba-Łęcka-Paderewska L. 1963. Osadnictwo neolityczne nad dolną Nidą. In *Badania archeologiczne w okolicach Wiślicy*. Warszawa, 55–58.

Gromnicki J. 1965. Sprawozdanie z badań cmentarzyska kultury grobów kloszowych w Zagości-Parcelacji, pow. Pińczów w latach 1962-63. *Sprawozdania Archeologiczne* 17, 71–74.

Gruszczyńska A. 1991. Prace wykopaliskowe na osadzie neolitycznej w Łańcucie, stan. 3, w latach 1982–1984. *Materiały i Sprawozdania Rzeszowskiego Ośrodka Archeologicznego* za lata 1980–1984, 149–155.

Gruszczyńska A. 1992. Sprawozdanie z badań wykopaliskowych na osadzie neolitycznej w Łańcucie, w latach 1985–1990. *Materiały i Sprawozdania Rzeszowskiego Ośrodka Archeologicznego* za lata 1985–1990, 119–130.

Grygiel M. & Pikulski J. 2006. Archäologische Forschungen von 2001–2002 an der multikulturellen Fundstelle 1 in Zagórzyce, Gde. Kazimierza Wielka, Woiw. świętokrzyskie. *Recherches Archéologiques*. Kraków, 136–159.

Grygiel M., Pikulski J. & Trojan M. *in press*. Archäologische Forschungen von 2003–2004 an der multikulturellen Fundstelle 1 in Zagórzyce, Gde. Kazimierza Wielka, Woiw. świętokrzyskie. *Recherches Archéologiques*. Kraków.

Gurba J. 1953. Drobne materiały do poznania kultury ceramiki wstęgowej. *Z Otchłani Wieków* 22/3, 98–100.

Gurba J. 1971. Najnowsze badania nad neolitem Lubelszczyzny. *Rocznik Lubelski* XIII.

Hachulska-Ledwos R. 1963. Osada kultury ceramiki wstęgowej rytej w Bieńczycach (Kraków-Nowa Huta). *Materiały Archeologiczne* 4, 75–89.

Howell J.M. 1983. *Settlement and Economy in Neolithic Nortern France* (= British Archaeological Report 157). Oxford.

Jakimowicz R. 1935. Sprawozdanie z działalności Państwowego Muzeum Archeologicznego za 1928 rok. *Wiadomości Archeologiczne* 13, 232–279.

Jamka R. 1963. *Kraków w pradziejach*, t. I. Wrocław.

Jaśkowiak P. & Milisauskas S. 2001. Wielokulturowe stanowisko 1 w Dziekanowicach, woj. świętokrzyskie. *Sprawozdania Archeologiczne* 53, 111–163.

Jersak J. & Śnieszko Z. 1983. Rozwój rzeźby miechowskiego płata lessowego w późnym vistulianie i holocenie. In *Przewodnik konferencji Późnovistuliańskie i holoceńskie zmiany środowiska geograficznego na obszarach lessowych Wyżyny Miechowskiej i Opatowsko-Sandomierskiej*. Katowice, 5–12.

Jeunesse Ch. 1997. *Pratiques funéraires au néolithique Ancien*. Paris.

Kaczanowska M. 1988. Materiały neolityczne ze stanowiska 41 w Nowej Hucie-Krzesławicach. *Materiały Archeologiczne Nowej Huty* 12, 27–72.

Kaczanowska M. 1990. Uwagi o wczesnej fazie kultury lendzielskiej w Małopolsce. *Acta Archaeologica Carpathica* 29, 71–97.

Kaczanowski P., Madyda-Legutko R. & Poleski J. 1984. Cmentarzysko kultury przeworskiej w Górce Stogniewskiej koło Proszowic. *Sprawozdania Archeologiczne* 36, 83–121.

Kadrow S. 1990. Osada neolityczna na stan. nr 16 w Rzeszowie na Osiedlu Piastów. *Sprawozdania Archeologiczne* 41, 9–76.

Kadrow S. 1991. *Iwanowice stanowisko Babia Góra*, cz. I. Kraków.

Kadrow S. 1992a. Badania sondażowe na osadzie kultury ceramiki

wstęgowej rytej na stanowisku nr 38 w Albigowej, woj. Rzeszów. *Materiały i Sprawozdania Rzeszowskiego Ośrodka Archeologicznego* za lata 1985–1990, 131–139.

Kadrow S. 1992b. Osada kultury lubelsko-wołyńskiej na stan. 35 w Kosinie, gm. loco, woj. Rzeszów. *Materiały i Sprawozdania Rzeszowskiego Ośrodka Archeologicznego* za lata 1985–1990, 141–150.

Kadrow S. 1997. Osada kultury ceramiki wstęgowej rytej na stanowisku 3 w Rzeszowie-Staromieściu. *Materiały i Sprawozdania Rzeszowskiego Ośrodka Archeologicznego* 18, 5–27.

Kadrow S. 2003. (ed.) *Kraków-Bieżanów, stanowisko 27 i Kraków-Rżąka, stanowisko 1, osada kultury łużyckiej*. Kraków, 273–284.

Kadrow S. & Okoński J. 2008. Materiały stylu zofipolskiego ze stanowiska 2 w Zagórzu, gm. Niepołomice. In J. Chochorowski (ed.), *Młodsza epoka kamienia – wybrane znaleziska* (= *Via Archaeologica. Źródła z badań wykopaliskowych na trasie autostrady A4 w Małopolsce*). Kraków, 1–21.

Kadrow S. & Zakościelna A. 2000. Evolution of Danubian cultures in Małopolska and Western Ukraine. *Baltic-Pontic Studies* 9, 187–255.

Kahlke D. 1954. *Die Bestattungssitten des Donauländischen Kulturkreises der jüngeren Steinzeit. Teil I: Linienbandkeramik*. Berlin.

Kamieńska J. 1963. Sprawozdanie z badań archeologicznych ekspedycji neolitycznej w 1961 r. *Sprawozdania Archeologiczne* 15, 47–50.

Kamieńska J. 1964a. Osady kultur wstęgowych w Samborcu, pow. Sandomierz. In Nosek S. (ed.), *Studia i materiały do badań nad neolitem Małopolski* (= Prace Komisji Archeologicznej PAN – Oddział w Krakowie 4). Wrocław-Warszawa-Kraków, 77–190.

Kamieńska J. 1964b. Sprawozdanie z badań archeologicznych w Samborcu, pow. Sandomierz, w 1962 roku. *Sprawozdania Archeologiczne* 16, 35–38.

Kamieńska J. 1965. Sprawozdanie z badań archeologicznych w Samborcu, pow. Sandomierz, w 1963 roku. *Sprawozdania Archeologiczne* 17, 76–82.

Kamieńska J. 1966. Sprawozdanie z badań archeologicznych w Samborcu, pow. Sandomierz, w 1964 roku. *Sprawozdania Archeologiczne* 18, 322–328.

Kamieńska J. 1968. Sprawozdanie z badań archeologicznych w Samborcu, pow. Sandomierz, w 1965 roku. *Sprawozdania Archeologiczne* 19, 431–435.

Kamieńska J. & Kozłowski J.K. 1990. *Entwicklung und Gliederung der Lengyel- und Polgar-Kulturgruppen in Polen* (= Zeszyty Naukowe UJ, Prace Archeologiczne, 46). Warszawa-Kraków.

Kamieńska J. & Kulczycka-Leciejewiczowa A. 1970. The neolithic and early bronze age settlement at Samborzec in the Sandomierz district. *Archaelogia Polona* 12, 223–246.

Keeley L.H & Cahen D. 1989. Early neolithic forts and villages in NE Belgium: A preliminary report. *Journal of Field Archaeology* 16, 157–176.

Kempisty E. 1962. Pierwszy grób kultury ceramiki wstęgowej rytej na Lubelszczyźnie. *Wiadomości Archeologiczne* 28, 284.

Koperski A. 2001. (ed.) *Dzieje Przemyśla*, t. I, cz. 1. Przemyśl.

Kowalewska-Marszałek H. 1981. Sandomierz, woj. tarnobrzeskie, Stanowisko Żmigród, *Informator Archeologiczny, Badania rok 1980*. Warszawa, 47–49.

Kowalewska-Marszałek H. 1992. *Osadnictwo neolityczne na Wyżynie Sandomierskiej*. Typescript of PhD dissertation in archive of Institute Archaeology and Ethnology Polish Academy of Sciences in Warsaw.

Kowalewska-Marszałek H. 1996. Faza I: relikty osadnictwa pradziejowego. In Tabaczyński S. (ed.), *Sandomierz: badania 1969–1973*. Warszawa, 50–87.

Kowalkowski A. 1991. Ewolucja gleb w holocenie. In Starkel L. (ed.), *Geografia Polski. Środowisko przyrodnicze*. Warszawa, 127–139.

Kowalski K. 1975. Wyniki badań archeologicznych w dorzeczu Obręczówki. *Materiały Starożytne i Wczesnośredniowieczne* 3, 471–500.

Kozłowski J.K. 1968. Materiały neolityczne i eneolityczne odkryte na stanowisku Nowa Huta – Wyciąże I (badania w latach 1950–1952). *Materiały Archeologiczne Nowej Huty* 1, 13–90.

Kozłowski J.K. 1969. Neolityczne i wczesnoneolityczne materiały krzemienne ze stanowisk Nowa Huta-Pleszów. *Materiały Archeologiczne Nowej Huty* 2, 131–149.

Kozłowski J.K. 1998. Neolityzacja Europy: pojawienie się rolnictwa i hodowli. In Kozłowski J.K. & Kaczanowski P. (eds.), *Wielka Historia Polski*, t. 1. *Najdawniejsze dzieje ziem polskich (do VII w.)*. Kraków, 99–114.

Kozłowski J.K. 2004. Problem kontynuacji rozwoju pomiędzy wczesnym i środkowym neolitem oraz genezy "cyklu lendzielsko-polgarskiego" w basenie górnej Wisły. *Materiały Archeologiczne Nowej Huty* 24, 11–18.

Konieczny B. 2008. *Modlnica 5. Badania Krakowskiego Zespołu do Badań Autostrad. Obiekty kultury ceramiki wstęgowej rytej*. Poster on round table: *The Interactions between different models of the Neolithization north of the Central European Agro-Ecological Barrier: Eastern and Western Linear Complexes*. Kraków 1-2 XII, 2008.

Kozłowski J.K. & Kulczycka A. 1961. Materiały kultury starszej ceramiki wstęgowej z Olszanicy, pow. Kraków. *Materiały Archeologiczne* 3, 29–50.

Kozłowski L. 1923. *Epoka kamienia na wydmach wschodniej części Wyżyny Małopolskiej*. Lwów.

Krause R. 1999. An enclosed Bandkeramik village and cemetery from the 6th millennium BC near Vaihingen/Enz. On the WEB SITE http.//helena.s.bawue.de/~wmwerner/grabung/vaih 99_e. html

Krauss A. 1964. Grób kultury starszej ceramiki wstęgowej ze Szczotkowic, pow. Kazimierza Wielka. In Nosek S. (ed.), *Studia i materiały do badań nad neolitem Małopolski*. Wrocław-Warszawa-Kraków, 69–76.

Krauss J. 1970. Wielokulturowe stanowisko w Kowali, pow. proszowicki. *Materiały Archeologiczne* 11, 157–174.

Kruk J. 1969. Badania poszukiwawcze i weryfikacyjne w dorzeczu Dłubni. *Sprawozdania Archeologiczne* 21, 347–373.

Kruk J. 1970. Badania poszukiwawcze i weryfikacyjne w górnym i środkowym dorzeczu Szreniawy. *Sprawozdania Archeologiczne* 22, 271–301.

Kruk J. 1973. *Studia osadnicze nad neolitem wyżyn lessowych*. Wrocław-Warszawa-Kraków-Gdańsk.

Kruk J. 1980. *Gospodarka w Polsce południowo-wschodniej w V-III tysiącleciu p.n.e.* Wrocław-Warszawa-Kraków-Gdańsk.

Kruk J. 1983. Wczesne rolnictwo i jego wpływ na kształtowanie się środowiska naturalnego wyżyn lessowych dorzecza górnej Wisły. In *Przewodnik konferencji: Późnovistuliańskie i holoceńskie zmiany środowiska geograficznego na obszarach lessowych Wyżyny Miechowskiej i Opatowsko-Sandomierskiej*. Katowice, 21–34.

Kruk J. & Milisauskas S. 1999. *Rozkwit i upadek społeczeństw rolniczych neolitu*. Kraków.

Kruk J. & Przywara L. 1983. Roślinność potencjalna jako metoda rekonstrukcji naturalnych warunków rozwoju społeczności pradziejowych. *Archeologia Polski* 28/1, 19–43.

Kukułka A. 1997. Badania sondażowe w Gwoźdźcu stan. 2, gm. Zakliczyn, woj. tarnowskie. *Materiały i Sprawozdania Rzeszowskiego Ośrodka Archeologicznego* 18, 161–168.

Kukułka A. 1998. Drugi sezon wykopaliskowy na osadzie wczesnoneolitycznej w Gwoźdźcu, stan. 2, gm. Zakliczyn. *Materiały i Sprawozdania Rzeszowskiego Ośrodka Archeologicznego* 19, 175–198.

Kukułka A. 2001. Wczesnoneolityczna osada w Gwoźdźcu, gm. Zakliczyn, stan. 2 na Pogórzu Wiślickim. In J. Gancarski (ed.), *Neolit i początki brązu w Karpatach polskich*. Krosno, 11–40.

Kulczycka A. 1961. Materiały kultury starszej ceramiki wstęgowej z Zofipola, pow. Proszowice. *Materiały Archeologiczne* 3, 19–28.

Kulczycka-Leciejewiczowa A. 1964. Materiały kultur z cyklu wstęgowych z badań ratowniczych w Targowisku, pow. Bochnia. *Materiały Archeologiczne* 5, 103–115.

Kulczycka-Leciejewiczowa A. 1965. Z badań nad osadnictwem kultury starszej ceramiki wstęgowej w Targowisku, pow. Bochnia. *Materiały Archeologiczne* 6, 197–200.

Kulczycka-Leciejewiczowa A. 1968. Ze studiów nad kulturą ceramiki wstęgowej w Polsce. *Archeologia Polski* 13, 56–124.

Kulczycka-Leciejewiczowa A. 1969. Nowa Huta-Pleszów – osada neolityczna kultury ceramiki wstęgowej rytej i lendzielskiej. *Materiały Archeologiczne Nowej Huty* 2, 7–124.

Kulczycka-Leciejewiczowa A. 1973a. Niektóre problemy osadnictwa kultury ceramiki wstęgowej rytej w dorzeczu górnej Wisły. *Archeologia Polski* 18, 73–90.

Kulczycka-Leciejewiczowa A. 1973b. Wczesnoneolityczne osadnictwo w dorzeczu Raby. In Nosek S. (ed.), *Z badań nad neolitem i wczesną epoką brązu w Małopolsce*. Kraków 19–64.

Kulczycka-Leciejewiczowa A. 1979. Pierwsze społeczeństwa rolnicze na ziemiach polskich. Kultury kręgu naddunajskiego. In Hensel W. (ed.), *Prahistoria ziem polskich*, t. II *Neolit*. Wrocław-Warszawa-Kraków-Gdańsk, 19–164.

Kulczycka-Leciejewiczowa A. 1983. O zofipolskim stylu ceramiki wstęgowej rytej w Polsce. *Archeologia Polski* 28/1, 67–97.

Kulczycka-Leciejewiczowa A. 1993. *Osadnictwo neolityczne w Polsce południowo-zachodniej*. Wrocław.

Kulczycka-Leciejewiczowa A. 1997. *Strachów. Osiedla neolitycznych rolników na Śląsku*. Wrocław.

Kulczycka-Leciejewiczowa A. 1988. Erste Gemeinschaften der Linienbandkeramikkultur auf polnischem Boden. *Zeitschift für Archäologie* 23, 137–182.

Kulczycka-Leciejewiczowa A. 2000. Early Linear Pottery communities to the North of the Sudeten and Carpathian Mountains. Recent researches. *Památky Archeologické – Supplementum* 13, 196–204.

Kulczycka-Leciejewiczowa A. 2002. Some remarks on the Stroke-Ornamented Pottery Ware culture in Poland. *Archeologické Rozhledy* 54, 179–190.

Kulczycka-Leciejewiczowa A. 2008. *Samborzec. Studium przemian kultury ceramiki wstęgowej rytej*. Wrocław.

Lech J. 1981. *Górnictwo krzemienia społeczności wczesnorolniczych na Wyżynie Krakowskiej*. Wrocław-Warszawa-Kraków-Gdańsk-Łodź.

Lech J., Rook E. & Stępniowski F.M. 1984. Archeologiczne badania poszukiwawcze i weryfikacyjne w dorzeczu Prądnika w latach 1976–1980. *Sprawozdania Archeologiczne* 36, 213–266.

Lenneis E. 2001. The beginning of the Neolithic in Austria – a report recent and current investigations. *Documenta Praehistorica* 28, 99–116.

Lenneis E., Neugebauer-Maresch Ch. & Ruttkay E. 1999. *Jungsteinzeit im osten Österreichs*. St. Pölten-Wien.

Liana T. & Piętka-Dąbrowska T. 1958. Osada z okresu wpływów rzymskich w Gródku Nadbużnym, pow. Hrubieszów. *Wiadomości Archeologiczne* 25/4, 373–382.

Liguzińska-Kruk Z. 1982. Poszukiwania archeologiczne w dorzeczu górnej Nidzicy. *Sprawozdania Archeologiczne* 33, 220.

Lorenc E. 1998. *Neolityczne materiały ceramiczne ze stanowiska Babia Góra I w Iwanowicach, woj. Kraków*. Typescript of MA in Institute of Archaeology Maria Curie-Skłodowska University in Lublin.

Lüning J. 1982. Research into the Bandkeramik settlement of the Aldenhovener Platte in the Rhineland. *Analecta Praehistorica Leidensia* 15.

Lüning J. 2000. *Steinzeitliche Bauern in Deutschland. Die Landwirschaft im Neolithicum* (= UPA B 58). Bonn.

Machnik J. 1957. Sprawozdanie z badań powierzchniowych na lewobrzeżu terasy Wisły na odcinku Igołomia-Sandomierz. *Sprawozdania Archeologiczne* 4, 152.

Machnikowie A. & J. & Kaczanowski K. 1987. *Osada i cmentarzysko z wczesnej epoki brązu na "Górze Klin" w Iwanowicach*. Wrocław.

Madej P. & Valde-Nowak P. 1997–1998. Stanowisko 10 w Czchowie w świetle wyników prac wykopaliskowych w 1997 roku. *Acta Archaeologica Carpathica* 34, 5–24.

Madej P. & Valde-Nowak P. 2001. *Badania wykopaliskowe na stanowisku Czchów 10/38, woj. małopolskie w 1999 roku*. The typescript of report in PSOZ O/Tarnów.

Madyda R., Stoch B. & Parczewski M. 1971. Wyniki badań powierzchniowych powiatu Dąbrowa Tarnowska z roku 1969. *Sprawozdania Archeologiczne* 23, 183.

Michalak-Ścibior J. M. & Taras H. 1995. Wczesnoneolityczna osada w Sandomierzu-Krukowie, stan. 20. *Sprawozdania Archeologiczne* 47, 69–135.

Milisauskas S. 1986. *Archeological investigations on the Linear Culture Village of Olszanica*. Wrocław-Warszawa-Kraków.

Milisauskas S. 1989. Specialized Activity Areas at Olszanica. In Rulf J. (ed.), *Bylany Seminar 1987*. Praha, 233–242.

Milisauskas S., Kruk J., Ford R., Lityńska-Zając M. & Tomczyńska Z. 2004. Neolithic forest composition as reflected by charcoal analysis from Bronocice Poland. *Sprawozdania Archeologiczne* 56, 271–288.

Mitura P. & Zych R. 1999. Sprawozdanie z badań stanowiska 20 w Olchowej, gm. Iwierzyce, woj. podkarpackie w 1999 roku. *Materiały i Sprawozdania Rzeszowskiego Ośrodka Archeologicznego* 20, 261–274.

Modderman P.J.R. 1986. On the typology of the houseplans and their European setting. In Pavlů I., Rulf J., Zápotocká M. and coll. *Theses on the Neolithic site of Bylany. Památky Archeologické* 77, 288–412.

Modderman P.J.R. 1988. The Linear Pottery Culture: Diversity in Uniformity. *Berichten van de Rijksdienst voor het Oudheidkundig Bodemonderzoek* 38, 63–139.

Moskwa K. 1961. Problemy archeologii województwa rzeszowskiego. *Biuletyn Wydziału Kultury WRN*, 19.

Moskwa K. 1963. Badania wykopaliskowe w Albigowej, powiat Łańcut (neolit, kultura łużycka). *Sprawozdania Rzeszowskiego Ośrodka Archeologicznego* za rok 1963, 14–15.

Moskwa K. 1964. *Pradzieje powiatu rzeszowskiego*. Lublin.

Moskwa K. 1974. Z badań nad pradziejami Rzeszowa. *Rocznik Muzealny Województwa Rzeszowskiego* 3, 7.

Nawrocka M. 1998. *Neolityczne materiały ceramiczne ze stanowiska Góra Klin w Iwanowicach, woj. Kraków*. Typescript of MA in Institute of Archaeology Maria Curie-Skłodowska University in Lublin.

Neustupný E. 1956. K relativní chronologii volutové keramiky. *Archeologické Rozhledy* 8/3, 386–406.

Nieszery N. 1995. *Linearbadnkeramische Gräberfelder in Bayern* (= Internationale Archäologie, Band 16). Espelkamp.

Nosek S. 1955. Wyniki badań terenowych w rejonie Igołomia-Wschód prowadzonych w latach 1953 i 1954. *Sprawozdania Archeologiczne* 1, 29–46.

Nowakowska M. & Jaremek A. 2008. *Wojnicz, stanowisko 34, gm. loco, woj. małopolskie*. Typescript of study in archive of The Cracow Team for Archaeological Supervision of Motorway Construction, Institute of Archaeology and Ethnology Polish Academy of Sciences, Museum of Archaeology Crakow, Jagiellonian University.

Nowosad A. 1998. *Neolityczne materiały ceramiczne ze stanowiska Babia Góra II w Iwanowicach, woj. Kraków*. Typescript of MA in Institute of Archaeology Maria Curie-Skłodowska University in Lublin.

Ossowski G. 1880. Sprawozdanie z badań geologiczno-antropologicznych dokonanych w 1879 roku w jaskiniach okolic Krakowa. *Zbiór Wiadomości do Antropologii Krajowej* IV, 38.

Pavlů I. 2000. *Life on a Neolithic Site*. Praha.

Pavlů I., Rulf J., Zápotocká M. and collaborators. 1986. Theses on the Neolithic site of Bylany. *Památky Archeologické* 77, 288–412.

Pavúk J. 1969. Chronologie der Želiezovce-Gruppe. *Slovenská archeológia* 17, 269–367.

Pavúk J. 1980. Ältere Linearkeramik in der Slowakei. *Slovenská archeológia* 28, 7–90.

Pavúk J. 1994. *Štúrovo. Ein Siedlungsplatz der Kultur mit Linearkeramik und der Želiezovce-Gruppe*. Nitra.

Pavúk J. 2004. Early Linear Pottery Culture in Slovakia and the Neolithisation of Central Europe. In Lukes A. & Zvelebil M. (eds.), *LBK Dialogues. Studies in the formation of the Linear Pottery Culture* (= British Archaeological Report, International Series 1304). Oxford, 71–82.

Podborský V. s kolektivem. 1993. *Pravěké dějiny Moravy*. Brno.

Podkowińska Z. 1959. Osada neolityczna kultury starszej ceramiki wstęgowej (rytej) w Jurkowicach, pow. opatowski. *Archeologia Polski* 3, 7–50.

Podkowińska Z. 1960. Sprawozdanie z badań powierzchniowych w Samborcu, pow. Sandomierz w 1957 r. *Sprawozdania Archeologiczne* 9, 9–20.

Posselt M. & Seile T. 2003. Early Neolithic settlements in Germany. Latest results of a magnetometr survey approach to the investigation of Early Neolithic architecture and settlement patterns throughout Central Europe. *Archaelogia Polona* 41, 254–256.

Proksa M. 1984. Próba analizy statystycznej kamiennych siekier neolitycznych ze zbiorów muzeów dawnego woj. rzeszowskiego. *Materiały i Sprawozdania Rzeszowskiego Ośrodka Archeologicznego* za lata 1976-79, 5–40.

Prusinkiewicz Z. & Bednarek R. 1991. Gleby. In Starkel L. (ed.), *Geografia Polski. Środowisko przyrodnicze*. Warszawa, 387–412.

Pyzel J. 2006. *Społeczności kultury ceramiki wstęgowej rytej na Kujawach*. Typescript of MA in Institute of Archaeology and Ethnology Polish Academy of Sciences in Warsaw.

Ralska-Jasiewiczowa M. 1991. Ewolucja szaty roślinnej. In Starkel L. (ed.), *Geografia Polski. Środowisko przyrodnicze*. Warszawa, 106–127.

Ralska-Jasiewiczowa M. & Starkel L. 1991. Zmiany klimatu i stosunków wodnych w holocenie. In Starkel L. (ed.), *Geografia Polski. Środowisko przyrodnicze*. Warszawa, 177–182.

Ramsey B. 2005. OxCal v.3.10. Internet Program.

Rauhut D. 1970. Materiały kultury ceramiki wstęgowej rytej ze Złotej, pow. Sandomierz. In Kozłowski J.K. (ed.), *Z badań nad kulturą ceramiki wstęgowej rytej (Materiały konferencji w Nowej Hucie dn. 22 IV 1969)*. Kraków, 61–72.

Reinecke K. 1982. Linearbandkeramische Siedlungen in Niederbayern. In Pavúk J. (ed.), *Siedlungen der Kultur mit Linearkeramik in Europa* – Internationales Kolloquium Nové Vozokany 17-20. November 1981. Nitra, 239–246.

Reyman T. 1931. Sprawozdanie z badań archeologicznych w Pobiedzisku i Tropiszowie w powiecie miechowskim. *Sprawozdania z Czynności i Posiedzeń Polskiej Akademii Umiejętności* 6, 30.

Reyman T. 1939. Zespół importów rzymskich z grobu ciałopalnego w powiecie krakowskim. *Wiadomości Archeologiczne* 16, 178–210.

Reyman T. 1947. Odkrycia w Zofipolu. *Sprawozdania z Czynności i Posiedzeń Polskiej Akademii Umiejętności* 48/3, 12–13.

Romanow J. 1977. Trapezowate budowle naziemne ludności kultury ceramiki wstęgowej kłutej na Dolnym Śląsku. *Silesia Antiqua* 19, 27–55.

Rook E. 1968. Osady z cyklu wstęgowych w Targowisku, pow. Bochnia. *Materiały Archeologiczne* 9, 91–121.

Rook E. 1980. Osadnictwo neolityczne w jaskiniach Wyżyny Krakowsko-Częstochowskiej. *Materiały Archeologiczne* 20, 5–130.

Rook E. 1981. Szyce, gm. Wielka Wieś, woj. krakowskie, stanowisko 1. *Informator Archeologiczny. Badania rok 1980*, 50–51.

Rook E. & Woźniak Z. 1968. Wyniki badań późnorzymskiej osady na stanowisku 2 w Łężkowicach, pow. Bochnia. *Materiały Archeologiczne* 9, 187–202.

Rulf J. 1983. Přírodní prostředí a kultury českého neolitu a eneolitu. *Památky Archeologické* 74, 35–95.

Rydzewski J. 1972. Badania poszukiwawcze i weryfikacyjne w dolnym dorzeczu Szreniawy. *Sprawozdania Archeologiczne* 24, 275–280.

Rydzewski J. 1973. Badania poszukiwawcze i weryfikacyjne w dorzeczu Małoszówki. *Sprawozdania Archeologiczne* 25, 243–260.

Saile T., Posselt M. & Bajer W. 2008. Zur Siedlungsarchäologie der Bandkeramik im Einzugsgebiet des San. *Neue Ausgrabungen und Forschungen in Niedersachsen* 26, 9–23.

Sielmann B. 1971. Der Einfluss der Umwelt auf die neolithische Besiedlung Südwestdeutschlands unter besonderer Berücksichtigung der Verhältnisse am nördlichen Oberrhein. *Acta Praehistorica at Archaeologica* 2, 65–197.

Sochacki Z. 1969. Materiały archeologiczne z Góry Chełmowej. *Wiadomości Archeologiczne* 34, 228–234.

Soudský B. 1954. K metohodice třídení volutové keramiky. *Památky Archeologické* 45, 75–105.

Soudský B. 1969. Étude de la miason néolithique. *Slovenská archeológia* 17, 5–96.

Soudský B. & Pavlů I. 1972. The Linear Pottery culture settlement patterns in central Europe. In Ucko P.J., Tringham R. & Dimbleby G.W. (eds.), *Man, Settlement and Urbanism*. London, 317–328.

Starkel L. 1991a. Ewolucja rzeźby gór i wyżyn. In Starkel L. (ed.), *Geografia Polski. Środowisko przyrodnicze*. Warszawa, 140–144.

Starkel L. 1991b. Rola holocenu w ewolucji środowiska i jego stratygrafia. In Starkel L. (ed.), *Geografia Polski. Środowisko przyrodnicze*. Warszawa, 105–106.

Starkel L. 2001. *Historia doliny Wisły od ostatniego zlodowacenia do dziś* (= Monografie 2). Warszawa.

Stryjowska M. 2007. *Stanowisko 26 w Spytkowicach. Materiały z badań przeprowadzonych w roku 1993*. Typescript of MA thesis in archive of Institute Archaeology of Jagiellonian University in Krakow.

Sulimirski T. 1961. Ziemianka kultury ceramiki wstęgowej starszej i mogiły kurhany w Rzeplinie, pow. Jarosław. *Acta Archaeologica Carpathica* 2/1-2, 161.

Szybowicz A. 1980. *Katalog zabytków archeologicznych Muzeum Żup Krakowskich w Wieliczce*. Wieliczka.

Ścibior J.M. 1986. Ćmielów. *Informator Archeologiczny. Badania 1985*. Warszawa, 17–18.

Ścibior J.M. 1993. Z badań nad osadnictwem najstarszej fazy kultury ceramiki wstęgowej rytej na Wyżynie Sandomierskiej. *Sprawozdania Archeologiczne* 45, 19–27.

Tabaczyńska E. 1972. Sandomierz-Żmigród. *Informator Archeologiczny. Badania 1971*. Warszawa, 37.

Uzarowiczowa A. 1964. Wyniki badań we wsi Gródek Nadbużny, pow. Hrubieszów, w 1961 r. *Wiadomości Archeologiczne* 30/2, 429–460.

Valde-Nowak P. 1997–1998. Badania osady neolitycznej w Łoniowej (Pogórze Wiśnickie). *Acta Archaeologica Carpathica* 34, 195–206.

Valde-Nowak P. 2007. *Sprawozdanie z badań wykopaliskowych w Żerkowie w 2007 roku*. Typescript of the report in archive of PSOZ in Tarnów.

Valde-Nowak P. 2008a. Dom ludzi żywych i umarłych sprzed siedmiu tysięcy lat. *Alma Mater* 99/2008, 51–54.

Valde-Nowak P. 2008b. Neolithic in the European Mid-Mountains case study from the Polish Carpathians. In S. Grimaldi & T. Perrin (eds.), *Mountain environments in prehistoric Europe: settlement and mobility strategies from Paleolithic to the Bronze Age. Proceedings of the session C31 UISPP* (= British Archaeological Report, International Series). Oxford, 131–136.

Valde-Nowak P. *in press*. Fruhneolithische Besiedlung in Wiśnicz Hugelland in den Karpaten. Die Siedlungen Łoniowa und Żerków. *Recherches Archaeologiques*, 2009.

Valde-Nowak P. & Madej P. 1997. *Badania wykopaliskowe na stanowisku 10 w Czchowie, woj. Tarnów, w 1997 roku*. Typescript of the report in archive of PSOZ in Tarnów.

Valde-Nowak P. & Madej P. 1998. *Sprawozdanie z badań wykopaliskowych na stanowisku 5 w Jurkowie gm. Czchów, woj. Tarnów* (AZP 107-63/73 X-328-Y-146). Typescript of the report in archive of PSOZ in Tarnów.

Vladár J. & Lichardus J. 1968. Erforschung der Früháneolithischen Siedlungen in Branč. *Slovenská archeológia* 16/2, 263–352.

Wiślański T. 1969. *Podstawy gospodarcze plemion neolitycznych w Polsce północno-zachodniej*. Wroclaw-Warszawa-Kraków.

Włodarczak P. 2006. Wyniki badań wykopaliskowych przeprowadzonych w latach 2003–2004 na stanowisku 16 w Targowisku, gm. Kłaj, woj. małopolskie. In Bukowski Z. & Gierlach M. (eds.), *Raport 2003–2004. Wstępne wyniki konserwatorskich badań archeologicznych w strefie budowy autostrad w Polsce za lata 2003–2004*. Warszawa, 585–592.

Wojciechowski W. 1981. *Wczesnoneolityczna osada w Skoroszowicach*. Wrocław.

Woźniak Z. 1966. Badania w Łężkowicach i Targowisku, pow. Bochnia w 1964 r. *Materiały Archeologiczne* 7, 269–271.

Wróbel H. 1982. Sandomierz-Kruków, woj. tarnobrzeskie. *Informator Archeologiczny. Badania 1981*. Warszawa, 55–56.

Wróbel H. 1983. Sandomierz-Kruków, woj. tarnobrzeskie. *Informator Archeologiczny. Badania 1982*. Warszawa, 55.

Zastawny A. 1997. *Sprawozdanie z nadzoru archeologicznego oraz badań ratowniczych na stan. 4 w Igołomi, gm. Igołomia-Wawrzeńczyce*. The typescript of report in Archaeological Museum in Kraków.

Zastawny A. 2002. *Sprawozdanie z nadzoru archeologicznego oraz badań ratowniczych na stan. 4 w Igołomi, gm. Igołomia-Wawrzeńczyce (2002 rok).* The typescript of report in Archaeological Museum in Kraków.

Zastawny A. 2003. *Sprawozdanie z badań sondażowych na stan. 4 w Igołomi, gm. Igołomia-Wawrzeńczyce, w 2003 roku.* The typescript of report in Archaeological Museum in Kraków.

Zastawny A. 2006. *Więckowice, st. 4, gm. Zabierzów, woj. małopolskie.* The typescript of report in Archaeological Museum in Kraków.

Zastawny A. 2008. Neolityczna plastyka gliniana ze stanowiska 3 w Dąbrowie, gm. Kłaj. In J. Chochorowski (ed.), *Młodsza epoka kamienia – wybrane znaleziska* (= Via Archaeologica. Źródła z badań wykopaliskowych na trasie autostrady A4 w Małopolsce). Kraków, 57–68.

Zych R. 2002. *Wielkie domostwa i grobowce typu kujawskiego w kulturze symbolicznej neolitu na ziemiach polskich.* Rzeszów.

Żaki A. 1948. Osada neolityczna w Boguchwale, pow. Rzeszów. *Sprawozdania z Czynności i Posiedzeń Polskiej Akademii Umiejętności* 49/2, 169–172.

Żurowski J. 1926. Nowe odkrycia przedhistoryczne. *Z Otchłani Wieków* 1/4, 45.

Żurowski J. 1929. Z badań archeologicznych w Złotej k/Sandomierza w latach 1927 i 1928. *Z Otchłani Wieków* IV/1, 1–9.

Żurowski J. 1934. Ogólne wyniki badań archeologicznych w Złotej pow. Sandomierz, w latach 1926–1930. *Sprawozdania z Czynności i Posiedzeń Polskiej Akademii Umiejętności* 39/5, 31–35.

131

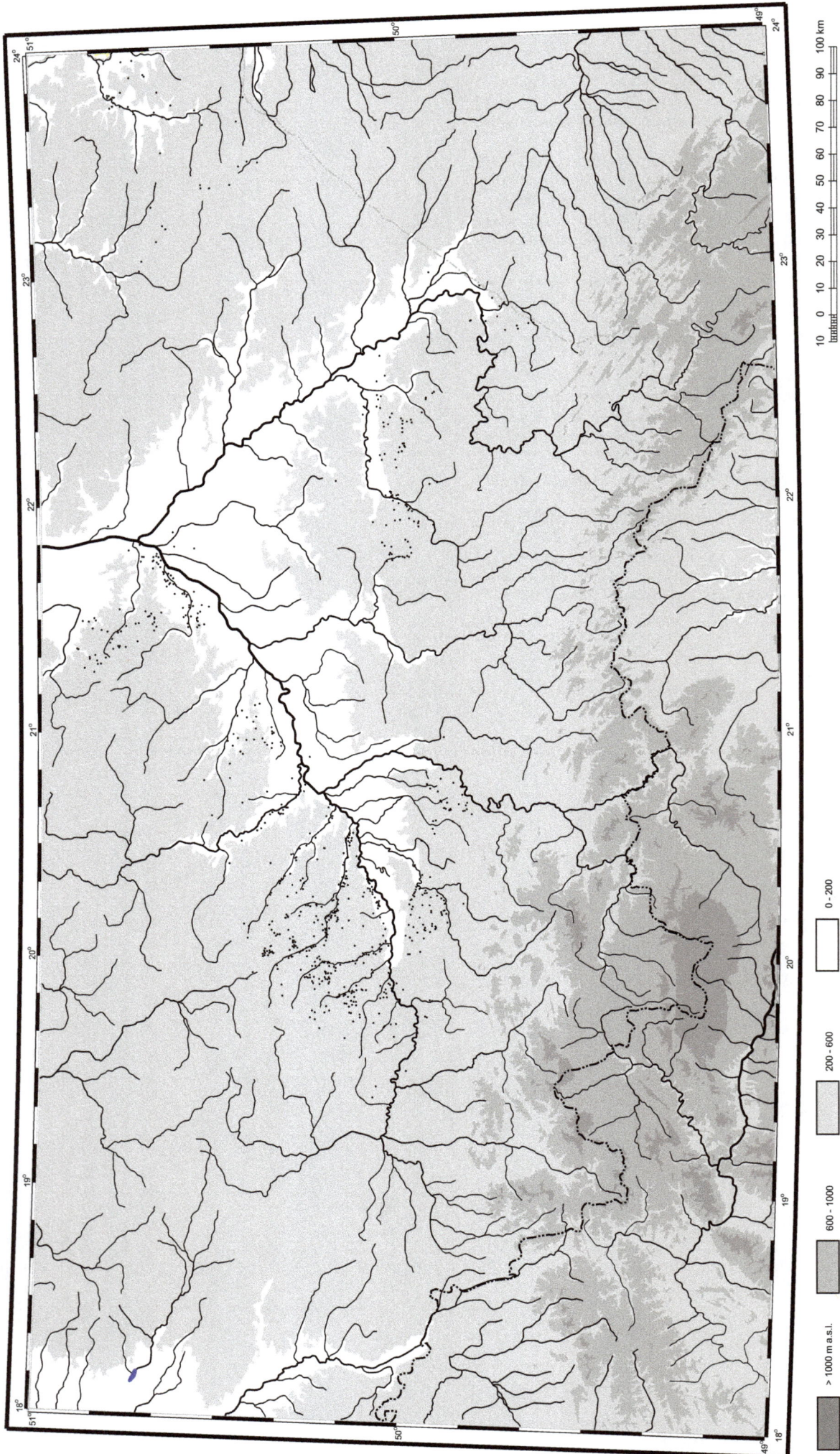

Fig. 3. Southeastern Poland. Distribution of LBK settlement. Drawn by I. Jędrychowski.

> 1000 m a.s.l.   600 - 1000   200 - 600   0 - 200

10 0 10 20 30 40 50 60 70 80 90 100 km

Please note that a full-size version of this image is available to download from www.barpublishing.com/additional-downloads.html

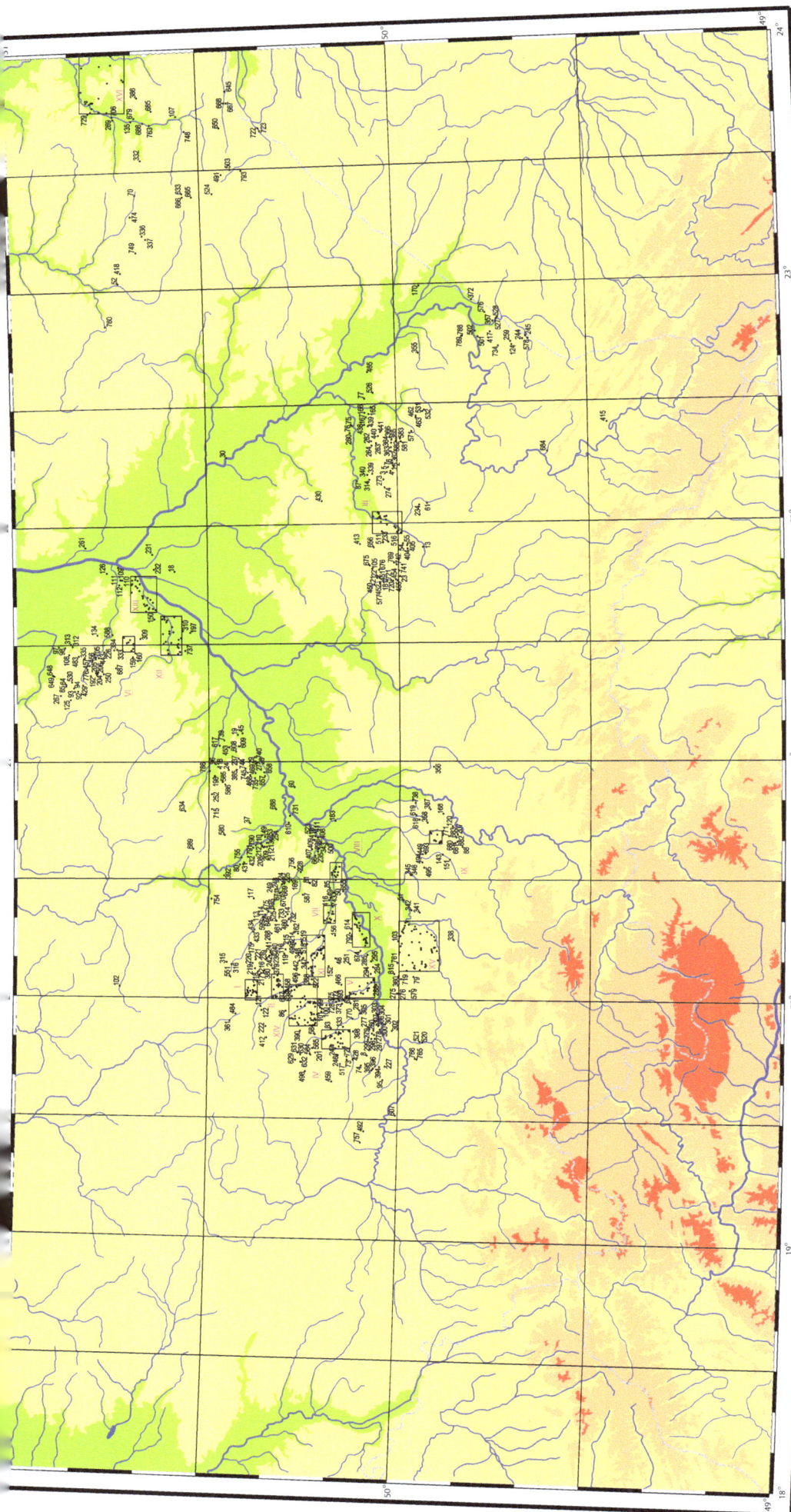

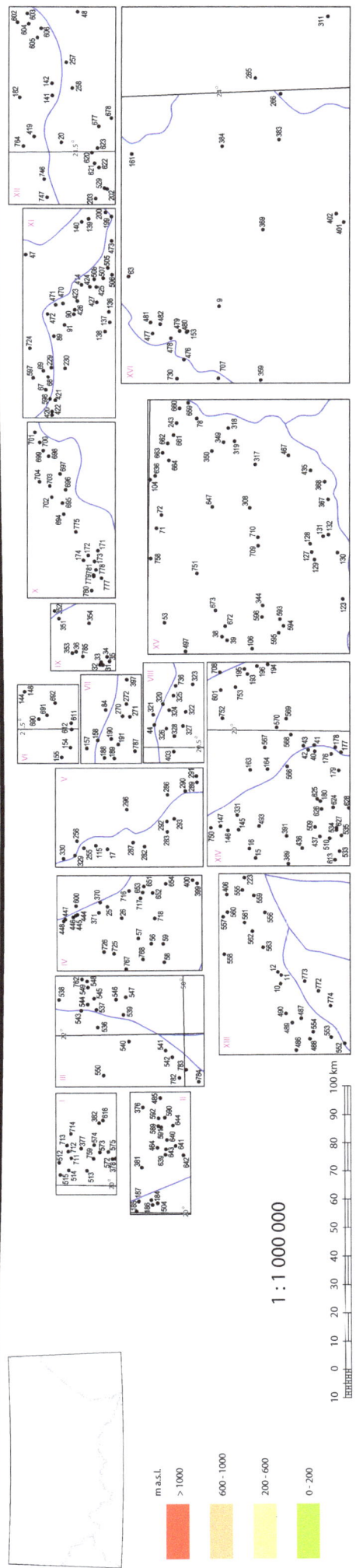

1 : 1 000 000

10 0 10 20 30 40 50 60 70 80 90 100 km

m.a.s.l.

>1000

600 - 1000

200 - 600

0 - 200

www.ingramcontent.com/pod-product-compliance
Lightning Source LLC
Chambersburg PA
CBHW061001030426
42334CB00033B/3317